The
Smart Woman's
Guide to
Starting a
Business

By
Vickie Montgomery

The
Smart Woman's
Guide to
Starting a
Business

By
Vickie Montgomery

CAREER PRESS
180 Fifth Avenue
P.O. Box 34
Hawthorne, NJ 07507
1-800-CAREER-1
201-427-0229 (outside U.S.)
FAX: 201-427-2037

Note: This publication is designed to provide accurate and authoritative information in regard to the subject matter covered. It is sold with the understanding that neither the author nor the publisher is engaged in rendering legal, accounting or other professional service. If legal advice or other expert assistance is required, the services of a competent professional person should be sought.

THE SMART WOMAN'S GUIDE TO STARTING A BUSINESS

ISBN 1-56414-129-2, $14.95

Cover design by Dean Johnson Design, Inc.

Printed in the U.S.A. by Book-mart Press

To order this title by mail, please include price as noted above, $2.50 handling per order and $1.00 for each book ordered. Send to: Career Press, Inc., 180 Fifth Ave., P.O. Box 34, Hawthorne, NJ 07507

Or call toll-free 1-800-CAREER-1 (Canada: 201-427-0229) to order using VISA or MasterCard, or for further information on books from Career Press.

Library of Congress Cataloging-in-Publication Data

Montgomery, Vickie, 1956-
    The smart woman's guide to starting a business / by Vickie Montgomery.
        p. cm.
    Includes index.
    ISBN 1-56414-129-2 : $14.95
    1. New business enterprises. 2. Women-owned business enterprises-
-Management. I. Title.
HD62.5.M665 1994
658.1'1'082--dc20

94-2667
CI

Dedication

This book is dedicated to all the women who have been role models in my life, especially my mom, whose entrepreneurial spirit was the greatest inspiration of all.

Acknowledgments

As with any book, I could not have done it without the help and encouragement of many other people. First of all, my agent, Mike Snell, was wonderful. He believed in me and provided great support and patience as I learned the art of writing a proposal. It was a book by itself. It never would have happened without his direction and ideas. And to Betsy Sheldon and Lois Sherman, my editors, who provided guidance and suggestions as the manuscript began to take on a life of its own, I want to say thank you.

A special thank you needs to go to India, Bonnie and Phil for reading my manuscript and providing great insight and suggestions. I asked three of the busiest people I know if they would provide input and they kindly obliged. I am grateful that they did, because they each brought a different perspective to my presentation.

As with any research endeavor, I was met with ready assistance by most and with ambivalence by a few. Many of my conversations were with employees of various government agencies. While any source is as strong as the individual you are in contact with, I have found several agencies to be consistently excellent servants to the public. First, the Nashville office of the Small Business Administration (SBA) has been extremely accessible and helpful through many stages of my research. In particular, I want to thank Saundra Jackson, the Women's Business Ownership and Minority Business Owners Coordinator for the state of Tennessee. I also had numerous professional dealings with the Atlanta regional office in my banking days and found them to be just as helpful. Another agency, the Internal Revenue Service, continues to be excellent. Don't be alarmed. They really are an entrepreneur's friend.

Table of contents

Introduction
How this book can help you

This book is for every female who is considering starting or has started her own business. Whether you want to start part-time or full-time, at home or away, and in whatever industry you choose, the information shared in these pages can benefit you.

Did you know that women-owned businesses are starting at more than double the rate of men-owned businesses? Currently, women-owned businesses account for one-third of all businesses in the United States and are projected to total half of all businesses by the turn of the century. In addition, research has found that women-owned businesses are succeeding at a much stronger rate than all businesses combined, 75 percent compared to 20 percent.

Women are eager to fill themselves with the knowledge it takes to succeed in their own businesses. When I first began teaching small business courses, I realized that the majority of my students were female. The questions these women asked were very different from those of male entrepreneurs. Their objectives were more conservative. Their styles more supportive, less competitive. They shared their knowledge. They shared their fears. Family always came up as a major concern. From these experiences, I realized that women wanted a book that would provide information,

support and advice. As a female business owner, this is something I personally understand. And it's what I set out to do.

Today, the term "woman's work" can apply to any industry, any business and any job that a woman wishes to undertake. We do have choices. *The Smart Woman's Guide to Starting a Business* is designed to help you through the maze of options, providing specific tools for starting a business and managing the operations as well as juggling career and family demands. This book is not intended to be a substitute for seeking qualified professional help. Every woman business owner should surround herself with the most trustworthy, honest and knowledgeable advisers she can afford. Integrity should not (nor does it have to) be compromised.

My hope is that you will continue to use this book for many years. First I recommend reading it in its entirety. Later, as your business grows, you may find it helpful to refer to specific chapters that concern you. Start building your personal library of resource books. In addition, I hope you will share this book with a friend. As you advise new women entering these entrepreneurial ranks, share your lessons, your knowledge and your support.

The Smart Woman's Guide to Starting a Business is divided into two sections.

The first section (Chapters 1 through 9) addresses the startup phase of your business. The second section (Chapters 10 through 16) looks at operational and managerial concerns for small businesses.

Chapter 1 introduces statistics concerning women as entrepreneurs, as a work force and as a strong economic factor. The reasons for entering the entrepreneurial ranks are as varied as the women they represent. Success and failure are both discussed, as is the individualization of goals and objectives. The second chapter provides nine interviews with successful female entrepreneurs. Their businesses range from home day-care operator to retailer, from freelancer to builder. Their stories represent a wide variety of skills, reasons for starting a business and styles of leadership. I want to thank each of these women for sharing their story with me, for without these stories this book would have been missing an important ingredient.

The next few chapters show the steps necessary for deciding on, organizing and starting a business. Chapter 3 discusses how to identify successful entrepreneurial traits in others and how to take inventory of your own abilities. This chapter includes several discovery exercises as well as an "Entrepreneurial Test." Experience, education and formal training are identified as key ingredients for all entrepreneurs.

Starting a business from scratch is only one alternative. Chapter 4 discusses options of home-based opportunities, franchising and buying an existing business. Each choice is evaluated with regard to its advantages, disadvantages and costs. Chapter 5 outlines the nature of planning and presents both nonwritten and written business planning steps. Also included in this chapter is a detailed outline of topics that you might incorporate when formulating a business plan.

While the majority of women-owned businesses are sole proprietorships, that may not be right for you. Chapter 6 presents the three common forms of organization (sole proprietorship, partnership and corporation) and addresses costs and benefits under each style. Because of the importance of expert advice in this decision, this chapter also suggests how to find these advisers and provides questions to ask and boundaries to establish. Open, honest communication is a must.

Chapters 7, 8 and 9 discuss some of the statistical aspects of business. Chapter 7 identifies various marketing concepts, including market research and analysis. Both are critical elements in business planning. This chapter provides a listing of numerous sources from which to gather information. It also evaluates criteria for choosing a location, establishing a pricing policy, the effect of competition on your business and how to sell your product. Creating and maintaining your public image is also discussed, along with how to market yourself and your company effectively.

Starting a business often requires a capital investment. Chapter 8 assesses a business owner's need for capital and lists a variety of sources available for startup financing, including new SBA programs designed specifically to benefit and assist women. Establishing and maintaining good credit is emphasized along with the five Cs of lending: character, credit, capacity, collateral and credentials.

The next chapter is one of the most important. It deals with the numbers. Chapter 9 looks at the financial statements businesses generate and discusses how to interpret the data and identify trends. This chapter talks about cash flow analysis, budgeting and basic book-keeping. Both service and retail financial statements are presented at the end of the chapter, as examples.

The second section of the book concentrates on managing and growing your business. Chapter 10 focuses on the growing concerns of small business owners. Growing a business can be achieved through several different avenues, depending on markets and product life cycles. This chapter looks at growth through establishing credit policies and accepting credit card sales and checks, as well as at the impact computers may have on both productivity and expenses. Establishing a good relationship with your banker can go a long way towards meeting future (or current) financial needs, as Chapter 11 explains. Understanding what bankers expect from customers and realizing that different banks are looking for different customers can help you find a workable solution.

Networking is a characteristic of successful women business owners. The next chapter looks at guidelines for effective networking that gets results. Opportunities for networking include your circle of friends, creating a board of advisers, business associates, involvement in outside activities and having mentors. Networking can help small businesses in a variety of areas. Etiquette and the art of conversation are also discussed, especially given their impact on networking.

Another concern for managing and growing a business centers on employees. Chapter 13 looks at interviewing and hiring and firing practices, including legal requirements. Management styles influence business success. Most women operate with an inclusive style of leadership, sharing and encouraging others along the way. Rewarding employees is the foundation for building a cohesive, fun workplace. This chapter will help you see how to reward employees in the ways that matter to them.

Chapter 14 looks at the abundance of laws that complicate the operation of businesses. Included in this discussion are fair labor laws, regulations of the EEOC, OSHA and ERISA, as well as worker's compensation and many more. In addition, a checklist for keeping business records is presented. A list of free IRS publications is provided at the end of this chapter. These publications are excellent resource guides for business owners.

Starting a business today also means planning for your retirement. Chapter 15 presents a variety of retirement plans available for small business owners, including those specifically designed for self-employed individuals. It looks at how to calculate the amount you will need to live on during retirement. Given that women are living longer, retirement planning needs to be a part of every female owner's business plan. Estate planning and wills are an important focus.

And, finally, Chapter 16 ties it all together as we balance our work and home lives. Starting a business often brings about additional tension and stress. We have to look at how our life affects those we love. This chapter discusses the need for strong, open communication within the family. It addresses the additional pressures on those couples starting a business together (and the additional rewards). Finding time for ourselves is critical to this equation. The chapter provides guidelines for improving time management and reducing stress to better help us achieve our goals in life, at work and at home.

Best of luck to you in your professional business endeavor. May it be everything you hoped for—and more.

Keep your enthusiasm and sense of humor close at hand. Both can see you over many hurdles. My personal wish for you is that you are able to find the enjoyment and satisfaction in your business that I have found in mine.

Chapter 1

Small business charm: beauty or beast?

"We need more of that innovative thinking...Remember, it is small business that created 24 million American jobs between 1980 and 1991. And it is small business that employs nearly 60 percent of all Americans."

Rieva Lesonsky
Editor-In-Chief, *Entrepreneur Magazine*

"When women are having a hard time finding employment, when their potential is not being adequately recognized or used, when there isn't too much room within an established organization to move up...then there is only one option— do it yourself."

Lourdes Miranda
Author, *Hispanic Women in the United States*

Women are starting businesses in record numbers. They are starting small and large businesses. They are starting home-based businesses as well as those away from the home. They are recreating how to do business reflective of their personalities and strengths. And they are redefining how to measure their success in terms of quality, not just quantity. Finding and maintaining balance has been at the forefront of this march. *The Smart Woman's Guide to Starting a Business* is designed to help women through the maze of business acumen, to find their personal niche and succeed on their own merits.

This book is written with today's woman in mind. It addresses situations that she may have faced, problems unique to her, and utilizes those wonderfully "feminine" qualities she possesses.

Today's woman doesn't have to hide her gender in the business world. She can celebrate her individuality and find comfort in knowing she is not alone.

Why has it taken so long for us to realize that women are natural at juggling the demands of business? Unfortunately, it's because too few role models reached those pinnacles to show us how it could be done. And many of the females who did succeed in management ranks did so by conforming to their male mentors' styles, leaving behind as "unprofessional" and "unbusiness-like" the caring and sensitivity they felt. But female managers are now accepting their unique style and slowly changing the old system. No doubt we may feel resistance. We are in the minority. Bumping against the glass ceiling has prompted many women to seek other opportunities, such as starting our own businesses, to find ways to integrate our personal styles and abilities from home into the workplace.

Many of the obstacles facing female entrepreneurs are not unique to women. And to that extent, men may gain great insight and advice from reading this book. However, it is designed specifically for women because our upbringing, our values and our life experiences have been different from those of men. That is not to imply that men do not have values or feel it is important to be actively involved with women's concerns. The fact remains, though, that domestic issues are still primarily the woman's responsibility in most homes.

Adding to this reality, we see how women are handling businesses and families today. We are integrating our demanding roles, entering nontraditional fields and succeeding in record numbers. Finally, we have the role models we so desperately were missing in the past. Now we must listen to their stories, learn from their experiences, and create new opportunities and objectives for ourselves.

At no other time in history have the mood, the support and the opportunity existed for so many women to enter the entrepreneurial ranks. We are succeeding in record numbers, in *all* business fields. "Woman's work" can now mean anything. All fields are open to us.

Faith Popcorn, author of *The Popcorn Report,* predicts that women entrepreneurs will make up the majority of small-business owners in the next decade. We have strength in numbers even now. In 1987, according to the most recent Small Business Administration statistics available, there were 4.3 million women-owned businesses, generating receipts of $476.9 billion. The National Foundation

of Women Business Owners estimates that currently there are 6.5 million women-owned businesses. Women collectively account for $37 billion in federal taxes (a 1988 figure that has surely increased since then), and another $13 billion in state and local taxes. In fact, *Megatrends for Women* cites women-owned businesses as "one of the fastest-growing segments of the U.S. economy." One-third of all businesses are presently owned by females. Women-owned businesses employ 11 million workers, which is more than all of the Fortune 500 companies combined worldwide. We are strong in number. Strong in results. Strong in economic impact. We are gaining political clout as we continue to make a difference.

Women are entering the entrepreneurial market out of both economic necessity and personal gratification. Already we are starting businesses at more than twice the rate of men. And when you consider part-time home businesses, the figure increases to as much as three to one.

While the majority of businesses women start are likely to be small and stay small, not all of them are. There are some very large, visible and competitive female-owned businesses in the United States. Yet, for those businesses that decide to remain small, small does not imply inferior quality or products. And because of this conservative approach, women are less vulnerable to wide economic downturns, which remain a major reason for the demise of many small businesses.

Women are vital to our labor force. Currently, women represent 45.1 percent of the American labor force, according to the U.S. Census Bureau. Government statistics anticipate that, entering the 21st century, women are expected to represent over half the work force and that more than 80 percent of women between the ages of 25 and 54 will be working.

In addition, the numbers reflect that the changing makeup of families has played a significant role in why women work. Today, more than at any other time in history, more families are headed by single parents. In 1970, 40 percent of U.S. households with children under the age of 18 were made up of married couples. By 1990 that number had fallen to 26 percent. In 1987, there were 2.6 million women who had never been married and were raising children under the age of 21. Yet, only 20 percent of these women were receiving child support. As recently as 1991, the total number of single parents included 11.2 million women.

Even though more women are working, approximately 25 million mothers and their children now live in poverty in the United States. Women have to work. Women want to work. Whatever the reason, it is no wonder that women are taking control of their financial and emotional destiny.

Reasons for starting a business vary from woman to woman. Some seek personal freedom; others want financial independence. Some wish for flexibility in managing a work and family lifestyle, and others desire home businesses because of inadequate childcare options. Whatever your reason may be, timing, money, security and risk continue to be significant factors in this decision. With over 1.3 million new businesses emerging in 1991 alone, according to *The Popcorn Report*, small business ownership is on the rise. With a force of nearly 1 million, women are leading this movement.

And women are having better results than their male counterparts at small business ventures. Their success ratio has been quoted as high as 75 percent compared to the historical 20 percent for all businesses. Women are more likely to succeed in small business, according to Janet Harris-Lange, former president of the National Foundation of Women Business Owners, because "women will admit their weaknesses and when they need help." Women bring a real sense of enthusiasm to the entrepreneurial table and are not afraid to ask questions. They are, in fact, less likely to let their egos get in the way. They are building community within the workplace.

Women are starting all types of businesses, from day-care centers to construction companies, from travel agencies to retail outlets, and from freelance services to high-tech businesses. Whether they are college-educated professionals or single moms (or both), they realize that they have many skills and qualities that can benefit the entrepreneurial arena. They have chosen to enter this arena with enthusiasm and determination and are breaking new ground and reaching new highs.

What is a small business?

What did Faith Popcorn mean when she said that women entrepreneurs will make up the majority of small businesses in the next decade? First, what exactly is a *small business*? The term small business is used to represent different business shapes and sizes. The concept is tossed around in the media every day without reference to its definition. Actually, you may be surprised to learn that there is little consistency in how the term is used. This lack of concrete definition creates conflicting statistics and adds to the confusion. Some definitions are based on revenues. Others on number of employees. And still others use a combination of the two, depending on the industry.

The most consistent definition I have been able to find is from the U.S. Small Business Administration (SBA). While many think of the SBA as simply a lending source, in fact they have been charged by Congress to develop the parameters for what constitutes a small business.

The SBA divides businesses into a variety of categories and then classifies the requirements for each group. The following eligibility requirements were printed in 1991 and were still in effect at the time of this publication.

Retailing: Average annual receipts may not exceed $3.5 to $13.5 million, depending on the industry. (Automobile dealers are at the high end of the scale.)

Wholesaling: Maximum number of employees may not exceed 100.

Construction: General construction average annual receipts may not exceed $9.5 to $17 million, depending on the industry.

Manufacturing: Maximum number of employees may range from 500 to 1,500, depending on the type of product manufactured.

Services: Average annual receipts may not exceed $3.5 to $14.5 million, depending on the industry.

Special trade construction: The average annual receipts may not exceed $7 million.

Agriculture: Average annual receipts range from $1 to $3.5 million, depending on the industry.

Most people are surprised that "small businesses" can, in fact, be quite large. Do not become overwhelmed, however, if you do not desire to operate a million-dollar company or manage a business with 100 employees. For women, 85 percent of all companies are sole proprietorships, operated with no employees and earning less than $20,000 annually in profits (or salary as the case may be). The majority of all small businesses operating in the United States are sole proprietorships. They are considered *microbusinesses*, employing fewer than five people, with annual revenues under $1 million.

Government procurement and minority status

The SBA definition of small business becomes the basis for government procurements under contract bids. The government is, by far, the largest purchaser of goods in the United States, spending $210.7 billion in fiscal year '91. The federal government awarded 30 percent of these bids to small businesses ($62.9 billion). Historically, small firms have won more contracts at lower dollar values. More than half of those government contracts under $25,000 were awarded to small businesses. Yet, women-owned businesses only received 1.1 percent of government contracts ($2.4 billion) for fiscal year '91.

Surprisingly, women, on the basis of gender alone, do not qualify as minorities, or to be politically correct, as "socially and economically disadvantaged" persons. The importance of this fact is that many government agencies are mandated to award a certain percentage of contracts to minorities. The Department of Defense, for example, does not recognize women as minorities. Most federal agencies do have "goals" to award some contracts to women business owners. But only the Department of Transportation has a mandate for women-owned businesses. You will find some agencies have more aggressive goals than others and strive more actively to achieve their goals. Women need to tap into this market.

The opportunities are wide open for women to participate in this process and to win. The SBA now offers programs specifically aimed at women for education and assistance for increasing their presence in gaining government contracts. The advantages of government contracts to small businesses translates directly into longevity, resistance to economic downturns and increased profitability.

Advantages of small businesses for women

Women are finding many advantages to operating a small company, rather than working for (or running) a large business. Women are bringing a new management culture to the companies they own. Women's style is more nurturing. They operate by building teams. By tapping into their feminine qualities, women business owners are becoming closer to their customers, staying in touch with customer needs, and responding quickly to changing market conditions.

Succeeding in small business means being able to prioritize, integrate and juggle. And these are traits typically associated with what used to be termed "woman's work." Women have been prioritizing, integrating and juggling for years. It is no wonder then that women are succeeding at a higher rate than their male counterparts.

Small business allows women the opportunity to create a business environment more suitable for them. Women have a need to build, not conquer. Building community internally as well as participating in the neighborhood is important to women business owners. It means more than locating a business in the neighborhood. It means providing products and

services designed to meet the neighborhood's needs. It means reaching out and being a part of the community. And it means involving the welfare of the community in business decisions.

Women have been forced to make quick decisions in the home for years. They have the ability to adapt to the situation. In small business, quicker management decisions correlate to more flexibility in the products and services offered and allow the business to respond to changing market conditions faster. Market shares are often decided by who gets there first. Time is of the essence, especially when new products are being introduced. And women are learning to respond to market conditions in a decisive and timely manner.

Women are advocating a no-nonsense approach to business dealings. Women want enough information to make fast and informed decisions. A faster decision-making process creates less red tape to unravel, fewer hurdles to jump over and, therefore, a faster response time to changing conditions. Market conditions *are* constantly changing. To ignore this fact is business suicide.

Women play a different game when it comes to sharing information. They gladly share what they know and expect others to share also. The development of strong networks can go a long way in creating the channels and opportunities for shared information.

Small business: an answer to work-home conflicts

American business has been very slow to respond to the changing dynamics of work and family life. It has been slow to offer the support and understanding to provide women with sufficient opportunities to grow. Women have made significant personal sacrifices, worked hard, yet still have not reached true integration in the workplace. Nor can they reasonably expect to until there is equality on the home front.

Despite attempts by many employers to improve the quality of work life for families, women continue to bear the brunt of this dilemma. Quality childcare is still an issue for many working mothers, followed by guilt. Careers and children do not have to be destined for a collision course. Not when the two are openly integrated.

The strain of trying to fulfill multiple roles is one few male entrepreneurs have experienced. According to Louis Rukeyser's *Business Almanac*, "only one-third of all women who work full-time hire household help....Only about 14 percent of all husbands do half the housework—75 percent of married women have to do over three-quarters of the work." Women continue to pull double-duty by working full-time at work and at home. Having a two-income family may not make matters any easier.

This dichotomy of work and family may be at the very heart of why women must create opportunities that do not clash, but that combine their lifestyles. Women no longer want to make an either/or decision concerning work and family issues. Family remains the top priority. But it does not have to come at the expense of a career. Women are now creating flexible job opportunities that balance their multiple roles.

In fact, accepting and valuing our total lives actually enhances our business culture. And women-owned businesses work hard at including the whole family in their companies. They realize customers have families. Employees have families. Vendors have families. And being able to recognize and appreciate individuals and their families creates a happier and healthier work environment. Everyone comes out a winner.

The female style of leadership and support, which many women have found missing from the corporate world, can often be found in women-owned organizations. Women are entering the entrepreneurial ranks without preconceived notions and confining boundaries. Women are building businesses that are more humanistic and less hierarchical in nature. They frequently eliminate the policy and procedural rhetoric found in big businesses and opt instead for an inclusive environment built on mutual respect and trust. This kinder, gentler style has not gone unnoticed. As Tom Peters suggests (in his book, *In Search of Excellence*), those who wish to stay employed should study women's ways of leadership.

Many women have been stopped by the glass ceiling. Opportunities for advancement didn't exist for women because they didn't conform to the man's world. Now women are taking their experiences from the corporate world and building their own personal empires. Being stopped by the glass ceiling may have been a blessing in disguise. Now we are finding the courage to accept the risk and step out on our own.

The economic impact

Women make an economic difference. The United States economy is dependent on small businesses for new products and services, for employment and for production. Without small businesses, our total economy would disintegrate rather quickly.

The U.S. has changed from an industrial nation to an information society as it joins forces with the global economy. Since we have become increasingly reliant on global markets, the climate is more conducive for new small business opportunities to emerge. These new opportunities are very encouraging to the many women considering opening a business.

Small businesses account for over 99 percent of *all* businesses in this country, according to the SBA. In addition, they contribute 57.3 percent of our total employment, produce nearly 40 percent of the U.S. gross domestic product and represent 53.5 percent of total sales. Most new ideas and product innovations come from new and small ventures. Substantial evidence suggests that well over 60 percent of all new jobs created in the U.S. in the past 25 years were created by small businesses It is an understatement to say our economy is dependent on small businesses. In fact, our economy is based on small businesses. Small businesses are here to stay. They continue to play significant roles in our lives. And women are a thriving force in all of these statistics.

Since women are starting small businesses at between two and three times the rate of men, their economic impact is magnified. Currently women represent over one-third of all small businesses. Projections indicate that, given the current rate of growth, women-owned businesses will account for half of all small businesses by the turn of the century. Women must understand the power they hold. They must also accept the responsibility that accompanies this power. All while they continue pursuing their dreams.

Women have concentrated primarily in service sectors because of the low cost and ease of entry. The service industry represents 38.7 percent of women-owned businesses, followed closely by wholesale and retail trades and finance-related businesses. Service businesses generally can be started with lower capital investments (which remains a limitation for women), have fewer assets (a factor of financing), can often be started at home (where the majority of women-owned businesses are located) and are less cumbersome to enter.

On the other hand, retail and wholesale trade businesses are often the outgrowth of women's work experience. According to *The State of Small Business: 1993 Report to the President*, 59 percent of women business owners had at least six years of employment experience. Ironically though, the fastest growing sector for new women-owned businesses is in the traditionally male-dominant industries of mining, construction and manufacturing. These pioneers of nontraditional fields are making a strong impact. Today we see all markets opening for women if they are willing to pursue their ambitions.

According to government statistics, women-owned businesses garnered only 4.5 percent of total business receipts in 1987. Because women are concentrating in less capital-intensive businesses, revenues have remained compressed. In a government survey of 100,000 small businesses, women-owned firms had average annual receipts of $67,595, compared to total average receipts of $145,654. Women are operating smaller businesses and advocating a much more controlled growth pattern. Many attribute their higher success ratios to these formulas. It's obviously working.

The entrepreneurial spirit

The numbers show that women have definitely been captured by the entrepreneurial spirit. Whether affected by corporate downsizing, glass-ceiling limitations or seeking personal identity, women are plunging forward with their heads held high and accepting the challenges and risks of owning their own business.

Big business has helped fuel this growth in the U.S. With the increase in mergers, acquisitions, corporate downsizing and reorganization, employees are looking to take control of their job futures. The past decade resulted in 30,000 corporate mergers, eliminating five million industrial jobs and more than 500,000 management positions. And the news continues to be grim concerning more mergers and layoffs. The number of unemployed female managers has increased steadily since 1989. In 1992, the Bureau of Labor Statistics reported that 463,000 managerial and professional women were out of work. Women are finding limited re-employment opportunities, forcing them to create their own opportunities, often through self-employment.

The reasons for entering the entrepreneurial ranks vary from woman to woman. Some women feel forced into self-employment because of changing job skills or a tightening economy, while others choose independence for personal and financial considerations. And still others want to prove to themselves (or others) that they can do it alone and succeed. Each woman has her unique reasons for wanting to be an entrepreneur. Each is equally valid and important.

Avon Corporation conducted a national survey of successful women entrepreneurs in 1990 to determine why women were starting businesses. Leading the list was happiness/self-fulfillment (38 percent), followed by achievement/challenge (30 percent); helping others was next (20 percent), while twelve percent of the respondents named sales growth/profits. Although not a representative sampling, these results do reiterate that many women are entering the entrepreneurial ranks for personal gratification.

Women's motives for self-employment are often very different from men's. This has meant establishing new methods for measuring success: methods that allow for flexibility and personal satisfaction to be measured and that do not compare women's success to that of men's, or even other women's. Instead, they measure personal expectations against personal achievement.

You must decide why you want to be in business. You must define your personal expectations. Take time to identify your goals, those things that are important to you. And then measure your ability to achieve your goals. Believing in yourself is not enough; you must also be willing to accept the responsibility of being an entrepreneur.

The risk of small business

Whatever your reason for wanting to become an entrepreneur, the result is the same. Now you have become a risk-taker. Carefully evaluate all aspects of this risk before taking the plunge. Talk with others, especially those who will be affected by your decisions. Include family and friends in this process. Listen to their concerns and be willing to compromise. Without their support and encouragement, being in business for yourself becomes even more challenging.

What exactly is the risk of starting a business? Ultimately, it may not survive. You may be forced or you may choose to stop operating. Can you accept that outcome? When starting a new business, the most essential questions to ask are: What do I have to lose? And, am I willing to lose it? The answer is to never gamble more than you are willing to lose.

Business closures continue to increase annually. Businesses close for a variety of reasons. Under-capitalization remains a common pitfall. Lack of experience and incompetent leadership can also be factors. Or perhaps the business is in a bad location. And there's always the economy. Most businesses close for a combination of reasons. They include things that could have been avoided—and things that couldn't have been foreseen. Women's businesses are no different in facing these hurdles.

Perhaps the gravest risk is that of trying to do too much. Avoid the Superwoman syndrome. Avoid trying to be all things to all people. Prioritize. Accept your limitations. And proceed at your own pace. Under your own terms.

Closing a business doesn't mean failure

Society has placed predetermined values and expectations on what we should and shouldn't do. Society has also established rules for measuring our successes and failures in business. And, as women, we may feel and show our emotions more visibly, especially over a business closure. Given that society often equates closing a business to personal failure, we must be armed to fight this psychological battle if it occurs.

Closing a business doesn't mean we have failed. Instead we need to look for the lessons learned and appreciate our courage to take risk. It won't be easy. Mistakes will be made along the way. They always are. I know I've had more than my share. But, what's important is to be resilient and proud of each step you have taken.

Does this sound impossible? It isn't. Not if you take it in stride. Begin by following the passion in your heart and trusting your judgment. Don't let others discourage you, for they will try. And always believe in what you are doing.

Success doesn't have to be measured in terms of status or money. Success can be gained, instead, by personal satisfaction, more family time or flexible hours. It can be measured by what is important to you.

If it sounds too good to be true: the hype factor

Women have been targeted as victims in the growing industry of business scams. Too many women (and men) fall prey to scams masquerading as business opportunities. Entrepreneurs are targets for many get-rich-quick schemes. You know the stories; the ones that show someone, like you or me, who invested very little money into an operation, had virtually no training or special skills and made lots and lots of money almost overnight. The goal of businesses advertising these come-ons is *not* to provide you with a service. They are in the business of selling their product (a book, tape, club membership, etc.). That's how they make money. And that's the bottom line. Sometimes it seems as though the hottest business of the decade is the business of selling business opportunities.

The saying "If it sounds too good to be true, then it probably is," is a golden rule of common sense for entrepreneurs.

Nothing takes the place of doing the research yourself. It's your money, your time, and your name that is on the line. So *you* are the one who needs to research all markets completely. Be careful. Be thorough. Be practical. Proceed cautiously and with a little skepticism. Don't buy into the "get rich quick and easy" school of "send me your hard-earned money and you too can make millions!" Your time and money are better spent on developing your own ideas.

Reaching for the pot of gold

There is a lot required of us as entrepreneurs. The road is bumpy and the ride often treacherous, but the rewards are immeasurable. There is a certain satisfaction and pride in being on your own that cannot be gained in any other situation.

Female entrepreneurs are in search of their pot of gold. Each pot is made up of unique objectives and goals. No two are alike. What works for one woman may not work for another. You must decide what matters most to you. For some it may be fame and fortune. For others it might be personal satisfaction and pride. And still others are driven by

altruistic motives of doing "good" for all humankind, the ecology or perhaps future generations. Whatever makes up your personal pot of gold, remember to keep yourself focused toward its achievement.

Be ready for the ride. Do your homework first; know the facts. And then set reasonable expectations and time frames for achieving results. The two most important things for potential entrepreneurs to remember are: the great possibility of failure (business is inherently risky) and the importance of collecting as much pertinent data as possible before proceeding with your idea (although the learning never stops). Proceed carefully, cautiously and, above all else, enthusiastically.

Don't let the little things get you down. And never let the spirit die!

Chapter 2

Her story: entrepreneurs sharing their triumphs

"Stories are medicine. They have such power; they do not require that we do, be, act anything—we need only listen."

Clarissa Pinkola Estes, Ph.D.
Women Who Run with the Wolves

Today's role models

We now have role models, women who are setting new standards in all fields. And they are willing to share their experiences. We must take the time to listen to their stories and learn from their past. The results will lead to easier roads to travel for all of us.

The following stories are representative of today's female entrepreneurs. Their backgrounds are varied. Each has different skills and job experiences. Each has a unique and special story to tell. These business owners include married, divorced and single women. They represent retail, service, construction, home-based and freelance types of industries. They range in age from their 20s to their 50s. These are very special women who have triumphed in their personal satisfaction. I hope these stories are as meaningful to you as they have been for me.

These stories are not fictitious composites, but are from everyday entrepreneurs. All but one ("Kathy Peters") allowed her name to be used. I respect her decision for privacy but her story is still shared and her voice still heard.

Jenny Moss
Owner, Quilters Attic
Started April 1987

"Be sure to have enough money when you start. It takes twice what you think it will to start and operate. Even though I had been told that, I never really knew how true it was until I opened my shop."

Jenny enjoyed needlework as a hobby. Her creativity evolved into other needlecrafts and eventually led her to quilting. In order to fulfill her dream, she had to travel over 100 miles to take quilting lessons. Her instructor was a well-known quilter who owned a home quilt shop. Jenny learned that quilters relied on quality fabrics for their creations. She didn't know of any local fabric stores that provided the range or quality of cotton fabrics needed, so she traveled great distances to get quality material to quilt. Jenny's love of quilting flourished through her many new quilting friends and many completed projects. It happened that a few years later the instructor decided to close her shop and liquidate her inventory because her teaching schedule had become so demanding. What a perfect opportunity to make a dream become a reality, Jenny thought. With the encouragement of fellow quilters, she bought the liquidated inventory and started a home-based quilt fabric shop.

Locating at home provides a very cozy atmosphere that quilters appreciate. Quilting is considered an art form passed down from generation to generation. Creating a comfortable surrounding enhances the very nature of this idea.

Jenny brought excellent and established business skills with her into this endeavor. She had grown up in retail. Her father owned a grocery store and later a department store. Jenny had previously operated a beauty shop for several years and had also worked as a bookkeeper in her husband's business. She understood what was involved in the startup operation and what was required to keep a business going.

Over the years, Jenny has not taken profits out of her business. Instead, she has continued to reinvest her profits into the business and build up inventory. Jenny's previous business experience in other industries provides good advice for all business owners—whether or not you have employees, whether or not inventory is involved—there are a lot of costs associated with the operation of a small business. You are faced with expenses ranging from licensing to taxes, from accounting and legal fees to advertising budgets, and from association memberships to trade publications, not to mention overhead costs and deposit requirements.

Jenny's suggestion of doubling your expense figure is offered supportively from her own experience. She realizes her business could not have grown to what it is today if she had had to rely on her business to financially support her. Fortunately, she didn't need to. That is

an important consideration when deciding what business to begin.

Being at home allowed Jenny to spend more time with her youngest child. As her daughter entered her teenage years and began to spend less time at home, Jenny began to devote more time to her business. It was a perfect way to avoid the empty-nest syndrome.

As with many startup operations, her business grew slowly. She began by offering only fabrics and located her shop in an empty room above the garage. Through word-of-mouth advertising, the business grew and she expanded her operation. In seven years she has outgrown several rooms and today uses the entire triple garage to sell fabrics and other quilting supplies, including books, patterns and threads. The room above the garage has become the classroom, since offering quilting lessons is an excellent way to gain and retain customers.

Jenny reflects on her accomplishments with pride and satisfaction that she did it by herself. "It really has helped build my self-esteem," she says. "Not that it was an easy road to travel. It required a lot of time and energy." The downside to operating at home, she observes, is that sometimes it can be difficult to get away. Still, she insists she wouldn't change a thing.

Sheila Goode
Owner, Sheila Goode Studios
Started operating 1992

"My advice for women is what I tell my daughter. I want her to know she can be her own person; for her to cherish her own identity and know she has the right to be an individual."

At age 38, Sheila decided it was time to find her own identity. As a wife and mother, she felt others were defining her role. She needed to do something that would allow her to stand alone and be proud of her accomplishments. She wanted to say, "I did it by myself. It's all mine."

A strong work ethic was ingrained. Her first job, at age 14, was giving baton lessons. Commitment and drive are reflected throughout her life, including her commitment to finding happiness and a drive to do whatever it takes. In searching for her special niche, though, Sheila looked at hobbies and outside interests for possibilities. She had strong business, marketing and finance talents, but fell short when it came to work experience in areas that excited her.

As Sheila took personal inventory, she decided that photography was an area she would like to pursue. She was a hobby photographer and had never taken any professional classes. Her first step was finding out about classes, teachers and programs. Next, she enrolled in an 18-month program that allowed her to investigate the field more thoroughly to determine if this was really where her interests and talents were. As the program developed, Sheila recalls how surprised she was to learn that photography was so specialized. As she became more proficient, her field of expertise began to narrow to black-and-white portrait shots. She had a natural eye for portraits. In fact, an instructor approached Sheila with a business partnership proposition, which she eagerly accepted.

After three years, she had outgrown the partnership, gained excellent experience, had a small following and was ready to step out on her own. Her former instructor gave her his blessing. They continue to do contract jobs together. But the time was right for Sheila to move on.

Sheila wanted to fill a special niche with her artistic black-and-white portraits. She determined that location was essential to creating this image within such a specialized market. She needed to maintain a strong presence since the target market was small. When the perfect location became available, it was the moment of truth. Sheila signed a three-year lease. She was finally in business by herself. It had taken over four years. But now it was a dream come true. It was hers, and hers alone, to make or break.

Sheila's background in marketing and accounting have been key to her success as an entrepreneur. To create name recognition, she began a six-month selective marketing campaign, offering free portraits in exchange for promotion of her work and studio. The second plan involved sending postcards of her work to parents of children in local private schools. From these campaigns, Sheila began to develop the clientele base she was targeting.

She operates with a written business plan that she reviews and updates frequently. She cautions new business owners not to spend profits too soon, since the business might not break even the next month. Her business continues to increase, thanks primarily to referrals. Sheila knows the importance that word-of-mouth advertising plays in her business success.

Family remains a priority to Sheila, and she admits she has turned down business because there isn't enough time to do it all. "I make time for my family. I work at creating a balance in my life. My goals have changed since I was younger," Sheila reflects. "I'm still competitive and driven, but now I take time to enjoy the fruits of my labor."

Sandra Cartwright Morris
Owner, Cartwright Morris and
**   Associates**
Search & Recruitment Agency
Started 1987

"I knew I needed a business that offered unlimited earning potential."

As a single mom, Sandra was forced to find a career that offered the financial security necessary to raise three teen-agers and pay for college tuitions. Sandra's experience was centered on being a wife, mother and homemaker. Before she entered the job market, her first step was to evaluate her skills. She discovered her strengths were in orga-nization and people skills. Next she had to define her career objectives, which were to create a work environment that she had control over, that offered flexi-bility in hours and that had unlimited earnings potential.

Sandra knew she wanted to work for herself and that self-employment pro-vided the avenue for achieving her objectives. The next step involved iden-tifying those industries best suited to her skills and goals. After researching numerous possibilities and trends, Sandra narrowed the field to four poten-tial businesses: real estate, recruiting, stock brokering and insurance. Since each industry was commission-based, each provided the unlimited earning potential she was seeking.

Additional research revealed the ease of entry, startup costs, growth, as well as training, licensing and time necessary to gain experience. Sandra interviewed busi-ness owners and employees within these fields to determine the best choice for her. All but one of these interviews produced a job offer. This process helped Sandra make her decision—to start a search and recruitment firm. Since she lacked the actual business experience, Sandra knew

that working in the industry to gain ex-perience was an absolute necessity. Part of her employment contract included a noncompete agreement for customers, so Sandra realized from the start she was learning skills and not building a clientele base to move with her.

After only one year of experience Sandra felt she was ready to start her own business. She had learned the art of cold-calling, finding and following leads, customer service, selling, closing a sale, and the hard work and determination necessary to pull it all together. Sandra took out an equity loan on her house to capitalize her business. While she could have started the business from her home, she decided that working at home wasn't right for her. Instead, she wanted the interaction of others. She needed to "go to work." Sandra reminds entrepre-neurs of the importance of knowing your own limitations and work motivations.

The business has grown significantly since its inception. Each year revenues have surpassed the previous year's, despite the recession and declining in-dustry trends. Last year Sandra had an 80 percent increase in revenues and net-ted income in the six figures (for the third straight year). She attributes this growth to her loyal customers, who place confidence in her ability to provide an excellent service at a reasonable price.

She stresses the importance of being honest and straightforward with cus-tomers. Being a wife, mother and home-maker taught her how to be a good lis-tener and to juggle multiple tasks. In the beginning, she couldn't afford to turn down any potential business. But, Sandra states that it is important to be able to know when to say no to cus-tomers, because it's not always in your best interest to accept every job. Sometimes jobs can be unprofitable.

Other times they can cost you in terms of your reputation.

Finally, Sandra's personal goals have changed as her needs have changed and her children have grown. She now is planning aggressively for her retirement. "That's what I'm working for today," she announces with pride. She wants to be "successful enough in business to invest a high amount in a retirement account. That's what I'm really working toward. And if I can sell my business down the road, then that's just a plus."

Sally Cheney
Partner, AAA Sewing & Vacuum
Started June 1, 1987

"Stay focused on your goals, and your means will be easy to see."

Sally has a marriage-work partnership. The Cheneys' business has grown to two local retail locations. The growth has not always been controlled or planned. They opened initially on a shoestring, with $5,000 in inventory. Profits were carefully reinvested, and the store began to grow. Their first and primary shop began showing a profit after its second year of operation. "Customers were very patient in the early years," Sally recalls, "offering advice and suggestions on new items to carry. It wasn't always feasible, but we listened. We kept centered on what was financially practical and in our plans. Our customers grew with us."

Then, during their third year came the good news—and the bad. A competitor was forced to close (the good news) but the suppliers wanted to keep the location open (unfortunately). AAA was offered the other store location. Sally recalls how difficult it was for them to make the decision to purchase the second site; they felt they had to do it to stave off competition.

What they failed to realize, however, was that their customers expected the new location to be a mirror image of their first store, which had grown to $40,000 in inventory by then. They could no longer start on a shoestring and expand slowly as profits allowed. The $20,000 inventory investment for the new store seemed scant by comparison. The new store became a cash burden to the main store and limited its growth.

Fortunately, as distributors for several different lines of sewing machines and vacuum cleaners, they had developed strong relationships with their suppliers. Their open communications and past track record prompted several major suppliers to offer favorable terms to help with their cash flow. The larger investment in inventory meant greater sales were necessary to reach the break-even point. After its second year of operation, the new location began to show a profit. Since then sales have continued to increase at both stores.

Word-of-mouth advertising has been one of the most effective marketing tools for AAA. Mailing quarterly newsletters and frequently appearing on a local noon television talk show adds to the company's name recognition and credibility. Customer service remains a top priority because happy customers refer friends. "Customer relations and goodwill are very important. They can make a business successful," says Sally. And thanks to a loyal and willing staff, Sally feels they have been able to keep customers satisfied.

Sally enjoys working with her spouse, but says that without a strong marriage it could never have worked. She stresses they each have very specific responsibilities within the company. The venture began with a mutual trust and open communication, something other partnerships must develop over time. Sally and her husband are extremely supportive of each other. No one is jealous of the time spent at the business. Both keep long hours. Neither partner feels they have a spouse competing with the company for time and attention. Instead, they have a shared vision and dedication to the business, which is a must for marriage-work partnerships to succeed.

Sally learned the business while working for a similar company on the West Coast. The experience and personal advice gained provided critical insight, especially during the initial stages of operation. Sally recommends finding an industry mentor whenever possible. Her long-term goal is to build a very strong and successful business and sell it to an interested (and trained) employee. Then she hopes to enjoy those golden retirement years. Sally's positive outlook keeps her going forward. She says, "I never think about failure; it isn't a choice." She just figures out how to make it work.

Helen Burrus
**Owner, Burrus Suburban House, Inc.
July 1984 - March 1991
Freelance photographer since 1991**

"I expected to succeed, and I didn't look seriously at failure."

Helen began her retail gift and specialty shop in July 1984. She gained strong experience from running a similar family retail business, but was eventually ready to venture out on her own. Location plays a major role, especially in retail operations, so she carefully chose a location after reviewing very promising statistics about the neighborhood and sales potential. She had done her homework and the demographics looked

encouraging, at least on paper. Those numbers were a deciding factor in her decision to open where she did.

When the sales didn't materialize, it was the beginning of a long, hard battle. Helen hadn't fully realized the strong competition facing small retailers—primarily from large discount chains. National statistics were actually encouraging specialty shop owners to open more locations. But it was too late for many industries. And complicating the situation further was a changing consumer—a consumer more informed, more apt to price-compare and no longer loyal to one store. Helen worked hard and created a refreshing and appealing store display, receiving frequent compliments from shoppers and staff. Unfortunately, their appreciation didn't translate into additional revenues.

Helen started her business, like many other entrepreneurs, never planning to fail. After four trying years, she finally saw a profit. The future looked promising. But then came the unexpected. First, there were two consecutive months of inclement weather, translating into low sales during the Christmas season, which traditionally represented one-third of her annual receipts. Then began the recession, and sales remained low, far below break-even. Helen called a meeting of friends and advisers to help redirect the business, salvage her investment and get things back on a positive track. Their consensus, however, was to liquidate inventory and close the operation. Helen was in shock.

Helen recalls this period in her life as one with great emotional pain and loneliness. Her image is vivid as she describes a dog that has fallen into a rapidly moving river, but who fortunately lands on a log. The log is the safety net, keeping the dog from drowning. Yet still the log is moving, out of control, down the river, the victim never knowing what's ahead, or where or when it would stop. Her life was out of control. It was moving swiftly down that river, and she wasn't sure when things would settle down. But they did.

Helen learned a great deal from this experience. She remains her own boss and now operates a successful freelance photography business. Helen has become more cautious and calculated in her risk-taking because of her experience. She knows the downside of taking on high risk. She realizes that uncontrollable events do play a major part in a company's success.

Her retail experience allowed her to develop many qualities that she has integrated into her service business. First, she appreciates the importance of customer relations, understanding customers' wants and expectations. She produces a quality product at a very reasonable price and stays competitive.

Marketing is another area where Helen's previous experience is valuable. While not officially adopting a marketing plan, Helen actively promotes her name and services. She donates many hours of her time and talent to various groups and organizations in exchange for recognition and the chance to build networks. Money couldn't buy the publicity she receives, not to mention the referral business she gains. While her motives are not profit-driven, the results have been very positive. Helen's photography business continues to grow and prosper.

Brenda Wilson
Home day care
Started 1974

"I only wish it hadn't taken me ten years to learn what I now know."

Brenda has operated a home day-care business for 19 years. After the birth of her first child, she and her husband agreed that she would stay home. They agreed it was important for one parent to be at home, and it was easier for Brenda to quit her job. However, a second income was essential to maintain their current lifestyle. Brenda reviewed their financial situation carefully and realized that by staying home she saved money on work clothes, gas, food, car, meals and child care. Any money she made from day care was a big help to the family budget. She didn't need to replace her salary dollar for dollar to show a net gain. The business was started with one child, and within a few years she was keeping six preschool children.

Her two children have enjoyed growing up around other children. And they help whenever they can. Brenda established the primary ground rule that her children's bedrooms were off-limits to the day-care children. She said her children never felt invaded or ignored by having a working mom at home all the time. Nor were they embarrassed. And she was able to enjoy flexible hours, so she could be available when her children needed her. Fortunately, Brenda had several other day-care moms in her subdivision who could swap hours if she needed to change her schedule for doctor's appointments, school meetings or band functions.

Looking back, Brenda refers to the first ten years as her "trial and error" period. She didn't see herself as a professional; nor did she treat her business as a professional operation. But she does now. Networking with other day-care operators and joining an industry association taught Brenda about pricing, writing contracts, paid holidays and ultimately how to build self-esteem.

Brenda started small and grew slowly. Now that her second child has graduated from high school, her reasons for remaining at home have changed. She realizes there's nothing she could do that gives her as much freedom and flexibility, pays as well and provides the personal satisfaction. Her only regret is that it took 10 years to learn!

Kathy Peters, CPA,
Freelance tax consultant
Started operating 1993

"Don't skimp on resources; your time is much more valuable. I knew the importance of computers for my business, but I wish I had spent a little more on the hardware. Now I see the difference."

Kathy started her career with a Big Six accounting firm. "There is no substitute for what I learned," she says, acknowledging the importance of her time spent with a large firm. "I couldn't do what I'm doing today without that experience." The demanding work schedule imposed by someone else helped Kathy to decide to take the self-employment risk. She wanted more control over her time. So, with her experience as a tax specialist, she decided to begin freelancing her services.

Kathy anticipated business would start slowly, but it didn't. She has grown through word-of-mouth advertising, networking and referrals. Kathy left her corporate employer on good terms, which has proven to be mutually beneficial. Several former clients followed her into private practice. She did not solicit any of her clients; they came in search of her. Fortunately, her former employer did not object. In addition, her former employer has provided leads on smaller companies it is unable to handle. Likewise, Kathy refers business to them.

When starting her business, Kathy knew that computers were going to be essential to her operation. She also knew that it would be impossible to project when cash would begin coming in, so she tried to conserve initially as much as possible. There is always an amount of cash outlay necessary to start any business. And projecting cash flow is extremely difficult in the initial stages. Kathy looked at several different types and price ranges of computers. Her decision to buy one that wasn't top-of-the-line was influenced by her need to be fiscally conservative. Now, she realizes that a few more dollars would not have made much difference. "And if it does, then perhaps you shouldn't be going into business. At least not right now," Kathy cautions. She advises new business owners not to skimp on resources, when your time is more valuable. "Time is money," she says.

Thelma Kidd, Karen Davis
Co-owners, Davis-Kidd
Booksellers, Inc.
Began 1980

"Don't take no for an answer. Keep on until you get a yes."

Thelma Kidd and Karen Davis have created a community-supported bookstore far beyond their initial dreams. They have grown to three stores. Building a successful retail bookstore, according to Thelma Kidd, was the result of hard work, commitment, supportive mentors and a long-standing friendship and partnership that still exists.

The two women met in Lubbock, Texas, and their friendship continued through the years as each pursued graduate degrees in social work.

During this time, Thelma lived in Ann Arbor where she first began to develop her entrepreneurial spirit, focusing finally on the idea of opening a bookstore. She wanted to create a large, open, friendly bookstore, a store patterned after Borders Bookshop, a local Ann Arbor bookstore she frequented. Karen had moved to Tennessee to pursue her career. As Thelma and Karen developed their business idea, they picked Nashville as the perfect location, because it had an untapped market for books. Their research included gathering as much information as possible from Borders, as well as from other business owners. The founders of the Borders store became both mentors and friends as they forged an invaluable supplier relationship that lasted for over a decade.

Neither woman had retail or previous business experience, but both brought a passion, understanding, drive and determination that contributed to their success. Knowing the importance of a strong inventory and the right location, they planned a store that would become a resource to the community. They sought the financial backing to start their venture from commercial banks. Bankers were slow to be won over, Thelma recalls, because of the women's lack of expertise in the business. Being female didn't help, but she says their naiveté kept pushing them forward. Thelma remembers one banker who commented that he'd never financed an 8,000 square-foot bookstore before, but he had seen several large liquor stores and he thought he had a good idea of what they were planning to do.

Eventually, their persistence paid off, and they received a six-month commitment for an SBA 90-percent guaranteed loan, subject to finding a location. But space was limited in the one particular section of town that was ideal for their store. It had the customer base that could support a bookstore, and any other location was less than perfect.

Determination and perseverance was then and continues to be the backbone of their business. The first loan commitment expired, and they began the process over again. A second loan commitment was obtained but expired and still no location was found. Then a third commitment was received. Thelma said the 18-month search was complicated by landlords' reluctance to lease space to inexperienced women. Finally, however, they found a location half the size they had originally intended, but in the right location. They opened their first store in October of 1980.

Thelma feels their social work background played a significant part in their success. Both women felt the need to develop a strong community presence, to be more than a bookstore, to create a strong relationship and name within the community. They continue to build on that image and excel in customer service, community relations and atmosphere. The store is now in its third location in Nashville and has grown from 3,500 square feet to 23,000 square feet, including a cafe on the second floor. Davis-Kidd has expanded to stores in Memphis and in Knoxville as well.

Thelma recommends, "If you want to grow, you can't have the day-to-day operational control you once had. You must learn to delegate and use the expertise of others." She notes that this can be a difficult step, but is necessary for growth to happen.

Thelma reflects on her 14-year journey, saying it wasn't easy but she always knew it would work. She and Karen were determined to make it work. Through difficult times, they stayed focused on their goals. Learning to deal with the uncontrollable aspects of business can be fatiguing, but she developed a strong network of friends, family and business associates who supported her during this learning process.

Sharon Lester
Owner, Sharon Lester Builder
Started 1974

"I am different than most. Most are men."

Sharon Lester is definitely different than most. She has spent the past 20 years excelling in an industry dominated by males. She has succeeded against the odds. A true pioneer, Sharon credits her success to her determination, experience, family support and being a perfectionist. "I have a keen eye for the details and can conceptualize the whole picture," Sharon professes.

At age six, Sharon received her first tool set. By eight, she had built her first house, a small one in her back yard. She describes it as "a log house, chinked with mud and grass, and it had a straw roof." As a child, she built several more little houses and often begged her mother to let her move out of the family home into one she had created.

Sharon tried to conform to societal expectations in her early years. She went to college, received a master's degree in educational psychology and taught in public school for eight years. Yet, this role wasn't fulfilling for her.

The pivotal time for Sharon came when she wanted her own home, but couldn't afford to buy one. Instead, she decided to build it herself. Her building career began as a personal and practical achievement. The skepticism of others only served to deepen her commitment and solidify her drive. Sharon carefully and thoroughly learned everything she could about building a house. After she built her own house, the learning process continued. Major experience was gained when she gutted an old house and converted it into a multi-unit apartment. It was a slow process, but one that taught her many lessons in how things could and should be done for efficiency and quality.

After Sharon had built a second house for herself, a friend and co-worker who had monitored her progress asked if she were ready to build a contract house for an acquaintance of his. Her challenge was to build a 6,000 square-foot house on what turned out to be unstable soil. Her perception and attention to detail resulted in altering the plans as the construction progressed. A year later, after unusually heavy rains, a house next to her contract home had come off its foundation and moved down the street. The house Sharon built stayed firm. She passed the test with flying colors, and her new career was launched.

Sharon relies on referrals and happy customers. Business remains steady because of her reputation for quality and excellence. She builds only one or two houses per year and maintains control over projects.

There have been many obstacles in her career path over the years. First was the fact that she was a woman. "Women couldn't be builders. At least that's what everyone kept telling me in the '70s. Women were not welcome in nontraditional roles then," Sharon recalls. No one took her seriously in the beginning. Fortunately, she had the support of her family and friends.

The second obstacle for Sharon was earning respect within the industry. To gain this respect meant that she had to be better, more knowledgeable and more prepared than the men. Sharon recalls a subcontractor on her first house who provided what he thought were words of wisdom by saying, "You'll never make it in this business; you want things too right. The best thing you can do is clean up and leave the building to us." After 20 years, Sharon says they do respect her now. She couldn't get by with being as good as her male counterparts, though. She had to be better in everything she did.

Today, Sharon's subcontractors know she means business. She reminds them she's not their mother, their girlfriend, wife or lover... she's their boss. Her style of managing and motivating is very different from the industry norm. Compliments and financial rewards are frequently provided to those who do exceptional work and get the job done early. Nothing is guaranteed, so it doesn't become another form of salary and expectation. Being able to share the fruits of the labor with others is important to Sharon. She builds a strong sense of community in her projects.

As the industry and consumers have changed, Sharon says she's getting close to retiring. She is looking forward to it and has invested for that day. Now, she's ready to give back her time and energy to help those in need. She has just completed volunteering as general contractor for Nashville's first Habitat for Humanity home built by an all-female crew. It was completed in just under two weeks.

Sharon encourages women who want to enter this profession to go ahead. But she advises them to learn everything they can about the business. They will have to know more than any man. She also recommends operating with back-up plans. Plans must always be flexible and open to change. If you are prepared for the unexpected, things will not get you down as easily. Since everyone will be watching you much more closely, you can also gain respect during the process.

From her speech to a large group of excited women helping with the Habitat House, Sharon said "There may be some of us who are afraid we may not be successful, but I'm here today to say to you, we will be successful. I did it. I'm still doing it. And you can do it too."

Chapter 3

Entrepreneurial characteristics: taking a personal inventory

"Thus learning to understand our dreams is a matter of learning to understand our heart's language."

Ann Faraday
The Dream Game

"Wolves and women are relational by nature, inquiring, possessed of great endurance and strength. They are deeply intuitive, intensely concerned with their young, their mate and their pack. They are experienced in adapting to constantly changing circumstances; they are fiercely stalwart and very brave."

Clarissa Pinkola Estes, Ph.D.
Women Who Run with the Wolves

Identifying entrepreneurial success traits

To mirror success, you must first be able to identify it. Is it different (or harder) for females to be successful? Traditionally women have achieved acceptance in a man's world by acting like a *man*; denying our feminine qualities. Now, the tide is finally changing. While as women we need not limit our mentors to only females, there exists a common female bond we cannot ignore. At the same time, not all women are positive role models. We should find successful entrepreneurs we admire and then listen to their stories. Ask questions. Watch their style. Integrate those characteristics we most admire into our own style. Mirroring the positive reflections of what we see. It's the best way to learn.

Numerous studies outline some admirable characteristics for entrepreneurs.

Generally, entrepreneurs should be driven, optimistic, visionaries who are highly motivated, well-organized, independent thinkers, strong leaders, able to handle pressure and blessed with both a good sense of timing and luck. Not every successful entrepreneur meets all these criteria. Instead, individual personalities are meshed with form and purpose to produce unique management styles. It is hard to separate the natural personality from the learned characteristics in most cases. Women add a sensitivity, passion and nurturing touch to their styles that has previously not been highlighted.

Admittedly, most of the successful role models used for studies have been men because men reached visible leadership positions in abundance. Now, we are understanding more about the actual differences between the sexes. Not that one is better than the other, but that the two often operate in very different manners. Recent studies identify two parallel styles, between thinking and feeling, intellect and intuition, and objective analysis and subjective insight. In the past, the success traits were presumed to reflect the thinking, intellectual, objective analysis style. However, successful women in leadership roles have forged a new dimension in these general classifications.

The yin and yang of things

The ancient Chinese recognized the differences between the sexes' approaches to life. Stereotyping emerged even then. For the world to be in balance though, both yin and yang must be present. The philosophy of yin and yang dates back to around 500 B.C.E. Yin (earth, female) carried weaker qualities. Yin was associated with darkness, yielding, warmth, autumn, winter, unconsciousness, emotion, passivity and absorption. Yin was present in even numbers, in valleys and streams, and was represented by the tiger, the color orange and a broken line.

Yang (heaven, male) on the other hand, presented a stronger image. Yang was associated with light, aggression, cold, spring, summer, consciousness, reason, activity and penetrating characteristics. It was represented by odd numbers, in mountains, and seen as the dragon, the color azure and an unbroken line.

Left-brain, right-brain dominance tendencies

Today, we look to science to understand the differences between the behaviors of men and women. Studies of the brain indicate that while people utilize all four quadrants of the brain at all times, many favor one half or the other.

Unlike yin and yang, society has predetermined which is the "better" half.

Left-brain people are logical, analytical, quantitative and fact-based. They are organized, planned, detailed and sequential. Right-brained individuals are holistic, intuitive, synthesizing and integrating. In addition they are emotional, interpersonal and feeling-based. The left brain controls verbal and linguistic skills, while the right brain controls the abstract, overall picture we have. One side is not better than the other. However, society has given a strong positive support to the left-brain dominant features.

According to a recently released study (July 1994) by the National Foundation for Women Business Owners (NFWBO), women and men have different styles of success and leadership. Their survey found that 53 percent of women business owners emphasize intuitive or right-brain thinking. "This style stresses creativity, sensitivity and value-based decision making." Whereas 71 percent of men business owners emphasize logical or left-brain thinking. "This style stresses processing information methodically and developing procedures."

"Up to now, models for business success have been largely male-defined, often forcing women into a mold in which they did not feel comfortable," comments Laura Henderson, chair of the NFWBO. With the growth of women-owned businesses, however, these non-traditional models are gaining force, credibility and popularity.

Anne Moir and David Jessel, authors of *Brain Sex*, say there are real differences between the thinking processes of males and females that are reinforced by society. The authors note that female businesses are stronger in labor relations because they frequently eliminate the petty rules and hierarchical structures that males have established as essential. "Women often run businesses like they run their households, without waste and extravagance."

Carol Tavris, in *The Mismeasure of Women*, reports that "women have interconnected hemispheres, which explains why they excel in talk, feelings, intuition and quick judgments." While both men and women operate within all spheres, there are more males with extreme scores. In fact, many of our success stories and models came from men who were dominant in left-brain qualities. We are realizing that both right-brain and left-brain characteristics are important to leadership. Our objective is to use our whole brain. To seek balance.

Marianne Williamson (author of *A Woman's Worth*) describes "the masculine as active, the feminine passive; the masculine is dynamic, the feminine magnetic. The masculine does while the feminine is." Nothing is wrong with either. Nor should one be perceived as better than the other. Simply stated, the two are different.

The whole brain approach

Finding balance is not easy. It requires identifying our weaknesses and giving more attention to those areas. It means knowing our strengths and using them to our advantage.

Extremes in either right-brain or left-brain dominance can be limiting. Businesses require a lot of attention to detail, a left-brain trait. People need caring and nurturing to perform at their optimum, which is associated with right-brain tendencies. Businesses require creativity, again a right-brain feature. Handling the daily operations requires organization, another left-brain trait.

The NFWBO survey also found that "women business owners' decision-making style is more whole-brained than that of their male counterparts, that is, more evenly distributed between right- and left-brain thinking." It takes utilizing both sides of the brain to have success and longevity in today's competitive marketplace. Even with the strength of the whole brain, women and men still perceive the other's differences as strengths. Women view men as being stronger in delegating, while men see women as being better in perception and caring attributes.

Entrepreneurs are a special breed. They are driven by an inner force, a need to create something. Female entrepreneurs carry that creativity beyond the drawing board and into the daily business operation. According to the April 1994 *Business Week* Special Report, "many experts believe that women business owners often seem to emphasize employee training, teamwork, reduced hierarchy and quality far more than their male counterparts." They are adding flexibility and creativity to their systems by integrating characteristics from both sides of their brain.

While society attempts to classify traits as "better" or "preferred," we must remind ourselves that individuals (both males and females alike) have unique and special gifts and abilities. Management characteristics of females are often different from the norm, especially when the norm has been set by males. While we need to enhance our natural gifts (team-building, people skills, organization, creating community, listening, etc.) and continue to see them as positive attributes, women must also develop complementary skills. There are different (not better) paths available to take to the same results: being successful in your own business. What's important is to find a path you are comfortable with and then proceed.

Experience

First, before starting a business, make sure you have the ability to *create* success. This requires more than tenacity, organization and drive. It centers on your attitude and outlook, your experience, knowledge and your discipline. It's the difference between trying to make it work and finding a way to make it work. If you are lacking in experience, education or formal training, take the time to accumulate these tools now, before you start. These tools represent knowledge that cannot be gained through outside observation. These skills require your participation.

Many women are starting businesses in areas where they lack experience but have strong passion and commitment. The lack of previous experience doesn't need to limit your options, however, if you realize the importance of experience.

Experience offers insight into the nature of products or services, customer needs, employee relations, purchasing power, trends and much more. It's more than just working experience and business skills; it is gaining industry knowledge and in-depth understanding. Experience can be gained from part-time work, volunteer activities, internships or temporary full-time opportunities, depending on your specific situation.

I learned the importance of experience in my first business venture—the hard way. My decision to leave bank management and start a retail travel agency was the result of a yearning for independence and the possibility that an upcoming merger would eliminate my position. Although I had strong business and management skills, I had never worked in the travel industry. I lacked industry knowledge and the local contacts that books couldn't provide. For example, since I didn't know any employees personally, I couldn't pick the best ones from within the industry to start with me. Even though I knew this industry was plagued with a high personnel turnover rate, what I didn't know was that most potential employees lived far from my location. Strong competition made it difficult to persuade quality employees to travel the additional distance. I fell victim to a mistake that could have been avoided had I started with industry experience.

The nature and complexity of your industry will dictate how important experience is in your business. Some businesses, particularly those requiring licensing, have specific experience requirements. For other industries, however, such as home-based or retail-related ones, it may be an individual option. Try to be creative in your search for work opportunities. Sometimes retail experience, although in a different industry, will suffice. Other times it provides little help. Your best choice is to look for businesses that are like yours, that target the same (or a similar) market and sell the same product or service. Depending on your location and amount of competition, this may or may not be possible. Improvise when you have to. And, like Sandra Cartwright Morris in Chapter 2, when you sign a noncompete agreement, you may be learning general know-how and not specific names and contacts.

For most businesses, experience is not enough. You need to have additional education and training to complement the experience. Since the world is constantly changing, it will be to your benefit to continue to refresh yourself on these skills.

Education and formal training

Recent studies published by Myra and David Sadker (*Failing at Fairness*) indicate that females may confront gender bias as early as their first years in grade school. Studies suggest that when girls begin school, they are intellectually equal to or even superior to their male classmates. But by the time they graduate from high school, they've fallen behind. And this gap appears to continue through college. This inequity has been perpetuated by teachers, both male and female, who have discouraged girls from excelling in math or science because it has been perceived that these are areas of difficulty for females. But such practices are changing as we become more aware of inequities. Today, women are entering math and science fields in record numbers.

Whether you've decided to blaze your way into a traditionally male-dominated area, such as engineering or construction, or whether your business interests lead you elsewhere, you'll discover the importance of a broad-based business education as well as formal training in your industry. Most female business owners cannot afford the luxury of hiring "specialists" in each field needed. Since, ultimately, you are responsible for all of your business decisions, you need to be armed with a broad knowledge to be successful. Of course, you may not be in a position to do everything yourself. But how will you be able to determine if someone is qualified to provide advice if you know nothing about their duties? You must know

enough to communicate your expectations, your procedures and your goals.

The best method for gaining information is through education and formal training in a variety of subjects. To be successful in business, it is essential to be knowledgeable in such subjects as accounting, finance, production, marketing, advertising and law, not to mention the significant benefits of staying abreast of technological advances, as well as industry trends and regulations. Gaining knowledge doesn't have to be expensive. Look into programs at community colleges, local business seminars, self-study courses and adult or community education classes for a variety of course topics at reasonable prices.

Deciding which business fits you

Chances are, if you've considered going into business for yourself, you already have some idea of the type of business you want to start. But if you have a variety of skills or interests or if the only thing you're certain about is that you want to be your own boss, you may have some thinking to do before you determine exactly what it is you're best suited to do.

When narrowing your potential business opportunities, first evaluate your strengths and weaknesses. Take an honest look at yourself. Assess your interests, skills, abilities, including skills gained from volunteer work. The practice exercises in this chapter are designed to encourage this discovery. Next, define your personal values and evaluate whether your prospective business works with or against them. It's hard to find the enthusiasm and energy to devote to a new venture when it isn't "right" for you. In addition, consider what education, skills or other training you might need before you can pursue your goals.

Let's look back at some of the women in Chapter 2 and see how their skills and backgrounds influenced their decisions. Jenny Moss, along with several of the other women interviewed, chose a business from a hobby. Jenny had taken private lessons and met many quilters who shared knowledge, ideas and the passion of quilting. Having worked in a small retail business, Jenny brought established business and bookkeeping skills with her that were easily transferable. On the other hand, Sandra Cartwright Morris, a recently divorced mother of three, had very limited business experience. She took inventory of her transferable domestic skills and saw her strengths as good people skills, listening and being able to juggle multiple tasks. In choosing her business, Sandra knew gaining work experience was a must. Sandra also knew she needed to get out of the house and "go to work." There would be additional costs for overhead that had to be considered as well. She named four potential business opportunities and then continued her research. Brenda Wilson, however, decided to make a career of her home and family skills by starting a home day-care business. Brenda speaks to the need to look at yourself as professional in whatever you do. And finally, Kathy Peters elected to continue her licensed career by freelancing her services. As a certified public accountant, specific qualifications in education and experience are required, which Kathy had previously met. Freelancing was a natural transition and fit better into her lifestyle.

It's important to consider your values as you identify the type of business you want to create. Money, time, family— depending on their importance to you, they'll influence your commitment to various businesses. For example, I wouldn't recommend setting yourself up as a seminar leader if spending time with your growing family is your number-one priority. If making a lot of money is important to you, industries that pay based on commissions are more likely to bring the financial rewards you desire; whereas a business in which you make a product (labor-intensive) is constrained by the number of products made.

Also, you must consider how much you're able to invest toward your new venture. There are some businesses that can be started on a shoestring, with minimal capital investments, and expanded slowly as profits are reinvested. Other businesses require large cash outlays for equipment, inventory, furnishings and the like. Know how much money you can invest in your business. Identify and accept your financial limitations (or resources) as you assess each potential business. Be realistic in your projections, expectations and goals.

Accept that each business opportunity includes benefits and hazards. List the advantages as well as the disadvantages for each choice. Then state your personal feelings about each prospect. Listen to your instinct.

Few businesses make money right away. So, if you are your sole source of income, you may need to modify your lifestyle initially. For some businesses, it may take two or three years (or longer) before the company's profits can provide your income. To help bridge this gap, keep some savings separate from your new business. This money will help cover your living expenses until the business can afford to support you. Always be conservative in your projections to preserve your cash as long as possible.

Accentuate the positive and eliminate the negative

Remember that the most important ingredient in starting and operating a business is *you*. *You* with all your pride and glory. *You* with fervor and flaw. *You* with the enthusiasm to overcome whatever obstacles lie ahead. You are the crux of your business; its single most important asset. And, you are made up of a combination of strengths and weaknesses, of knowledge and experiences unique and special to only you.

This is an opportunity to discover (or uncover) some of your many gifts and talents. We all have a lot of potential. Sometimes we need help seeing it, though. It's like the story about Michelangelo. It is said that a neighbor saw him pushing a large marble rock down the street to his shop. Michelangelo was working very diligently at moving the marble. The neighbor called out to him and asked why he was working so hard at moving just a rock, to which it is reported that Michelangelo replied, "Because there's an angel in that rock that wants to come out." We, too, have angels inside us that want to come out.

Taking inventory of your strengths and weaknesses can be a challenge. It requires being honest with yourself about the process and the results.

The following practice exercises are designed to assist with this discovery. This process is akin to gathering information for a resume. I recommend reading *The Smart Woman's Guide to Resumes and Job Hunting*, by Julie Adair King and Betsy Sheldon. They do an excellent job of walking you through the various steps of communicating paid and unpaid experiences. The steps are similar. During this process you create a sense of personal awareness and self-discovery that is often overlooked.

Exercise 1

A. List personal characteristics you consider to be assets, along with strengths and skills you have acquired. For example, are you a good listener? A good communicator? Do you have fund-raising experience? Any accounting or bookkeeping experience? Marketing experience? Management or supervisory skills? This exercise may take a few days to complete. Give yourself ample time. Begin by looking at your paid work experience, then volunteer duties, organizations, clubs and hobbies that you've been involved in. Don't overlook anything. For example, don't dismiss yourself as "just a housewife." Consider yourself, instead, a domestic engineer, transportation specialist, function coordinator, conflict resolutionist, peace negotiator and master chef!

_____
_____
_____
_____
_____

B. Next, list areas in which you need to improve—skills you need to learn, weaknesses you need to overcome. Refer to past performance evaluations for help if you're having difficulty with this one. How proficient are you with computers? What about accounting? Management? Marketing? Do you work well with others, or prefer to work alone? Are you a delegator? Organizer? How well do you handle stress? Are you in strong financial, physical and emotional shape right now?

_____
_____
_____
_____
_____
_____
_____

Exercise 2

A. List five businesses that appeal to you and then rank them according to personal preference. If you are unable to come up with five different businesses, don't worry. List as many as you can. And what if you have more than five ideas? That's great, too. Make as complete a list as possible; let those creative juices flow.

_____
_____
_____
_____
_____
_____
_____

B. Then list five (or as many as possible) businesses you are not interested in. This step is often more difficult, so don't get discouraged. Both aspects are integral in evaluating your options.

_____

_____

_____

_____

_____

C. And finally, highlight any common threads you see emerging in both lists. Do you prefer service businesses? Or retail? Or helping the ecology? Do you detest manufacturing? Do you want to work alone? Do you need to go to an office away from home to get motivated? Is your forte in highly technical areas? Or perhaps you enjoy the freedom of freelancing?

_____

_____

_____

_____

_____

_____

_____

The entrepreneurial test

The purpose of this test is to further your self-discovery process and to help you anticipate potential problems or identify weak areas early. Think carefully about each question and answer honestly.

1. Why do you want to start your own business? (Are you looking for more money, freedom, career challenges, flexible work schedule, etc.)

_____

_____

_____

_____

2. What are your monthly living expenses? Can you cut back comfortably on some of these expenses? How will that change your lifestyle? Are you willing to adjust your lifestyle (at least temporarily) until the business is solidly operating? How much money do you have in savings?

_____

_____

_____

_____

_____

3. Do you want to start a part-time or full-time business? Can this particular business fit into your lifestyle? How much time are you willing to give to a new business? Know what your limitations are up front. More time does not translate automatically into greater success, but often the first few years of starting a business will take additional time commitments.

_____

_____

_____

_____

4. What are you willing to lose? How much risk will you take? Decide on a dollar amount ($5,000, $10,000 or $100,000) as well as items (house, company assets, car, other personal belongings). Do not list them if you are not willing to lose them! Include friends and family if you borrow money from them. All businesses entail a certain degree of risk.

_____

_____

_____

_____

5. Have you managed or supervised a staff before? How do you rate your management abilities? Did you enjoy managing people? If not, why? Not all businesses need outside employees, but if you are your only employee, you may be limiting your growth.

_____

_____

_____

_____

6. How do you rate your ability to delegate? The ability to delegate can be one of the most difficult for owners, but without delegating you are establishing an immediate bottleneck. Don't burn out because you feel compelled to do it all.

_____

_____

_____

_____

7. How easily do you accept and react to change? How well do you work under pressure? How comfortable are you operating in an environment that is unpredictable, and at times chaotic?

_____

_____

_____

_____

8. How organized are you? This becomes very critical with the heavy workloads and variety of hats that you will be wearing. Perhaps taking a time-management course will help if you are weak in this area.

_____

_____

_____

_____

9. Can you take full responsibility for both your successes and your failures? Are you goal-oriented? Are you overly critical of yourself?

_____

_____

_____

_____

10. Are you willing to work hard to acquire new skills, if necessary? And can you lead, inspire, motivate and share the limelight with others?

_____
_____
_____
_____

11. Do you enjoy selling? No product or service sells itself. However, some businesses require less effort for sales because of stronger markets, whereas commission-based businesses rely one hundred percent on your ability to sell.

_____
_____
_____
_____

12. Do you enjoy people? Selling, servicing, managing, networking...all require people skills. Unless you want to be an inventor and have someone else sell your product (highly unlikely scenario), you will be dealing with people. This includes phone conversations. When you're having fun, your happiness is contagious. You may want to review some of those positive mental attitude tapes you have, just in case you're a little rusty.

_____
_____
_____
_____

There are no right or wrong answers to this test. I detest grading someone else's life, just as I resent when it's done to me. Here, it is the process that is important. It is meant to stimulate your thinking, to help you determine what sort of work environment and business situation will best suit your goals, values, experiences and abilities. This is a very personal decision, one you must weigh carefully, given a host of variables. Ultimately, your dedication and perseverance may see you over many hurdles. What is important in this exercise, though, is to gain an understanding of why you want to take on this risk and if you are prepared for the journey.

No one can tell you the best business for you to start. You are your best judge. There may be several options to choose from, or only one that works for you. If it feels right, then follow your intuition. Intuition is not impulsiveness. Impulsiveness is an irrational action you feel propelled to do. Webster's defines intuition as the "quick perception of truth without conscious attention or reasoning." It has to do with the knowledge women have, that cannot be explained or readily taught. We just know what to do by following our heart. It's the right thing to do. We may not be able to explain why, but we just know. Others may refer to this as your sixth sense. Intuition can lead you into the right decision about hiring or not hiring someone.

People who love their work will have a better chance of succeeding. Now you are ready to move to the next step and look closer at the various start-up options. The process has begun.

Chapter 4

Startup options: home-based opportunities, franchising and buying an existing business

"Opportunities are limited only by your imagination."

Carole Hyatt
Shifting Gears

"There is a potential heroine in every woman."

Dr. Jean Shinoda Bolen
Goddesses in Every Woman

If you're considering or are in the process of starting a business, expect a lot of work. Expect a lot of pressure. Expect a lot of questions. Prepare yourself for the roller-coaster ride of a lifetime, providing thrills and chills, fears and tears, joys and toys, excitement and horror—all in a day's work.

Women have a variety of opportunities available to them today. To accommodate hectic lifestyles, many women are choosing businesses that can be started from home. Of the 6.5 million women-owned businesses, nearly 65 percent are home-based. Most women will start businesses from scratch, with the majority of them being at home. However there are also the options of franchising or buying an existing business. Women should carefully explore all options to evaluate the requirements (both personal and financial) before ruling out any opportunity as unlikely.

Home-based business

Over the past decade women began spending more time at home. Books such as *Women and the Work/Family Dilemma*, by Deborah Swiss and Judith Walker explore this phenomenon. We went out to work, but tried being "Superwoman" initially. Now, we are downshifting and reprioritizing.

This was a choice we fought hard for. It hasn't been easy or without compromise. Women were told they had to choose between family and career. They couldn't have both. Today, women are speaking out for what they want. We have taken family and career off its collision course and created a working dynamic that incorporates both. Home-based businesses provide such avenues. Finally, women can have their personal satisfaction, financial independence and supportive family lifestyle working together.

Home-based business is the trend of the '90s, an option more and more Americans are choosing, especially women. Many home-based businesses can be started with limited financial investments, which make them more appealing to women. Estimates suggest that by the year 2000, nearly 40 percent of the North

American work force will operate from their homes. These home-based entrepreneurs are seeking flexibility in the work force and are gladly leaving behind the regimen of nine-to-five as they blend their dreams and ambitions into creative business opportunities, often with lower risk and greater personal satisfaction.

The financial risk has been reduced for home-based businesses, but saving on rent and overhead does not guarantee success. Running a business from home requires the same drive and skills demanded of any business. Maybe more. Working at home requires perseverance, self-motivation and a talent for time management beyond that needed for other entrepreneurs.

Today's advancements in technology make it easier for anyone to work at home and still communicate with the world. A single employee can now perform the tasks of several employees, with the assistance of computers. This allows for greater freedom in creating and sustaining small business operations.

Setting up a home office

Privacy at home may be difficult to achieve. Can you find a room where you can work undisturbed? How quiet and private will phone conversations be? Can you physically and visually separate yourself from household chores? Is the environment conducive to work? The answers to these questions will start you on your quest for deciding whether a home-based operation is agreeable with your lifestyle. It isn't for everyone.

As a home-based business owner, you must integrate work and family more carefully. Often, conflicts and problems arise when you try to blend the two. Open communication is critical to home-business success. Make sure you have the support of your spouse, children and other family members whose lives may be disrupted by your new schedule. Include them in your routine whenever possible. And be willing to make concessions yourself, if needed. Everyone needs to work toward the same goal when living under the same roof. Otherwise, the anger or jealousy may tear down everything you are working to build.

Complying with local regulations

Make sure you comply with all local state and federal regulations for operating a business. For home-based businesses, an additional concern is "may I operate this *type* of business from *my* home?" Unfortunately, many restrictive zoning laws, designed to keep out manufacturers and high-volume traffic, limit the current trend in at-home businesses. Laws and ordinances vary widely from community to community.

Check local zoning laws *before* you start your business. This includes county and city ordinances. Since these regulations are enforced at the state, city and county level, they vary from state to state, including which departments to contact. Ignorance is no excuse. If you are close to an SBA field office, call them for direction and assistance. They may know which offices to contact for appropriate approvals in your area. Also try the local zoning board for regulations, guidance and information.

Current IRS guidelines provide a test to determine whether deductions for the use of your home can be taken. You can take a limited deduction for business use if you use part of your home exclusively and regularly:

• As the principal place of business for any trade or business in which you engage.

- As a place to meet and deal with patients, clients or customers in the normal course of your trade or business.
- In connection with your trade or business, if you are using a separate structure that is not attached to your house or residence.

Before taking a tax deduction, though, it is advisable to seek the interpretation of a professional accountant who is familiar with home business deductions.

Currently there are numerous tax laws favorable to businesses operated from home. However, because tax laws change, you should calculate your cash needs as if there were no benefits beyond the savings on rent and utilities. When approached in this manner, a more conservative method, the tax savings become a "benefit" instead of an expectation. They can be taken away just as quickly as they are given. An accountant, however, will guide you through the requirements of record-keeping for deducting certain percentages of your household expenses (including rent, utilities, phone, etc.) as they apply.

Home-based businesses are faced with the same requirements as away-from-home operations, plus more. Almost all businesses need a license to operate. You may need a seller's permit and federal I.D. number, depending on your industry and local requirements. Other areas to check into include fire department permits if you use flammable materials; air and water pollution control permits if you plan to burn any material or discharge any waste into the waterways; liquor, wine and beer licenses if you sell liquor, even through the mail; and health department permits if your business involves food items or food preparation (this especially affects catering businesses).

In addition, verify local laws concerning sign permits or ordinances. While this is an affordable method for small-business advertisement, regulations are becoming more restrictive. County permits are often needed in addition to city permits; check both offices. State licenses are becoming more common for certain occupations, especially for those persons who must pass a state examination to qualify. And federal licenses are required for a few trades, such as meat processors, common carriers and radio and television stations.

Depending on the type of business you are starting, you may not need additional insurance coverage. You may be sufficiently covered under your existing homeowner's (or renter's) policy. Check with a reputable insurance agent, as well as your state's insurance commissioner's office to determine industry specific requirements, however. Certain types of insurance coverage may be mandated for your industry by your state or by the federal government. Insurance coverage may be obtained on risk for fire, theft, health, life, errors and omissions, disability, liability and worker's compensation, to name a few.

The first step in assessing your insurance needs is to determine what you have to lose (assets, loss of business, income, etc.), whether you can afford to lose it, and what the cost is to cover that risk (the premium amount). You should list specific items and their value, as well as calculate various "what if" scenarios: What if...I had a fire? I had a robbery? I became disabled? Decide whether this loss can be absorbed by you or your company. If not, the gap should be covered by insurance. Home-based businesses that require little initial capital and have few assets will probably have a low exposure to significant losses.

Following the checklist below will help you in researching the regulations before starting a home-based business. Make a list of the phone numbers and offices you have contacted, along with the date and the name of the person you spoke with. Keep this list as a permanent record for personal reference. Ask other home-based businesses what licenses they have acquired. However, just because they have failed to meet the legal requirements doesn't excuse you from compliance.

Checklist

1. Do I qualify to operate in my house under current zoning ordinances?
2. Are any changes anticipated for zoning in city, state or federal legislatures?
3. Have I picked out a name for my business?
4. Will I need to file a doing-business-as (DBA) statement or fictitious name filing statement?
5. Is a business license required?
6. Are other licenses required by state, county or city offices?
7. Have I chosen a legal form of business operation?
8. Do I have a business attorney?
9. What insurance is needed for my industry?
10. Can I add on to my current home-owner's policy?

Advantages of a home-based business

- Flexible hours, allowing you to work when it's most convenient for you to work.
- Increased productivity because you have more focused time, with fewer interruptions and wasted meetings.

- Reduction in business overhead costs.
- Additional tax deductions.
- Reduced transportation costs and commuting time.
- Minimized involvement with office politics.
- Savings on wardrobe.

Disadvantages of a home-based business

- Requires strong time-management skills and additional discipline to get going.
- Long hours, especially when you start.
- Isolation. No one to share ideas with around the water cooler.
- You never leave your business.
- Family life may be disrupted.
- Work space may be limited.
- Difficult to maintain social interactions. You must consciously create networks.

Others may not consider you a professional because you work at home. They may also make constant demands and interruptions to your work schedule.

Franchises: another business option

Starting a business from scratch is not the only option available for those who want to be their own boss. Another option is to buy the expertise and experience of someone who's done it before you by buying a franchise business. In essence, a franchise is a business agreement in which one party, the franchisor, allows another party, the franchisee, to distribute a licensed product or service. The franchisee owns the business, but the franchisor controls what you can and cannot do. A franchise is a licensing and distribution agreement between a parent company and an independent business.

According to the Federal Trade Commission (FTC), a franchise relationship is one in which the franchisor provides significant assistance or exercises significant control over the franchisee's method of operation.

Franchise operations do have higher success rates than most startup businesses, as high as 90 percent. They achieve this higher success rate because much of the groundwork has already been done. The trial-and-error learning process has been undertaken by someone else, at their expense, and is minimized for you. In addition, many franchisors offer training programs for management and/or staff that further reduce the risk of a new venture, especially in labor intensive industries.

Still, the high entry cost may be exclusionary for some women. Franchising fees can range from $4,000 for tax preparation services up to $425,000 for hotels and campgrounds. In 1992, the median cost was between $60,000 and $70,000, according to a franchise owner survey by the Gallup organization.

Most people associate fast-food chains, such as McDonald's and Burger King, with the concept of franchising. However, the industry has grown significantly in the past decade to encompass a large variety of business types and sizes. Franchises can now be found in nearly every industry, in various sizes and requiring a wide range of financial investments. Many franchisors are making ongoing efforts to increase ownership among women and minorities.

Franchising is not for everyone. There are distinct pitfalls that all potential franchisees should investigate. The cost of franchises varies significantly but is generally higher than startup ventures.

Among the other pitfalls: Not all franchise operations are honest and ethical, although legislation has helped weed out many of the leeches. Also, owners may find the franchise contracts too restrictive. High costs associated with franchising continue to discourage many. For this additional investment, however, franchisors profess the risk of starting and operating a business is greatly reduced. Other benefits include stronger buying power, competitive prices, advertising campaigns and product recognition. Bankruptcies of franchisees are extremely rare, and franchisors will often go to great lengths to avoid having one of their operations shut down, even if this means investing more money or buying back the business under the parent umbrella.

Women are finding greater flexibility in franchised businesses. They are also finding more access to capital financing, either through commercial banks (because of name recognition and track records) or through the parent company financing part of the purchase.

Franchising is well on its way to becoming the dominant form of retailing in America. As of 1990, there were more than 533,000 franchises in the U.S., generating combined revenues of $716 billion. In fact, more than 10 percent of American businesses with employees are franchises, and they account for 34 percent of the total retail sales in this country. Evidence suggests that very small franchises are slowly gaining market share, especially in such areas as day-care and house-cleaning services. Women-owned franchises totaled 131,000 in 1987, according to the Department of Commerce Bureau of the Census, and the number continues to increase.

Who should own a franchise?

Franchises are good for people who have capital to invest, want to minimize risks and want to reduce decision-making responsibility. Franchising is best-suited for personality types who are happiest with structures and order, versus those "free-spirited" individuals who seek new and better paths. Women should be especially cautious when considering franchise options because most are still owned and run by males. They tend to be structured in hierarchical ways and to look first at money—and then at credentials. Potential franchisees should research their choice of franchises carefully, consider their personal financial resources as well as the financial stability of the franchisor, and be committed to selling, managing and hard work.

In addition, before committing to a franchise business, you should ask yourself some questions. Do you personally like the product or service? Do you believe in what you will be selling? Are you committed to this venture? Your enthusiasm will make or break any venture you undertake. Even though there is a track record, carefully review the company's marketing and financial success. Talk with other franchisees before you sign—including some ex-franchisees, who've gotten out of the business. Don't limit yourself to the names and phone numbers the franchisor supplies for references.

Franchise regulations

Unfortunately, the law does not always protect you from unethical franchise operations. Stricter regulations have evolved to help both investors and consumers, but this does not mean buying a franchise is always safe. Although much has been done in the past decade to enact legislation that eliminates or discourages bad operators, you must proceed carefully to determine the legitimacy of the operation and its ability to deliver the services and benefits offered. Some franchisors may make misleading statements about the income potential of a franchise. This is against the law, but is frequently employed during high-pressure sales meetings. Franchisors are required to detail estimated costs, but often the costs are buried deep in the contract and legal forms. Do not peruse through papers quickly! Read carefully and understand all the fine print before signing.

The Federal Trade Commission requires franchisors to file disclosure statements. These statements contain a wealth of information, including the backgrounds of the franchisor's officers, the organization's financial footing, obligations placed on the franchise, responsibilities of the franchisor, lawsuits filed against the franchisor and the names and addresses of the company's other franchisees.

However, many franchisors have found loopholes in the filing requirements, so a thorough investigation is a must. Commonly, franchisors establish numerous side companies that manage and run franchise operations, leaving the parent company as a "shell." This can make it difficult to ascertain the financial stability and exposure of the parent company, since it has probably guaranteed financial obligations for many of these related companies. Related company information does not have to be disclosed.

Over the past decade, there have been numerous large, nationally known franchise operations that have failed. Some of the more recent failures include Chuck E Cheese Pizza, Minnie Pearl's Chicken, Jerry Lewis Theaters, DeLites Restaurants, Lums and Arthur Treacher's Fish and Chips.

Buying a franchise should never be attempted without an attorney and accountant who specialize in franchise operations. Make sure they perform audits and assist with the investigations and negotiations. Franchisors frequently discourage these interventions. However, you need to protect yourself and your money. All contracts will be written with the franchisor's interest protected, which is limiting (if not suffocating) to you. If you sign a contract, remember, you are bound by what you sign.

Franchise agreements

The franchisee is required to follow the franchisor's dictates, regardless of her individual desires or markets. Everything will be outlined in the franchise agreement. Franchise agreements often contain provisions on the fees for buying a franchise, royalties that may be due the franchisor on an ongoing basis, the franchisee's investment requirements, inventory, record-keeping requirements, promotional and management services offered by the franchisor (sometimes at additional costs), the territorial rights of the franchisee (if any), the terms of the agreement, conditions for canceling the agreement and the sale of the franchise license. The franchise agreement can give the franchisor the right to cancel the agreement for ambiguous, sometimes petty reasons. Many agreements run up to five years, requiring a renewal and sometimes additional payments upon expiration. Expect the agreement to be written in very confusing *legalese*, which is another reason to employ the services of an attorney.

Pay close attention to the fees and costs of buying the franchise. Franchisors often fail to present the whole story in the beginning. Instead, they simply offer information on the cost of using their name and way of doing business. Check into other costs, such as those for equipment, lease deposits, inventory, credit policies, staff salaries, advertising and royalties to be sure that all costs are outlined and within your budget.

Not all franchisors are wolves. Many strong, supportive and successful franchises exist today. However, my skepticism calls for caution, especially for women. The growth of the franchising industry has spawned numerous shady operations. This has been most prominent in those franchises requiring lower cash investments, although not isolated to smaller franchises. The lower cash investments have been more attractive to women, who have sometimes become vulnerable prey. Follow the advice offered in Chapter 1 about the hype factor: "If it sounds too good to be true, then it probably is." If a franchise is a good business idea without the franchisor's support and assistance, then proceed. But the business decision should be based on facts, not weak promises.

Advantages of owning a franchise

- A ready business package that may include set-up, training, operations and often marketing programs.
- Public recognition of franchise logo and product achieved through uniform standards in color, design, taste, clothing, etc. This includes quality control measures imposed and enforced by the parent company.
- Lower costs through collective purchasing power for suppliers because of the economies of scale.

- Ongoing financial relationship that may include assistance and training in budgeting and financial management for your business.
- Finely tuned operating system where the bugs have been worked out at someone else's expense.
- Training and guidance, often in the form of an ongoing program for employees and/or managers.
- Financial assistance, such as startup financing packages. Nearly one-third of parent companies offer startup financing to qualified potential franchisees.

Disadvantages of owning a franchise

- The high cost (franchise fee, royalties, advertising, etc.) may prevent you from looking at several franchise opportunities.
- Royalty fees appear to be never-ending, often as high as four to six percent, and are tied to gross revenues (not profits). Royalty fees are a variable operating cost and often become a cash drain to small businesses.
- Lack of control; someone else tells you how to run your business.
- Borrowing money may be difficult (not all franchisors offer financing packages). Banks that have had bad experiences with franchises may be less willing to participate in a franchising arrangement.
- The franchisor's ability to terminate the franchise agreement may be somewhat arbitrary.
- The franchisor often reserves the right to place new and more restrictive financial commitments on the franchisee at the franchisor's discretion.

Buying an existing business

Another option available to entrepreneurs is to buy an existing business. Have you compared the total costs of starting a business on your own with the costs of buying somebody else's business? Acquiring an established business requires a greater financial outlay than starting from scratch, which is not as feasible for most companies started by women, since two-thirds of them are capitalized with $5,000 or less. Not as many women buy existing businesses as men because of the cost, but it remains an option to explore and evaluate.

Buying an existing business is intrinsically less risky than starting from scratch. It allows you to realize profits faster and receive a quicker return on your initial investment. A major advantage to buying an existing business is having a track record to review. The business already has its financial and marketing plans put into action. It already has an established location, inventory, customer base and trained staff. At least, it should. And these features are what you are paying for—so be sure they are benefits.

The risk

It is just as easy to inherit ill-will as goodwill from a previous owner. The location may be bad, too expensive or inadequate for expansion. The facility or equipment may not be up to modern standards for quality and cost-saving benefits. Inventory may be obsolete and useless. The staff and management may be incompetent. Poor quality and bad customer service are difficult, if not impossible, to turn around.

In order to avoid these pitfalls, entrepreneurs wanting to buy an existing business will have to do as much (or more) research and careful analysis than is required when starting from scratch. Carefully evaluate the opportunity cost of entering various industries through acquisition.

How to select a business

When deciding on what business to buy, consider your strengths, expertise and training. Don't buy a business simply because it is for sale, it's making a profit and the price is right. Make sure that you're the right person for that particular business. Make sure the business is something you enjoy, something you feel passionate about. Be sure you are focused on your objectives, and not buying into a high-powered sales pitch.

Experience is essential when buying an existing business operation. Unlike the entrepreneur who starts her business from scratch, you'll have to step right in as owner and manager. There's no time to learn on the job. Business is already in process. And without expertise in the field, you are more apt to miss major problems, thus making a poor evaluation of the business proposal.

Remember, no matter how smooth the sales pitch, the seller is always selling for a reason. And, most likely, it is because there's something wrong with the operation. These areas may be well-concealed and may require careful analysis and research to uncover.

Objectivity is important when evaluating business purchases. Do not become so emotionally attached that you're unable to remain objective, that your biases cloud your judgment, that you cannot walk away from a questionable transaction. Outside advisors will also help you stay focused on the facts and away from your impulses.

Buying a business anticipates an aggressive negotiating practice for price and other items. Again, you are strongly encouraged to have both an accountant and attorney represent you to protect your interests.

Questions to ask

The actual questions to ask will be representative of your personal needs and expectations. Here is a list of sample questions to begin the process. This is not meant to be a comprehensive list, only to start you in your investigative mode.

1. Would I be comfortable in this business?
2. Do I have the necessary temperament, education, skills and experience to operate this type of business?
3. Do I have enough money to buy and operate the business and still have a reserve fund?
4. What am I actually buying? Physical assets? Name? Customer list? Existing business or projected business?
5. Is this business a highly personal one? Keep in mind that customers may be loyal to the present owner and not to the company itself. How long is the current owner willing to spend making sure the customers make an easy transfer? If the owner is in failing health, how will that affect my decision?
6. Why is the owner selling?
7. Is the business profitable? If it is losing money, why? Is it in a bad location? Producing an inferior product? Facing strong competition?
8. Does the business need an immediate cash infusion? Will that solve the problem?
9. Is the owner reluctant to provide details and answers? If so, move on to another opportunity. Don't waste your time.

There are several methods you can employ to gather this information. Financial questions will primarily be answered through financial statements, tax returns and supporting documents, such as inventory reports and accounts receivable and accounts payable schedules.

You may also find some answers through employees of the business. Depending on the reason for the sale, the employees may or may not be aware of the pending transaction. When they are not aware, your discovery process is greatly impaired. If you are permitted to talk with employees and to observe their routines, much information can be gathered. If employees are not happy, that will be easy to determine. Customers as well as competitors can shed information in this process.

Ask for personnel records, customer lists and supplier contracts to review. Some sellers may not want to reveal much information until they are convinced you are a serious buyer. It will be your job to convey that you are a trustworthy, serious buyer, but that you must have sufficient information to make a well-informed decision.

How to find a business for sale

Businesses are put up for sale every day. The best place to begin is through your own contacts. Look within your networks. Ask friends, relatives and professional advisers if they are aware of any businesses for sale. Both your accountant and attorney may be aware of potential opportunities.

Many businesses for sale are represented by brokers. The businesses may be either advertised in the newspaper or listed with a brokerage firm. Caution should be used in following brokers'

leads. Often, high-pressure sales tactics are employed.

Finally, there are some entrepreneurs who have found success by locating a business they want to operate and talking to the owner personally. The owners may be ready to move on, but just not motivated enough to advertise the business yet. You never know unless you ask.

Owners treat businesses like their children. When they look at you as a buyer, they want to be sure you are interested in preserving the business they have built. This requires convincing them of more than your ability, interest and enthusiasm. Factor in enough time to build trust.

The negotiating process

Assuming that you have found the business you want to own, the next step is making an offer. Be sure to have an attorney review all contracts first. Also, your attorney should negotiate the details on your behalf.

Be especially thorough in your evaluation when dealing with a broker. Brokers are salespeople who work on commission. They make no money unless they close the deal. I have found most brokers pushy and biased on how they present the business. Don't feel pressured into a big decision. If a decision has to be made before you've completed your research, then pass. If someone else is about to write a contract, let them. Don't make an offer until you're ready. And, especially, do not take a broker's numbers and projections without investigating further.

Sellers normally list their businesses at a premium price. They use the most lucrative method of calculating its value and then add some cushion. You (with the help of your accountant) should take a much more conservative approach.

Remember, at this point everything is negotiable.

To determine the value of the business, you need the past five years' audited financial statements as well as tax returns. In addition, you should review the most recent interim financial statement for consistency. Any company less than five years old is a substantial risk because it lacks a track record. Pass on those.

Methods for valuing businesses vary within industries and frequently look at market trends (growth, size, position) as well as the age of the business. One method is to base the value on the assets you are actually buying. This is more difficult for service businesses. Also look beyond the physical assets, to the systems that are in place. Are the employees highly trained and productive? Is the company faced with poor morale and high personnel turnover? What is the value of those benefits? Another common valuation method looks at the earnings ratio, in conjunction with projected earnings. Future earnings is a very risky method of valuation, since you do not know if the customers will remain with you after the owner sells. Your accountant should review the financial data and determine a price to offer for the company. I recommend the *Small Business Valuation Book* by Lawrence W. Tuller for understanding how to value different types of businesses. He specifically addresses service, retail and manufacturing businesses and professional practices.

Numerous conditions may be inserted in the contract by either party. Items you may want to consider include having the owner staying on board (perhaps in a consulting capacity) for an agreed-upon period of time to help with the transfer of ownership; not determining the final price until six months to a year after the purchase, based on actual revenues (not projections); requiring noncompete agreements for the owner and senior management personnel; and having the seller finance all or part of the purchase price. Ask for terms that will help you with an easy and profitable transfer of ownership. Remember that negotiating means being willing to compromise. Know what items you are willing to concede and which you are not.

Advantages of buying an existing business

- Obtaining outside financing may be easier because of an existing track record.
- There should begin an immediate return on your investment.
- Projections should be more accurate because of known historical trends.
- You will have an established customer and supplier base.
- The target market has already been defined.
- Trained employees will (hopefully) continue the operation.

Disadvantages of buying an existing business

- The loss of an owner or manager may lead to disruption for the operation.
- The present location may be limiting.
- You may be locked into the existing policies and practices of the business, at least for the foreseeable future.
- You may inherit inept employees or employees who are loyal to the previous owner and not to you.
- Equipment may be obsolete for current industry standards, and updating may be prohibitive.
- The market may anticipate strong regulation that you had not projected. And the cost of implementing these regulations may be high.

Whatever option you choose for starting your business, buying a franchise, buying an existing business or starting from scratch at home or away, remember that all businesses require dedication, determination, enthusiasm and perseverance. Being in business for yourself is hard work. Find a business that utilizes your strengths, so that you can continue to grow personally and professionally. Find a business that's fun!

Chapter 5

Roadmap to the future: creating a practical business plan

"If you don't care where you're going, any road will get you there."

Unknown

"One moment of patience may ward off great disaster; one moment of impatience may ruin a whole life."

Chinese wisdom

Sheila Goode knows the importance of business planning. Even though her photography business is small, she constantly reviews and revises her plans. It is her way of keeping her finger on the pulse of her business. Sharon Lester also relies heavily on the process of planning. Both women use planning in very different ways. Both women use planning effectively and to their benefit.

Writing formal business plans remains an activity not often practiced by small business owners. Educators contend that a business cannot operate successfully without a business plan. Yet, when you speak to owners of small businesses, many confess they do not have formal plans. But they are successful. So, why the discrepancy? What does this mean when we consider that women-owned businesses are succeeding at a much higher rate than those of males? It means that women are finding results in the new formulas they're creating. And that the old methods may be outdated or even flawed. This new, more realistic approach is a welcome change.

Typically, female owners are less inclined to formalize their plans because they don't need to seek outside financing, which would require a plan. Recall from Chapter 4 that approximately two-thirds of companies started by women are capitalized with less than $5,000, according to SBA research. In fact, when the cash risk is low and the expected return not overly ambitious, the benefits from long hours of research and evaluation may not substantially increase the bottom line. It may be a wise decision to forego this tedious process.

Planning is essential to all businesses, however. Without it, you risk repeating the same mistakes other entrepreneurs have made—mistakes that could be avoided or drastically reduced through the process of planning. Business planning must be viewed differently than writing a formal business plan. One is the process; the other a tool. Not every business needs the tool, but every business does need the process. Business owners should assess their risk and potential reward to determine the benefits of writing a plan. For some it may be useful. Others will be able to keep a conceptualized plan in their head.

What is a business plan?

A business plan is an entrepreneur's road map to the future. As you journey across the country, you not only plot a course, you also verify your current position and, if you are not on track, you make the necessary adjustments. The same is true of a business plan. A well-prepared business plan will provide market research, allow you to gain control over your company and promote a competitive advantage over industry rivals. A plan should contain information concerning marketing, finance and the management of your business. A plan also helps define concepts, evaluate competition, estimate costs, predict sales and determine risk.

Business plans should allow for unexpected interruptions in your daily routine. No matter how prepared you are, things will go wrong. If you are not prepared, then a crisis could turn into a disaster. It's not the problem that's important as much as it is how you handle it. Potential crises include fires, floods, theft, losing a major customer, the death of a partner or key employee and so on. Think through these situations carefully and develop various plans of action in the unfortunate event one should occur.

Preparing a business plan requires attending to details, something you probably do with ease. Understand, however, that planning is a never-ending process. Accept that fact in the beginning and don't become frustrated with the job of planning. If you stay focused on your objectives, listen to your findings and learn from your results, then it becomes both a meaningful and fun process.

Should every business have a plan?

Yes. All businesses should have a plan. Maybe not a written plan, but they should have a plan nonetheless. The amount of detail required in that plan will vary among businesses as well as within industries. First, determine your financial risk as a gauge for deciding how much time and energy to devote to planning. The lower the risk, or less cash needed to start the business, the less time should be allocated to prepare a workable business plan. Even though a business may have minimal risk (for example, one started at home, in your spare time, with no inventory), it is recommended that you still undertake some degree of research and evaluation of your industry and competition. It is just smart business. Women should carefully weigh the whole situation before deciding how much planning is beneficial for their business. While there is a great deal of truth to the fact that the more you learn, the better prepared you become, often the cost of time and energy are too high and cannot be justified by small operations. This is not to downplay the importance or benefits received, only to be realistic in today's competitive environment. The amount of planning directly correlates to the risk and financial rewards of the business. Be realistic in the amount of time applied toward planning.

Don't expect a fancy, detailed business plan to make a business successful. The reason for creating a business plan is to learn more about your business, your industry and the competition. The business plan is only a vehicle. It gives options, not answers. And it is as limited in use as the information it represents. If inaccurate assumptions and false or weak data are used, then the results will be distorted.

A major problem occurs when entrepreneurs assume they know the answer and then try to prove their answer through research. This mistake often results in overlooked critical information and ignored findings that could save money and headaches down the road. Keep an open and objective mind when you research. Allow the research to reveal the answers instead of forcing it to support your hypotheses.

When should you prepare a business plan?

Women often ask if it's too late to prepare a business plan once they've started the business. Preparing a business plan can be implemented at any stage of operation. However, the sooner a plan is integrated, the sooner results will be seen. For example, if you are considering a new business opportunity and want to determine if it is a cautious, sensible investment, you can evaluate the risks and rewards through business planning research. If you are looking at expanding your market and adding new products, the financial analysis and industry data from planning can help determine a less risky decision.

Of the minority of women-owned businesses that do operate with a written business plan, most businesses fail to update or revise the data with any regularity. That's too bad. Too often, the formal business plan is thought of as a necessary step to humor bankers or appease outside investors and is rarely utilized for its potential value. Since your marketplace is never static, you should constantly be aware of new developments and potential changes within your industry, competition and your target market's buying habits.

This requires, at a minimum, semiannual revision of your plan, but being most effective means constantly researching and learning more and better methods of operations.

Basic steps for all business plans

Creating a business plan involves defining the problem—asking the questions. It involves doing your homework to determine solutions. Once information gathering has started, you should refine your initial questions. Continue collecting detailed data to resolve your questions. Analyze the answers and their feasibility. Then put your plan into action. The steps sound simple enough:

1. Ask questions
2. Gather research
3. Observe competition
4. Evaluate the data
5. Propose solutions
6. Implement the findings

Step one: ask questions

Pose the questions: **Who, What, When, Where, Why and How** on all aspects of business life and business operations. The more questions you ask, the more detailed the research. Realize that for every piece of advice or information discovered, there will be another story written to contradict or dispute those findings. What is a person to believe? Hint: Ask very simple questions and note the different answers you find and the frequency.

Begin by identifying your product, defining your target market and identifying the competition. Questions are best asked in a very simple, direct manner. **Where** should I locate the business? **When** will the product be ready to enter the market? **Who** is my target market? My competition? **How** should I market to them? **What** are the seasonal trends of this industry? And **why** do I personally want to take such a risk? Questions may be very specific: Should I introduce widgets? Or they can present a what-if scenario: What if a competitor lowers her price?

Step two: research

Once you have created a detailed list of questions you want answered, it's time to begin the research. This will help you further evaluate and define the market. Begin to accumulate data from a variety of reliable sources. The first place to begin researching should be your local library. Don't be overwhelmed by the amount of material the library contains. Ask for assistance, especially in the reference department. Let the reference librarians know what you are doing and ask for their input and recommendations. They can become a valuable source for finding hidden information and providing suggestions on publications to use. In addition, most libraries participate in inter-library loans. If there is an existing book that your library doesn't have, you may be able to borrow the book through another library. Ask to see a copy of the *Books in Print* series (by author, title or subject). I have found the subject section to be the most useful for general research.

Realize, though, that the library houses primarily historical data and that your research is trying to predict future trends. History is not always the best indicator of future events, but it may be the best source available. Look at today's economists and you can see how predictions based on the same historical data differ. Each economist, however, justifies her prediction. This

should be your objective as well: to present your case with compelling confidence and strong argument based on what you know and what you believe. You are not searching for "the truth" as an absolute. Instead, you are learning more about options available and how to respond quickly to change. Your predictions are ultimately a guess. But your objective is to present the "best-guess" based on what you know. Small business operations still rely on luck!

Library data may be too broad and general for your research. For example, your market may be identified geographically, by age, sex and race, as well as by other buying characteristics. Buying habits differ within regions, and that is often not reflected in national statistics. Finding relevant data requires using good judgment, common sense and a lot of creativity.

There are many other sources to consider when gathering data. Read industry and business periodicals and newspapers for the latest trends and market changes. These sources will better reflect the sensitivity within your industry and often address regional patterns too. In addition, information can be obtained from unrelated industries that offer parallel findings. All small companies have similarities. Other sources for reference include local data banks, such as the Chamber of Commerce, SBA or industry associations. Ask questions concerning trends or patterns of growth for your community, unemployment statistics, road construction or expansion and so on.

Collecting data is an ongoing process. Businesses that downplay its importance are often stagnant and destined to shorten their life. Chapter 7 goes into further detail on how to research markets.

Step three: observe

Some of the best research is done through simple observation. This is my favorite and a frequently overlooked tool. Observe what the competition is doing right and then mimic or perfect those good qualities. Observe what the competition is doing wrong and then avoid those mistakes. Assessing one's position among peers is an important vehicle of evaluation.

Observe your competition relentlessly. Ask questions and take notes. If you are not too obtrusive, you may be surprised how willing people are to share information. Entrepreneurs have tremendous pride in their business and are excited when someone shows interest. They enjoy talking so long as they do not perceive you as a threat to their business or bottom line.

Don't forget to ask your customers what they want; then listen to their response. When they're angry, they will tell anyone within earshot what has upset them. Unfortunately, to spread good news requires going beyond just being satisfied. Today's consumers are more sophisticated and informed than they were a decade ago. And they are more demanding. Women have some advantage in this situation because we have been consumers of a variety of products for years. We know to treat customers like we want to be treated, to ask for their input, listen to their concerns and honor their opinions.

Step four: evaluate

Listing questions is the first phase of the business-plan process. Next, you should begin researching for answers (or various solutions) in your local library, through trade magazines or with local data banks. After observing your competition, your customers and your overall market, the next steps involve analyzing, evaluating and interpreting the results.

Evaluating findings requires listening to your results as well as following your intuition. A good tool for evaluation can be created by listing all your findings and then rating them on probability of outcome, frequency in finding and reliability of resource. Probability of outcome looks at the degree of risk involved with a particular finding (very likely, possible, doubtful/high risk); frequency deals with the number of times you have found the same material in different resources. There is a great deal to be said for repetition of data. While not always accurate, frequency of occurrence does imply lower risk. There is safety in numbers. Finally, the grapevine may be unreliable as a sole source of information. However, the grapevine may support the findings of other research and provide a strong favorable evaluation. Where you found the information is as important as what was found.

If you were evaluating what child-care shortages exist in your neighborhood, possible questions might be: How many children are in this neighborhood? What are their age groups? How many mothers work outside the home? What other child-care provider services exist? What are other similar-sized communities doing in innovative, new market approaches to child-care needs? What child-care services have a high failure rate? What licenses are required? From these questions you would research statistical data on your market through the library, the local chamber of commerce or government agencies that may have such information readily available. Licensing requirement questions may be answered through other business owners and establishing local networks.

Talking with working mothers may provide some insight into needs and shortages in the community. If a day-care center has a long waiting list and is always at capacity, there is a ready need for more day-care providers. Observing their traffic patterns can be very revealing. Talking with other day-care operators may produce information concerning upcoming legislation that may prove costly to your business.

The questions about new services may produce a flood of responses. As you evaluate these answers, you will eliminate those that seem highly unlikely, too risky or not something you are interested in pursuing.

Step five: propose solutions

Once you have evaluated your findings, you will have a list of possible solutions, each of which has been assessed on the basis of its probability. Being prepared with more than one alternative will help you respond to changing markets more quickly. If your particular market conditions change, and the suggested outcome seems doubtful, you will be able to implement plan B or plan C without much additional research. You will already know that you have a plan B and C, so half the battle has already been fought, and you are way ahead of the game.

Choose the solution you feel most comfortable with. This comfort zone will be based on the amount of risk you are willing to undertake, given your market and your financial condition. Some solutions take more time to produce profits—time you may not be able to afford because time means money. Even though a solution has strong ratings on your sheet, it may not be possible, due to your personal situation, to implement

that plan now. Therefore, you will have to pass, at least for the time being, on that solution. Instead, other alternatives with lower ratings will need to be implemented.

The important thing here is simply knowing that you have solutions.

Step six: implement

Once the information has been researched and evaluated, you must implement the plan of action that affords you an acceptable degree of risk. It is one thing to understand the results and another to listen and respond to the information. If you have done detailed research and feel comfortable with your findings, then change will be a more natural step. If you are still leery, ask yourself why. It may be because more research is needed. Or perhaps the risk is greater than you are willing to undertake. Or then again, it could be time to rely on your female intuition. If it doesn't feel right, don't do it. You have to believe in what you are doing for it to work. You remain the single most important ingredient in your business.

Set goals for the business, establish realistic timetables for their achievement. And then periodically review these results. Be sure to revise your goals accordingly. Do not become frustrated with the constant state of flux businesses operate in. That is simply a condition of the world we live in, which is changing quickly in response to production, technology and information.

And finally accumulate your findings. Identify what trends are emerging. See what products or services are becoming obsolete. Change your business direction according to these results by adding new products, changing services, responding to consumer needs, etc. Then continue with the planning process. It never ends.

Alternative plans

All business plans should include a back-up plan of action in case the business doesn't survive. Businesses do close. But closing a business doesn't mean failure. Having a plan for closing your business doesn't mean you are planning to close. It may mean that a choice was made to no longer operate, for whatever reason.

The choices available will be representative of your particular situation. The choice to sell, liquidate, dissolve or elect bankruptcy are all viable options depending upon your immediate circumstances.

Closing a business can be as involved as starting one, or even more. Keep a list of everyone you contacted for starting a business. Closure includes the reversal of many of these steps. Closing a business is much more than simply ceasing to operate. Protect your name, your assets and your exposure. Communicate with others who are affected by the business closing, which includes customers, employees, vendors and government regulatory agencies.

All closings, but especially forced closings, can be psychologically draining to female business owners. The feeling of lack of control that Helen Burrus described in Chapter 2 is commonly identified with forced closings. One of the most difficult steps is acknowledging the situation and accepting your options. Allowing oneself time to heal is not only healthy, it also opens up new opportunities. Grieving is a natural step in this process. Supportive friends and family members can ease the pain during this journey. Don't be afraid to lean on others, especially during trying times.

The written plan

In its most ideal sense a business plan is the written document that describes the basic elements of business operations and projections. The steps identified are all part of this process plus one additional step, that of composition. The final result becomes the tool with which you, and others, can gauge your business direction.

Formal business plans are often required to obtain loan financing or other small business considerations. In these cases, the risk/reward factor becomes secondary to achieving the main objective, usually financing. Funding sources other than family and friends will prefer having something concrete to review. A significant amount of time is necessary to research and prepare a detailed, written business plan. Start early. This doesn't mean that a written business plan should be long. In fact, it should be written in the least amount of space necessary to convey the information required to achieve your objectives. Brevity is fine if the plan is complete.

There are definite advantages to writing a plan. First, it illustrates that you have thought through the process, made assumptions, researched the product's marketability, reviewed the competition and then analyzed the results. It also shows the direction anticipated of the company, for all to see and read. In addition, a written business plan can help you sell the business to outside investors, especially bankers, for financial considerations. And finally, it shows that you have done your homework and that you know your business.

There is no right or best method for creating a business plan. There are many ways of assimilating the information. This chapter offers a general guideline that may be followed or adjusted to meet your specific needs. However, if you wish to learn more about creating business plans, there are many books on the market that address this topic specifically. Some of the more popular books are: *The Entrepreneur's Planning Guide: Building and Implementing Your Own Business Plan*, rev. ed. by Robert M. Donnelly (1991, Van Nos Reinhold); *The Total Business Plan: How to Write, Rewrite and Revise*, by Patrick D. O'Hara (1990, Wiley) and *Why the Best Laid Business Plans Usually Go Wrong*, by Harry Browne (1989, Fireside). Find a book that serves your style and your needs and one that you are comfortable with. Adapt an approach to fit your mission.

Step seven: composition

The final phase involves compiling the information you've researched, documenting the findings and writing it in an easy-to-follow format. Be sure to write down your assumptions (or questions) as well as your results.

If it seems difficult to sit down and organize your thoughts on paper, you are not alone. Writing takes patience, time and practice. To get started, try reading several styles of business plan writings to complement your own writing style.

If, however, you do not feel proficient in writing, there are sources available (for a fee) that provide these services. Certified Public Accountants (CPAs) and business consultants both frequently prepare business plans for clients. Fees vary as does the quality of work.

Computer generated business plans are available, but they are very limiting

and do not reveal an individual's personality very well. True, they may help with some of your financial analysis and assist in the presentation format, but I would not rely on one alone to do the job.

A good business plan should be prepared in both two- and five-year periods. These windows into the future allow for a variety of scenarios to be developed and explored. Adjusting to volatile markets during business operations becomes a planned alternative and less an anxiety attack. Revise business plans frequently. At the very minimum, they should be revised semiannually to see how sales and expenses compare to projections and to identify emerging new trends. The more frequently they are revised, the quicker you can adjust your plan of action to fit current markets.

Outline of a business plan

Business plans come in a variety of shapes, sizes and colors. They reflect the owner's style, her goals and her direction. The following is an outline of typical areas covered in formal business plans. However, you should adjust your topics to meet your specific needs.

I.   **Table of contents**

II. **Introduction**
   A. The proposed type of business
   B. Products or services offered
   C. Mission statement
   D. Description of the industry

III. **Market Research**
   A. Total market
      1. Size
      2. Trends
   B. Target market
      1. Customers' ages
      2. Customers' trends
      3. Target market size
      4. Is the target market growing?

Roadmap to the future: creating a practical business plan

C. Competition
1. Industry competition (direct and indirect)
2. How many players?
3. What are the competitions' weaknesses?
4. What are the competitions' strengths?

D. Growth
1. Where is the product in its life cycle?
2. Will the introduction of your product alter the life cycle?
3. If so, why? And how?

E. Predictions
1. About the market at large
2. About your target market
3. About your entry in the field

IV. **Marketing Plan**
A. General strategy
1. Governmental regulations
2. Technological trends
B. Pricing philosophy
1. Sensitivity
2. Flexibility
C. Sales
1. Point of sale
2. Method of sale
3. How developed?
4. By whom?
5. Dependence on one purchaser?
D. Suppliers/Vendors
1. Dependence and reliability
2. Variety
3. Quality control
E. Customer Service
1. Who will handle?
2. How will routine problems be resolved?
3. Who will have decision-making authority?
F. Advertising
1. Objectives
2. Types or forms of advertising used within the industry
3. Forms of measuring the success
4. Flexibility
G. Sales
1. Forecasts
2. Variables

3. High/low parameters

V. **Operations**
A. Plant and equipment
1. Purchase versus rent
2. Minimum versus maximum
3. Obsolescence factors
B. Growth
1. Building expansion
2. Equipment additions
3. Impact on overhead and salaries
C. Projected time frame
1. Purchasing and expanding
2. Leasing and acquiring
3. Risk of too much too soon
4. Controlled growth

VI. **Financial Plan**
A. Projections
1. Income Statement
2. Balance Sheet
B. Break-even analysis
1. Projected sales
2. Sales growth
3. Minimum sales
4. How quickly can you make adjustments?
C. Startup and operating cash needs
1. Personal money
2. Outside investors
3. Loan proceeds
D. Use of proceeds
E. Repayment plan

VII. **Management**
A. The management team
B. Organizational chart
C. Responsibility and authority of key personnel
D. Resumes of key personnel
E. Resumes of major shareholders (if different)

VIII. **Outside Advice**
A. Legal
B. Accounting
C. Marketing/Advertising
D. Banker
E. Others

71

IX.   **Conclusion**

X.   **Supporting Documents**

I.   **Table of contents:** Readers will prefer a business plan enhanced by a table of contents listing the topics included.

II.   **Introduction:** The Introduction addresses the business, product, mission and industry. "Business" has to do with whether you are a service, retail, wholesale, manufacturing, engineering or construction concern. Often people think of industry and product as synonymous. Do not make this mistake. This can be especially damaging (or limiting) when you select a name to describe your company. If you use a product name as your business name, you may find growth is limited. Once you have decided what product(s) to manufacture or sell, define your industry separately. For example, a company in the 1960s may have decided its product was selling eight-track tapes, but how it defined its industry could determine its longevity in a changing market. History tells us that an eight-track tape company would be obsolete now. But, if the industry were defined as music or entertainment, you can see how flexible they could become for responding to change. Complications arise when you choose a product name instead of an industry name to promote your business. We do not have the fortune of operating with hindsight vision for our businesses. I only wish we were so lucky.

Every business should identify its mission. To find your mission, answer the following questions: Why does the business exist? What is the purpose of the business? Is it for profit? Is it for personal gain and satisfaction? Is it for the good of the community? Then try establishing what your mission is not. While profit is a necessary by-product of business, it should not be your goal. Profit represents the successful achievement of your mission. When stated as a mission, profit implies greed and loss of target market.

III. **Market Research:** Marketing research looks at the total industry, however it is defined. Analyze the data for both the total market and your specific customers. Your target market represents your potential customers, who may be defined by age, sex, race, education, affluence, location, etc. Quantify your target market. Is it growing? How aggressive is competition? What are the spending habits of your targeted consumers?

IV.   **Marketing Plan:** The Marketing Plan identifies how to get the product to the consumers. It looks at potential obstacles, such as government intervention, industry regulation, technological advancement and obsolescence factors. Price your product based on its sensitivity within the industry. Undercutting competitors may cheapen your company image by giving the appearance of a "lesser quality" than the competition. This is especially true for service industries where product comparisons are difficult.

V.   **Operations:** Operations incorporate the physical plant, its capacity and ability for growth, and your needs in terms of contract and equipment purchases (or leases). How adaptable is the plant for updating its process? Is the industry rapidly changing and improving quality? What is the minimum you can manufacture (or sell) to avoid losing money? What salaries are necessary to operate the business? How quickly can you respond to a dynamic market? These are all good questions to ask.

VI.   **Financial Plan:** The financial plan looks at the quantitative projections as well as the supporting documents and creates a pro forma (future) balance sheet and a profit and loss statement. It shows when you expect to see profits and how long you can afford to absorb losses. It is important to estimate your expenses carefully and show your cash needs thoroughly. This section may be the most scrutinized by bankers and investors.

VII.   **Management:** The management section provides an overview of the management team, their work experiences, education and strengths, along with their expected roles within the organization and philosophy. Women tend to operate with a flattened organization chart, sharing responsibility and authority among many.

VIII.   **Outside Advice**: List those individuals you plan to employ for outside consultations. Usually this will include attorneys, accountants, insurance agents and bankers, although others may be involved in the company's operation.

IX.   **Conclusion:** Write a brief summary concerning the company, its potential, management abilities and the probability of success. The conclusion is often read first by investors to determine their interest. Summarize all sections.

X.   **Supporting Documents:** Attach documents you feel are important in your business operation. Copies of any contracts, especially equipment and building contracts (leases and purchases) may be included, along with copies of lending agreements.

To start or not to start? Practicality v. passion

Women must prepare themselves mentally, emotionally and financially before accepting the responsibility of owning and operating a business. If you haven't done all your homework, stop and take a look at the information you still need to gather and the steps you need to take before you dive into it. It takes more than passion to make a business a success.

Learn the facts. Listen to the results. Many small businesses have failed not because it wasn't a great idea, but because it was not possible to make a profit. Others have failed because it wasn't the right time for either them or the product. Careful market analysis is essential. Often entrepreneurs ignore the warning signs. I know I did. Even though others have tried and failed, the new (blindly optimistic) entrepreneur feels her idea is different and better. If only she will take the time to learn from others, she may avoid a crushing blow.

Chapter 6

Legal forms of organization: styling and filing

"Anticipating a new reality is the beginning of the process of creating it."

Faith Popcorn
The Popcorn Report

Identifying your options

After you decide what type of business to open, then comes the decision of how to organize your business. There is no best structure for all situations. The three primary forms of ownership in the U.S. have different requirements and costs of entry. These forms are sole proprietorship, partnership and corporation. For businesses that have little debt and low risk of financial failure, a sole proprietorship might be recommended. However, if the potential exposure involves personal assets, the corporate structure might provide additional protection. Because most women start small, they tend to elect sole proprietorship status with greater frequency. In fact, 80 to 85 percent of all women-owned businesses are sole proprietorships. As businesses grow and needs and exposure change, the sole proprietorship may no longer be suitable; fortunately, it is the easiest form to change.

Let's look at what is involved with each type, as well as the benefits and disadvantages of each form of ownership. Keep in mind that your actual determination of the form of business ownership should be made with the guidance of professional advisors, both an accountant and attorney, who can review your specific needs and advise you accordingly.

Sole proprietorship

This is the most uncomplicated form of legal structure to develop, and the most common. Simply stated, you are the business and the business is you. But this can only happen if you are in business by yourself. The term "yourself" can apply to married couples when they file a joint tax return. See the section "Spousal business partnerships" later in this chapter. You may still hire employees in a sole proprietorship, but you must own 100 percent of the business.

You, the individual, own all rights and control all decisions of the business. You are owner of the company's assets (furniture, inventory, equipment, etc.) and you are financially responsible for the debts incurred by the business. Your personal assets are *not* separate from those of the company. Therefore, you are placing all your household assets at risk for the business, including your home, car and other personal items you may own. For example, if someone sued your company for breaking a contract and they won, you would have to pay the damages awarded by the court. If you did not have sufficient cash, you would be forced to liquidate other personal assets (house, car, boat, etc.) to pay the costs. Under a sole proprietorship, nothing is protected from company exposure. This is very different from corporate status, which offers a shield of protection.

There are few formalities to establish a sole proprietorship. The company usually uses the owner's Social Security number for the required company tax number.

Advantages of sole proprietorships

- You have complete authority concerning business operations without the need to involve others, such as stockholders, directors or partners.
- It is the easiest form to create and to terminate.
- Startup costs are less.
- All profits are retained by the individual.
- It can easily be changed to a partnership or corporation, if desired.
- There is less government regulation.

Disadvantages of sole proprietorships

- You are unable to protect your personal assets from business obligations.
- You are limited by yourself and your financial resources.
- You are completely responsible for the business, and getting time away may be difficult.
- The limited life of a proprietorship precludes passing the business to a designated heir and can complicate its sale.

Partnerships

Partnerships, when they work well, can bring a strong energy to a company. They can provide a built-in support mechanism—a confidant; a person who is committed to the business and its objectives just like you. Partnerships are a less popular form of business organization, and they aren't for everyone. When they don't work, they can be messier than the ugliest divorce you know. However, thoughtful selection of partners has produced a high success rate for partnerships. In fact, *Forbes Magazine* reported that in a study of 2,000 entrepreneurs whose businesses were founded since 1960, partnerships were four times as likely to succeed as sole proprietorships.

The common classifications of partnerships are general and limited. A partnership is not a taxable entity; it is the *relationship between two or more individuals who are involved in a trade or a business*. Partners typically contribute time, money, expertise and property or any combination of these to a business. The profits (or losses) from the partnership are reported on personal income tax returns. Partnerships are regulated by state government, and filing requirements and interpretations vary from state to state. Contact your Secretary of State's office to determine your state's legal requirements.

To form a partnership, there must be a clear understanding by all partners of what is expected and permitted within the company. It is strongly recommended that this understanding be written in the form of an agreement. A partnership agreement is the legal document filed by the partnership that lists specific understandings within the partnership, such as a partner's share of income (or loss), percentage of ownership, rights to sell, buy-back agreements, liabilities and dissolving the partnership. The more items spelled out in an agreement when the partnership is being formed, the less confusion later.

Partnerships have better results when they are based on common elements. Building a relationship, especially in business, takes time, energy, dedication and a willingness to compromise. There should exist a shared vision, a mutual respect and a trust. The rewards, however, of having someone to share in your triumphs, to divide the numerous responsibilities and to support you during those bumpy roads can make partnering a very attractive form of business organization.

The key to its success is finding the compatible match. This means knowing yourself, knowing and communicating what you are looking for in a partner, being honest, open and flexible, and having a willingness to share. Knowing your strengths and weaknesses will help you identify what you are looking for in a partner. First you must know what is important to you and the business. And then know that you can work well with someone else.

There are several kinds of partnerships. But all partnerships are formed by first having a general partnership. Let's look at the two most common forms of partnerships, general and limited.

General partnership

A general partnership consists of two or more individuals who are in business together. And unless otherwise stated, all partners are personally and equally liable for the company's debts and for any potential judgments against the partnership. In other words, the partnership's creditors (such as banks) can collect from any one of the partners without regard to their percentage of partnership involvement. Potential liability can be great since a single partner can

legally bind the partnership by signing a contract in the capacity of the partnership. A partnership ceases when any one of the partners dies, retires or declares bankruptcy, unless prior arrangements have been made.

Since a partnership is not considered a separate taxpayer, all profits (and or losses) are passed through individual income tax returns proportionate to the percentage of ownership. The partnership files an annual information return with the IRS, showing income and expenses for the business operation from the previous year. A partnership schedule is then filed with the partners' individual returns, which allows the partners to pay taxes or use the losses to offset related income.

Tax laws are constantly changing and being revised. I strongly recommend that your accountant prepare your tax returns (both company and personal) to allow you to take full advantage of current laws.

Advantages of partnerships

- Shared power and responsibility for business operations.
- Partnerships offer the potential for additional capital to be raised from multiple sources (partners' investments).
- Each partner can bring different strengths to the business. This works best when partners have complementary skills.
- Since income taxes are based on percentage of ownership, they may be lower than a corporate income tax might be.
- Partnerships offer the ability to have others (financially connected to the business) who can act as a sounding board for ideas and opinions. The financial well-being of the business is shared.

- Partnerships can be easily changed to corporations.

Disadvantages of partnerships

- All general partners are liable for the debts of the partnership.
- Each partner, individually, becomes exposed to the partnership's liabilities.
- Each partner can legally bind the partnership.
- A partnership terminates upon the death or incapacity of one member, unless prior arrangements are stipulated in the partnership agreement.
- Lack of equal involvement may make a partnership difficult to operate.
- Financial investments are limited by the partners' personal financial strengths.

Limited partnership

A limited partnership is based on a general partnership. It consists of one or more general partners, and one or more "limited partners" who have *limited* responsibilities and liabilities. General partners have management rights, which limited partners do not have. The term "silent partners" is often used to describe this arrangement because limited partners have no voice in the business operation. However, as an added benefit, limited partners are not fully exposed to partnership liabilities. A limited partner's loss is *limited* to her investment in the partnership. Another special feature for limited partners is their exposure to lawsuits. While general partners can sue or be sued for partnership problems, limited partners can only sue the partnership—or be sued by it—for problems that arise out of the limited partnership

itself. Outside entities or individuals cannot sue a limited partner.

Why create a limited partnership? Primarily they are created for the benefit of outside investors. Investors may believe in your concept, but not be willing to risk total exposure. This type of arrangement provides the vehicle for their protection while allowing you management flexibility and freedom.

Creating a limited partnership involves more formalities and legal constraints than a general partnership. And unless great care is taken, a limited partnership may find itself being treated as a general partnership. Therefore, it is especially important to seek professional advice in the creation of a limited partnership.

Spousal business partnership

One of the fastest growing areas for women-owned businesses is starting a business with her spouse. This partnership form qualifies also as a sole proprietorship when the partners (spouses) file joint tax returns. From an operational standpoint, then, you are completely exposed personally to all liabilities of the business. The psychological benefits and pitfalls are discussed in Chapter 16. Spousal business partnerships should only be undertaken when you have a strong, healthy marriage. Communications and trust are at the very core of their success.

Corporation

As women's businesses grow, they frequently seek the protection provided by corporate status. A corporation is a legal entity that has a life of its own. It is an organizational structure that has been established in accordance with the laws of the various states and endowed with rights and responsibilities. A corporation is owned by shareholders (or stockholders) and managed by a board of directors who are elected by and answer to the shareholders.

Corporate status is not for big businesses only. Small companies can form corporations with great ease. In the least complicated form, a corporation may have only one shareholder (you) who owns 100 percent of the issued stock. And that one shareholder (you) may also act as the chairwoman of the board, and be the president of your company. You may nominate and elect those individuals who you would like to serve on your board of directors. As you are the sole voting stockholder, their nomination should pass with ease.

Even though you may be the sole stockholder, there are numerous regulations you must conform to and forms you must file, as do all corporations. Legal counsel should be obtained to verify that state and federal procedures are followed completely. These procedures include stockholder meetings, keeping notices and minutes of all board meetings, electing officers to the board of directors and appropriate board approval for various decisions affecting the operation of the business, such as applying for a loan, purchasing large equipment, etc. When procedures are not strictly adhered to, you risk losing the protection provided by corporate status. Your corporate charter will outline authority and proper procedures to follow.

Stock is sold to raise capital for the business. And as owners of stock, the stockholders own a part of your company. If you are the only stockholder, the potential for problems is eliminated. However, if you use stock to raise more capital, reward employees or share responsibility, you must be very cautious.

Minority stockholders, those with less than controlling interest in your company, have many rights, too. And their involvement in your business can wreak havoc on your corporation. They have the right to insist that the corporation conduct business formally, never mind the informal decision-making process you were accustomed to. In addition, if there is extra money in the business, minority stockholders have the right to insist that dividends be paid before salaries are increased. They have the right to ask for a court appointed "receiver" or "custodian" to look over the shoulder of the primary stockholder, which can be a nightmare, or at least an inconvenience. And a minority stockholder may have the right to sell their stock in your company to anyone, including your competitor, unless otherwise specified. You must be very careful who you sell stock to, especially as an investor.

In days gone by, the formation of a corporation protected an individual's personal assets and separated the person from the business. In an abstract sense it still does that today. However, the climate in the U.S. has created more accountability for board members. There have been several lawsuits filed against board members for their mismanagement of funds. Many judgments have been found in favor of the plaintiff. Also, in the past, small businesses had many off-balance-sheet financed benefits, such as take-home car usage and personal long distance calls paid for by the company. Tax laws have restricted many of these benefits, and requirements to account for corporate funds are more stringent. It is becoming commonplace to have the individual or primary stockholder of small businesses sign all obligations personally as well as in the company name. This occurrence dilutes a significant benefit of forming a corporation—and fully exposes you to the company's liabilities.

Corporate federal tax rates have historically been higher than individual rates. The 1993 tax rate was staggered for both corporations and individuals. Corporations that made less than $50,000 paid at a 15 percent federal tax rate. The rate increased to 39 percent for profits above $100,000. However, for those companies classified as personal service corporations, which includes attorneys, accountants, consultants, etc., the IRS has a flat rate of 35 percent on all profits. This flat rate charge could affect many of the women-owned businesses, if they elect corporate status.

Individuals (single, married and head of household) paid 15 percent on taxable income under $22,100. The rate increased to a top rate of 36 percent for taxable income above $250,000.

Profits are maintained in the corporation through retained earnings. If earnings accumulate beyond the reasonable needs of the business, the corporation can be subject to an accumulated earnings tax. These accumulated earnings are expected to be paid out to shareholders in the form of dividends.

Attorneys often recommend corporate status because of its protective basis. On the other hand, your accountant may be more objective in assisting with this assessment. Listen to both their arguments. But, ultimately the decision is yours.

I strongly encourage that corporate filings be handled by attorneys familiar with state requirements. However, books and filings forms are available in office supply stores or bookstores for do-it-yourself incorporating.

Advantages of corporations

- The shareholders' liability (frequently owners) is often limited to the amount of their investment. This provides the ability to separate your personal assets from company assets.
- The business will have a legal life of its own, which allows for the continuation of the corporation beyond your life. A corporation can be passed down simply by transferring stock ownership.
- Since shareholders are the owners of the corporation through their stock purchases, you have the opportunity to raise more capital by opening up the sale of stock to more people. Often small percentages are sold (or transferred) to key employees as an incentive or company benefit.
- Ownership can be conveyed through selling or transferring stock.
- Corporations are allowed numerous tax deductions not available to partnerships or sole proprietorships.

Disadvantages of corporations

- The complexity of starting and maintaining a corporation dictates higher costs and more guidance to conform to legal requirements.
- The board of directors dictates policy, while shareholders, who elect these board members, must be satisfied. The decision-making process is more complex.
- Corporate income distributed as ordinary dividends is double-taxed. The dividends are taxed first as profits in the corporation, and then as income to the shareholder.

• You may pay more taxes unless you elect S status. Corporate tax rates are generally higher than individual tax rates.

S corporation

Since federal income tax policy may strongly influence your legal form of organization, you may want to consider forming your corporation as an S corporation. The Internal Revenue Code provides a way to keep all the benefits of corporations, but to allow the corporation to be taxed at the individual tax rate. Under S corporate structures, the income, losses, deductions and credits of the corporation are passed through to its shareholders to be included on their personal returns.

An S corporation benefits from both personal and corporate entities. While the organizational requirements for corporate structure must be met and maintained, the profits are taxed on an individual tax basis (for each shareholder). The S status exists *only* for reporting taxes and can easily be changed to a regular corporate tax structure when it is deemed financially advantageous.

Some states do not recognize the S corporation status although the Federal government does. What this means is that while you may still get the individual tax benefit from the IRS, if your state has a state income tax, you may be taxed at the corporate rate.

To become an S corporation, you must meet the requirements of an S corporation and have the consent of the shareholders. The current requirements for S status are that you must be a domestic corporation, you may have only one class of stock, you may have no more than 35 shareholders, all shareholders must be individuals (partnerships and corporations that own your stock preclude you from electing S status) and all shareholders must be U.S. citizens.

The IRS requires that form 2553 be filed when a corporation elects S status. It is not sufficient to meet the requirements and note in your corporate charter the election of S status. Without filing this form, your corporation is not recognized as an S corporation.

Seek advice and recommendations from both your accountant and your attorney for this adaptation. They know your personal and financial needs and can provide recommendations on specific items and their effect on you.

Limited liability company

The newest form of organization, the limited liability company (LLC), is a hybrid of the positive aspects of both a partnership and an S corporation. LLCs are, as with other forms of business organization, governed by state laws. Therefore variances occur from state to state. The first LLC began in 1977 in the state of Wyoming. Since that time, more than 40 states recognize this legal structure.

Limited liability companies avoid the double taxation of dividends while protecting personal assets from the liabilities of the business. Commonly, they eliminate the maximum on the number of shareholders and the restriction on the class of stock offered, which currently restricts S corporations. LLCs are member-managed instead of being responsible to a board of directors as are corporate structures.

The cost of constructing an LLC is often as high or higher than that of forming a corporation. Legal counsel will advise you of the benefits, costs and ramifications, given your particular situation. Because of the newness of this form, many of the details are still being established in state legislatures.

Cooperatives

A cooperative, or coop, can be established as either a partnership or a corporation. They are generally formed for businesses in the areas of agriculture, housing, child care and craft design. To create a cooperative, you need a group of people having common economic or physical needs. The cooperative does not make money for itself, but for its members. Profits are shared according to a predetermined agreement. Some states have laws regulating coops. When a coop is incorporated, the coop members are not personally liable for any debts the cooperative incurs. If, however, the coop elects partnership status, all of its members are responsible for any business debt. Profits, under the partnership formation, are taxed as individual income.

Following the letter of the law

Starting a business involves a lot of paperwork. Do not think that by operating a business outside the law you are saving yourself money. Much of this paperwork is designed so that you gain tax benefits and (depending on the form of ownership) can limit your liability.

Start your business off on the right foot. Make the necessary calls to determine what is required by your state, county, city, as well as by federal regulations. Each state has different requirements. The following is a general list provided to start the process:

County court clerk: In your county of residence or operation (if different counties, call both—ask about necessary licensing for your specific business).

State department of revenue: In your state of operation, ask about state taxes and franchise and excise tax filing fees. They may be different based on the form of ownership.

State department of employment security: In your state, this office can provide you with an employer account number, which is needed for paying unemployment tax (on all employees, unless you are your only employee). Unemployment benefits are supported by state funds and paid through these taxes.

Internal Revenue Service: This Federal government agency will give you a Federal ID number and tell you tax requirements for your form of ownership.

Secretary of State: This office can provide information concerning your state's corporate license applications, fees and requirements.

Seeking expert advice

Be smart. Surround yourself with the best advice you can afford. It costs less to get qualified, expert advice in the beginning—even if the hourly rate is high—than cleaning up a mess later on. But who are these "qualified" professionals and how do you find them?

Realizing you are legally responsible for all decisions and actions of your company means you still need to make the final call. If you hire someone who fails to provide sound advice on an acceptable timetable, fails to file required forms, etc., it is you who must answer (and pay) for the mistake. For example, if your accountant does not file your quarterly federal tax returns when due, the penalty will be assessed to you. You hired the accountant; you should know her abilities. While you may have legal recourse, it is often too little, too late.

The two most important individuals who can help you in starting and operating a small business are a Certified Public Accountant (CPA) and a business attorney. Finding someone who is knowledgeable about your industry and about small business operations can be invaluable. They can save you time and money and avert many potential problems. They can provide the inside track. Find someone already experienced in areas that affect you and your business. That way, you won't have to pay for their learning.

Both your attorney and CPA should have defined roles and agreed-upon expectations. It is not uncommon for them to confer, since often their territories overlap. In fact, encourage them to frequently share information.

Although I use the female pronoun in referring to both the accountant and attorney, I do not recommend one sex over the other. I recommend finding the most qualified individual, regardless of gender, race or any other bias. Find someone who can do the best job for you at an affordable price.

If you already have connections with accountants and attorneys, this may save you money (or maybe not), but that doesn't mean they are the best-suited individuals for your business. It is costly to change, but not impossible. Recommendations and referrals remain the best method for finding advisors. Others you might add to your professional team include bankers, insurance agents, financial planners and marketing or advertising consultants. The purpose of your team is to provide you with objective feedback and to fill you with knowledge about specific issues. Always try to find individuals you are comfortable with in business dealings, individuals who will work in partnership with you, not in a dictatorship to you.

Certified Public Accountant

The question many entrepreneurs ask is should I pay the higher rate for a CPA? Or is a bookkeeper or tax preparer sufficient? It helps to understand the role a CPA plays to see why the rates may be higher. A bookkeeper records numbers; an accountant interprets data; and a CPA reads the numbers and turns them into statements and predictions. CPAs consider themselves consultants of your financial well-being. A good CPA instructs you on how to run your company so that she will not waste her time (billable time) cleaning up your mess. As your business grows, your need for additional services grows, and your CPA earns more money. She will grow with you.

Unfortunately, CPAs do not come cheap. Be prepared to spend as much as $3,000 for the first year's advice and service. Budget sufficiently and allow for the quality of service you expect. Future years' charges should be less since the first year includes your training as well as establishing proper accounting procedures. A good CPA doesn't want to act as your bookkeeper. She will help you to establish the appropriate accounting methods internally that will aid in her analysis. The less additional work she has to do, the lower your cost. If she's not willing to spend time training you on these procedures, find someone who is.

Business attorney

Did you know that the United States has more lawyers per person than any other country? Yet, because the legal field is so specialized, finding someone qualified in small business operations will be challenging. Do not use your real estate, trust or divorce attorney for this job. Seek someone who is knowledgeable in business law and the laws of your state and local government.

What is expected of a company's lawyer? A good attorney will take a leadership role in representing your company. In addition, she may participate in planning, organizing and controlling business operations. By being involved in various aspects of the business, your attorney can make sound decisions based on facts. Consider your attorney preventive medicine. She should keep you out of trouble and not have to spend her time (and your money) putting out fires that could have been avoided.

In seeking legal counsel you should establish what responsibilities will be given to the attorney to achieve your objectives. Once selected, the attorney should know and understand the firm's goals and be willing to assist in their implementation. Use an attorney prior to signing any documents, not after.

A good habit to get into is to never sign a document, no matter how routine, without having your attorney review it first!

Many contracts are written with the expectation that negotiations will take place. No document is too routine to have your attorney review. Have her explain the small print and its potential repercussions to your operations.

Entrepreneurs must adhere to many laws, such as business laws, tax laws, leases and contracts, labor laws, zoning laws, local ordinances on signs, health permits, licenses, OSHA standards and many, many more. Chapter 14 briefly highlights some of the more common regulations. But they are just the tip of the iceberg. Hire a qualified attorney;

have her (and help her) keep you informed at all times.

Finding the experts

How do you find these archangels? They are, unfortunately, not heaven-sent. The process involves interviewing and sifting carefully through information to determine your specific needs and how they can best be met.

First, find a source of potential applicants to interview. Yes, you should interview CPAs and attorneys just like you do any other potential employee. Being a professional doesn't make someone right for you or your business.

Finding prospective advisors can be accomplished in a variety of ways. Check with business acquaintances or friends who currently have a lawyer or accountant. Do they like and recommend their advisors? Referrals can save a lot of time. Also, other professionals (bankers, insurance agents, city officials, etc.) may have recommendations. Don't forget to network with small business owners and industry specialists. Ask for recommendations. Compile a list of names. Use the yellow pages only as a last resort.

After you have a list of candidates, prepare several questions that give you a consistent basis for reviewing each person's qualifications. Schedule a get-acquainted interview. Be sure there is *no fee* for this initial consultation or interview. Eliminate immediately anyone who charges an initial fee. Plan on interviewing several candidates before the list begins to narrow.

When designing your questions, weigh the potential answers. The sample questions on the next page will help you determine each question's importance and how negotiable the answer is. Eliminate those individuals who do not meet your minimum standards and expectations. For example, which is more important to you: small business experience or industry experience? Frequently, you must choose between them. Is there a fixed dollar amount budgeted for these professional services? How flexible is that amount? Ask the professionals to estimate the first year's costs for their services, and see whether they are willing to help you save money in their fees by allowing you to do some of the work yourself.

Here are some guideline questions you might include in your interview:

- **Have you represented small businesses before?** Historically you will find that experience will be an excellent indicator of qualification. Though lack of experience alone may not eliminate someone, it is good to listen to their practical experience and expertise as it applies to you. Also ask if they have worked with startup companies before or with franchise businesses.
- **Do you have any clients in my industry?** Again you want to understand their expertise as it applies to your business. Avoid paying for your professional team to learn. Not only will it cost you more because it takes longer, but it may not be the best advice available.
- **What is your billable hourly rate?** Also ask if there is someone in their office (perhaps an assistant) who can do part of the leg work at a lower rate? What you want to see is a willingness to be fair and not gouge you.

- **When you bill, do you send a detailed analysis of the charges?** Request this if it is not offered. It's your money, and you have a right to know the specific details of charges. Some professional may argue or say their firm is not set up to provide detailed bills. But in such a case, how will you know if they're saving you on the billing rate?
- **What are your office hours?** Will it be difficult to meet with them during those hours? Most professionals keep standard 9 to 5 hours. But make sure. Also, location may be a consideration.
- **Are you comfortable advising me on various situations?** First, decide how much authority you are *willing* to relinquish to these professionals and then see if they are comfortable with that much responsibility. Let them know specifically what is expected of them so that you will not be disappointed later. Are they willing to work in partnership with you?
- **How will you feel if I do not take your advice?** This is one of the most important questions you can ask. Can the person work in the role of advisor and not dictator? Often, the egos of professionals make this difficult to achieve. Since the repercussions will be on you, the decision should ultimately be yours. Hopefully, you will not have a difference of opinion, but you want to know going in that your authority is respected.

Chapter 7

Marketing concerns: more than selling, servicing and promoting

"The state of mind of today's consumers—their needs, their fears and the personalized benefits they're seeking—are more important than age or zip codes or numbers."

Faith Popcorn
The Popcorn Report

Marketing

Marketing is not just selling. It incorporates the selling function, but marketing is much more. Marketing looks at presence. Marketing searches beyond selling to get to the heart of having the right product, for the right price, in the right location. It includes research, distribution, pricing, advertising and promotion, as well as selling. It means convenience when convenience is important. It means quality service when service is required. And it means having the lowest price when cost is the deciding factor. Marketing means creating long-lasting repeat business.

At the root of planning, selling and organizing you must have information. In today's information age, however, the abundance of knowledge may overwhelm you as you struggle through stacks of material searching for relevant data. Information overload can easily be the result if you are not focused. Ironically, technology was supposed to make our lives less complicated. But, instead, it seems to have increased our work load, forcing us to absorb more information and put more

time and energy into trying to keep up the pace.

Marketing is the very essence of any business. Without a buyer, businesses cannot exist. Entrepreneurs have long realized that effective marketing doesn't happen by accident. It is the result of mindful and intentional planning. Marketing means knowing who your customers are, understanding how your company fits within the industry, identifying competitors' strengths and weaknesses, having a marketing plan (and following it), and then evaluating the results and making the necessary adjustments.

Women are accustomed to the role of consumer and understand that buyers hate to be talked down to. Buyers want to feel important, to know that *their* purchase matters (regardless of its size). And buyers want to know that you are an honest, caring business owner.

Successful entrepreneurs understand that people don't care how much you know until they know how much you care.

Women have frequently targeted other women as their niche markets, creating or improving on products or services to fill voids. In addition, women have created many new products and services reflective of our changing lifestyles and career choices. For example, women have found great success in day-care operations, child taxi services, gift-buying services, party planning and hostessing functions. All of these are the by-products of experience, need and a changing family lifestyle pattern.

Marketing research

After identifying one or more business opportunities you'd be interested in pursuing, your next step is to determine the market potential for each prospect. You'll have better results by *responding* to the market than by attempting to change the market to meet your particular product or service. The latter is a losing battle from the start.

There are a variety of sources women can consult for information. Some are free, others cost money; some are useful, others are a waste of time. Your challenge is to find the most beneficial information for the least amount of money. Sources (usually free) include your local library, the Small Business Administration, networking associations and various business seminars. Other options such as consultants and accountants charge fees. On-line information sources have made accessing a variety of data much easier, and the costs often vary with usage.

One of the most underused resources available is that of interviewing individuals currently in your industry. Talk to the competition if they appear receptive. Do not assume that, because they are competition, they will not share information with you. While some people are very protective of information, others are willing to share general knowledge. There's no need to reinvent the wheel when you don't have to. Instead, find business owners who will share their stories and experiences.

Ask open questions like, "I'm thinking about opening a small business and wondered if you would share some advice with me. Maybe something you wish you had known before you started the business." Or you might ask something more specific about how they see the industry changing or what the competition has done to their business. Use your judgment about how personal a question you can ask. Don't be offended if they don't share their information. Maybe they don't believe in the merits of networking. Whatever the reason, move on to the next story. There are always others who are willing to share.

Federal and state government agencies are an abundant resource for information and have numerous pockets of money for small business financing. The U.S. Department of Commerce collects statistical data that can be very beneficial for business planning. Your local library will be an excellent resource for material. Also, utilize the SBA and its side arms, The Service Corps of Retired Executives (S.C.O.R.E.) and the Small Business Development Centers (SBDC), whenever they're available. Most of their services are free to the public.

There is no question that marketing research is an integral part of business planning. It should encompass evaluating test markets and determining the total size of the overall market, as well as the target market, understanding pricing elasticity within the industry and knowing how to develop and evaluate sales techniques. Marketing research can be gathered by both statistical research and observation. Ideally, both are used.

You must first understand how consumers respond to your potential product or to the competitions' products. Each industry requires determining those factors that are most vulnerable in your business and concentrating on those areas. Sample questions you might ask are:

- Who will buy this product or service?
- What features are these customers looking for?
- What benefits can be offered? What cannot?
- How much competition exists within this market?
- How frequently do consumers purchase this item or service?
- Will I be dependent on repeat business?
- How much would consumers pay for this product?
- What are the competitions' prices?
- What is different about my product from the competitions'?
- Would consumers pay more for my product than competing prices?
- Is there more than one use for this product?

Research is a matter of keeping your eyes and ears open, but do not rely on your own judgment to make market-research decisions. Your opinion is important, but it is not the total picture. An optimistic assumption is that you will have enough information to make an informed decision half the time. This means that 50 percent of the time you will not have enough information to proceed. Businesses cannot stay in business long undertaking this much risk. The

way to lessen this risk is by researching your market carefully through a variety of sources. And listen cautiously to the results.

Will your target market support your ideas and products? No one item will motivate all of your prospects. But, are there enough customers to make going into business profitable? Research, along with personal observation, can help determine whether the potential market exists. You may develop a short questionnaire and take random samples from potential customers at specific locations. Remember, always listen to what the customers are saying!

The importance of statistical data

One of the best methods for obtaining information in marketing research is through statistical analysis. Statistical information can be confusing and overwhelming if we let it. Given the abundance of information available, we need a strong foundation for interpreting this data. The challenge becomes obtaining the correct (or best available) data to make informed, less risky decisions.

How do we know if the numbers are true? We may never know, especially since we are dealing with trends and human responses. However, the more research we acquire and the more frequently a number is repeated, then the more likely that the outcome can be predicted. Realize that it still boils down to a *best-guess* scenario based on assumptions and the past. While there is a great deal of emphasis placed on historical data, it may not predict the future with any degree of accuracy.

Do not look for absolutes. The world is constantly changing. People are constantly changing. And your market is constantly changing. Do not accept the written word as fact, simply because it is in print. Your objective is to discern its reliability. And that may be one of the greatest challenges to entrepreneurs. Your success with knowing garbage from facts will grow as you learn more about your industry and trends. The more you know, the easier information becomes to decipher.

Sources available

There are numerous places to go for research. Start with the public library. Most public libraries have copies of the U.S. Bureau of Census publications and abstracts available. Both are filled with statistical information concerning past trends and future projections and are excellent sources for obtaining marketing data.

The Bureau of Census in the Department of Commerce collects a wealth of census data on numerous aspects of business. Compilations are produced at varying intervals, as shown in the following list:

- Catalog of United States Census Publications (monthly)
- Census of Agriculture (every five years)
- Census of Business (every five years)
- Census of Government (every five years)
- Census of Manufacturers (every five years)
- Census of Population (every 10 years)
- Census of Retail Trade (monthly)
- Census of Selected Services (monthly)
- Census of Wholesale Trade (monthly)
- Statistical Abstract of the United States (annually)

In addition, local state, city and county agencies collect statistical data. You can look for the *State and Metropolitan Area Data Book* as well as county and city data books. The frequency of publication for these varies. Your reference librarian will be able to assist you.

Other federal agencies within the Department of Commerce that you may want to contact include the Bureau of Economic Analysis, Bureau of Industrial Economics, Domestic and International Business Administration, and International Trade Administration.

U.S. Small Business Administration

The U.S. Small Business Administration (SBA) can be a valuable source for guidance and information. It's an independent federal agency whose primary function is to assist, counsel and champion the millions of American small businesses. The SBA provides small businesses with financial assistance, management training, counseling and help in getting a fair share of government contracts. With over 100 field offices around, there may be an office in your city. The SBA offers a variety of general business counseling services either for free or for a nominal fee.

The SBA's Office of Women's Business Ownership offers a range of specialized resources, including financial assistance, publications, counseling and training. The Microloan pilot program (not yet available in every state) offers loans from $100 to $25,000. The Women's Network for Entrepreneurial Training is a year-long mentoring program that links startup business owners with seasoned entrepreneurs who offer advice on a variety of business topics. And the SBA's Procurement Assistance Office provides counseling, training and contract assistance for women interested in competing for federal government contracts. Local field offices have a person designated to provide assistance to women entrepreneurs.

The SBA realizes that in addition to financial assistance, small business owners need management advice, expertise and support. Who better to give this advice than someone who has been an entrepreneur? So, S.C.O.R.E. was created as an independent, voluntary, nonprofit association that provides business counseling and training. Training seminars are offered in business planning, marketing, finance, accounting records, advertising, inventory control, etc. This is an excellent place to find an industry mentor and friend and to build your network.

Small Business Development Centers, another SBA program, provides counseling, training and research assistance for all aspects of small business management. SBDCs are usually located on college campuses. They are one of my favorite sources for entrepreneurial information and are frequently overlooked.

As women business owners expand their companies, they become increasingly important to the local, regional, national and global economies. The SBA is working hard to participate in this dynamic market and to help women achieve their goals.

Finding other sources

In addition, local trade and community organizations are good sources of marketing information. These groups not only have the resources concerning local habits and markets, but they also have hands-on experience. Consider joining local merchant associations, trade groups or the Chamber of Commerce. Participate. Go to meetings. Get on committees. Meet a lot of people. Share information. And create interactive networks.

And finally, talk with professionals, such as bankers, attorneys, accountants and college professors, to see what information they have uncovered in their research and contacts. You'll never know what information others have unless you ask.

Analyzing raw data

Numbers can be confusing. Numbers can be boring. Numbers can be manipulated and massaged. However, numbers still paint the best picture of future scenarios, options and pitfalls to either follow or avoid. Without a doubt, numbers are extremely important to a well-prepared business.

Numbers can be confusing if you lack the mathematical background to interpret the results. Don't become overwhelmed by the multitude of numbers available, with different formulas and interpretations. Take it one step at a time.

Numbers can bring the abstract concept into tangible focus if you are willing to spend the time and listen to the results. Numbers are an extremely useful decision-making tool for small business owners.

Learning how to use numbers to create meaningful data takes time and practice, however. For example, if you are entering the service field of computer training, there are several sources of data to analyze for better understanding your market. First, list what it is you are trying to discover. The following questions are samples. Of course, the list could go on and on:

- How large is the computer sales market?
- How has it grown over the past five years?
- How many personal computers are in homes verses at offices?

- How frequently do individuals or companies upgrade their systems?
- What are the projections for computer sales for the next 5 years?
- How competitive is the computer training market?

Next, try to find out, as best you can, the answers to these questions. You will discover a variety of answers (often conflicting) from differing sources. Most sources will explain how they determined their answers. Mark each source as reasonable, conservative, liberal (overzealous) or unfounded. At the very minimum, your sources should include government documents and surveys, industry and trade publications and personal observation. The more you include, the stronger and more meaningful the results. Quite often, I have found that government statistics are very conservative, whereas industry and trade sources tend to be more liberal in their findings. The final analysis is a judgment call, but it should be based on sound findings and recurrence of data.

Look at what your research has produced. Were you unable to find a numerical response because some of your questions were not included in surveys? That is quite often the case. In these instances, you will probably have to assess a best guess. Try to find some industry or trade magazines that support your hypothesis.

Much available information is based on national averages. The next step requires determining your local market's relationship to national trends. Locally, if you are facing high unemployment numbers, large corporate downsizing (or closings) or a recession, your business may not follow national trends at all. Training may be considered a luxury item that companies and individuals can do without. Or, you may be in a location that simply lags behind national averages. For understanding the local market, your chamber of commerce should be able to provide resources that are available from government or private enterprise.

Another indicator is to note how other small-service businesses are doing in your market. Is the market not large enough to support your business locally? How many computer stores are there? Do they offer in-house training? Research from your local newspaper may indicate trends.

National trends can give you an indication of where your product or service is in its life cycle, how quickly change is introduced and accepted, and the size of the total market. Your local numbers, however, are more important in your final decision. Ultimately, all numbers can do is reduce some of the risk that is inherent in small business operations. And the more risk you can eliminate, the greater your opportunity for success.

A common problem for entrepreneurs is starting with the wrong set of figures. If the numbers do not work, don't expect the idea to survive—at least not for long. Numbers not only make you wiser to the business, they also communicate to others your knowledge and understanding of your business and your industry.

Location, location, location

Not all businesses are location-sensitive. Before starting a company, determine how important location is to your business. What image are you portraying? Where are your customers located? And how far will your customers travel to get to you?

Location is often more of an issue for retail operations than for service businesses. You must determine if customers (or clients) will be coming to you, and if so, how visible you need to be for them to find you. Many businesses have excelled based on choosing a strong, visible, high-traffic and accessible location. On the other hand, location may have little impact on revenues for your operation. Often prime locations come with prime price tags. Is that money well-spent for your business? Will you benefit from walk-in traffic? Or will walk-ins impede your normal operation and cost you more money than they produce? Analyze the effects of location for your business from a variety of angles before finally deciding its impact.

Studying market potential is important in selecting the right site. You may want to talk with your Chamber of Commerce about growth and economic feasibility within a specific area. In addition, you can utilize data from the U.S. Bureau of the Census, which provides general characteristics of the population, including age, race, sex, education, occupation, income, etc. One of the most successful methods for small businesses, however, remains observing traffic patterns and the competition. Be sure to evaluate the potential location from both a current and future market perspective.

Don't forget yourself. After all, work should be enjoyable, and this is more likely to occur if you do what you like where you want to do it. Do you and the location mix well together? Is it convenient to your home? Is it a safe area for working late hours, especially if you will be there alone. Determine what is important to you and how these decisions affect your bottom line. Analyze all results carefully before deciding on where to locate your business.

Competition

Competition exists for every product. Don't deny its existence in your industry. *Everyone* has competition, whether direct or indirect. You may be competing for dollars and time or you may be competing for convenience, price or service. But competition always exists.

Competition is not necessarily bad; it can also be healthy for your business. While you can win the competitions' customers over, realize that you can also lose your customers to the competition. Don't underestimate the power of competition. A price war may produce a long, harsh battle whose winner may exhibit financial staying power, not quality.

Direct competition may actually be a benefit. Some companies prefer to locate near competition, others are weakened by competition and still others are not affected significantly by where competitors locate. For example, automobile dealerships feel they are strengthened when they locate near other dealerships. On the other hand, print shops prefer to distance themselves from direct competition. Attorneys and accountants feel that competition does not affect their sales significantly.

If you expect customers to change to your product or service, be sure you know what customers want for that change. The average person usually resists change. To change, whether brands or companies, represents significant discontent with the status quo. Research has shown that it takes 22 repetitions of something before it becomes a habit. You cannot gain market share just by being as good as the competition. Conversely, being better may not be important to the customer.

The easiest way to gain market share is by entering new and growing segments. These markets have less competition, are increasing and often offer easier entry. Although there is an inherent risk associated with new, less proven markets, there may also be a significant opportunity for growth and expansion.

Pricing

Pricing is the one area new business owners feel most unsure of. Pricing is defined as what a business charges for its products or services. The dilemma involves maintaining prices low enough to compete in the market and generate sufficient sales and high enough to provide profits. Each industry varies widely as to price elasticity. Demand for a product is elastic when a small change in price significantly changes its demand. Demand inelasticity is reflected when changes in price do not alter significantly the demand for the products. Tobacco and liquor are considered to be inelastic goods. On the other hand, computers are considered to be elastic items. As prices have come down, the number of people owning computers has increased significantly.

Women frequently undervalue their products. Prices that are too low can translate into an unprofitable business. And increased sales may result in increased losses. Women too often place little importance on profitable pricing. This has been a significant problem for women who operate service businesses because product costs are more difficult to calculate.

Pricing for profit is vital to any business in a free-enterprise system. But pricing should not be driven by profit motives at the expense of fair, ethical tactics and competition. Profits should be the result of smart business, not the means toward an end. With good business relationships and products priced correctly, profits will occur naturally.

Different factors affect a company's pricing structure. Pricing may be affected by the perceived image, the price sensitivity of the market, the prestige of the product or the differentiation of products, quality, competition and profit. The three commonly used pricing strategies are: cost pricing, competitive pricing and market-value pricing. Your choice depends on several variables, but should always stay flexible and open to change.

The most commonly used pricing strategy is cost pricing. In cost pricing, simply stated, you calculate all your expenses, both direct and indirect, and then add a profit. The second strategy is competitive pricing. Competitive pricing meets the going price for similar products in your local market. It does not take into account costs as the primary factor. Finally, market-value pricing looks at what the market will bear. Market-value pricing is generally used for unique products or services that have few or no competing products on the market.

Adopt a pricing policy that integrates these strategies, but fits your needs. When you decide on a price, make sure you can still be profitable. Determining your company's total costs to operate can be a tedious and slow process, but it is imperative to assess costs when you are establishing pricing. You may be surprised to know that many companies have tried to increase sales to make a profit, when all they were actually doing was losing more money.

Unfortunately, you cannot control all items that go into the calculation of costs. For example, prices of raw materials may fluctuate frequently. Or your utility company may approve a rate increase for your service. How quickly you are able to respond to these items may strongly impact the viability of your business. The soundness of your assumptions should be carefully tested before you gamble all you have invested.

Service industries should follow these same guidelines. However, costs are often harder to determine. For service businesses, begin by evaluating your competition's prices and decide what customers are willing to pay for your service. Calculate your costs to see if the current market price will cover your expenses. What image does price connote to your clients? Some products suggest price and quality correlation. In other words, a less expensive product may be thought of as a poorer quality product. And finally, talk with other industry specialists to see how elastic pricing is for your market.

When you start a new business, you want to stand out from the crowd, somehow, so that you are noticed. Often the initial pricing structure will not be your long-term pricing strategy. Instead, you may find that by offering lower introductory prices, the consumers are educated to you, your product and your business. Also realize that you may have different prices for different customers, based on quantity, annual volume or other, perhaps competitive, factors.

Whatever your pricing theory and objective, remember that you must always be ready to react quickly to changes in market conditions. A successful pricing policy is sound, logical and, most importantly, flexible at all times.

Bartering

Bartering is one of the oldest forms of enterprise. And, it is one that women are finding extremely beneficial as they start and grow businesses on tight budgets. Don't be shy about offering your business's products or services in this type of arrangement. If another business has a product you are willing to purchase, you may never know whether they want to purchase your product (or service) unless you ask. Not everyone will be interested in bartering, but it can help a struggling business during a cash flow crunch. It is a definite advantage for service industries that have time as their biggest expense. Plus, when used selectively, bartering can be an excellent source of advertising and business referrals as more people try your product and tell their friends.

Ask about bartering for printing and duplicating costs, marketing, promotion and consulting as well as for other personal items.

For tax purposes, a bartering transaction is valued like a cash transaction (without the cash). The savings, however, come from not using your money. There are tax implications from bartering that your accountant will explain, depending on the actual transaction and the nature of your business.

Selling

Selling is a learned skill. To be successful at selling requires both a thorough knowledge of your product and a complete and sensitive understanding of your customer. Selling involves trial and error. It involves listening and learning. It also involves evaluating and changing.

Good selling includes several fundamental steps. First know your product and its features and benefits. Ask sufficiently probing questions of your potential customers to qualify them as buyers, not just shoppers. And finally, speak specifically to their needs through the product's benefits. Sales should be 80-percent listening and 20-percent talking. When asking questions, ask open-ended questions that allow potential customers to offer specific information about their concerns. Answer their concerns one by one. The questions are very important to your buyers. Therefore, they are very important to you.

After you have responded to a customer's concerns sufficiently, it is time to close the sale. Knowing when to close a sale takes perception, knowledge and confidence. If you are sheepish and unsure of yourself, customers tend to be hesitant; radiating a sense of confidence can go a long way in helping you close a sale.

Be sure to ask the prospect if they would like to buy your product or service. You may be surprised how many people lose sales simply because they haven't asked for them. Find a closing line you feel comfortable with, something that works for you, and then stick with it. Make it simple and direct. Sometimes, saying something like "Will that be cash or charge?" will work. At other times, customers will be put off by your smooth presumption of closure.

Depending on your product or service and your market, closing a sale may take time. Customers may want to go home and think over the purchase. In this case, you should have a follow-up procedure for letting the potential customer know that she is important to you—that you want her business. Whether that is done by telephone or in a letter, stay in contact with potential customers. Don't, however, go too far and have them think you are harassing them, or they will not buy.

Never assume that the customer knows you want her business. Always make it a point to ask for it. Realize that your product or service will not be right for everyone. Be sure to close the sale when it's time. And, don't take rejection personally. Not everyone will buy.

Keep track of your clients. Build a mailing list of customers. If you can't afford to mail anything now, at least you'll have the information for later. Then follow up after you've made the sale. Referral business is a major source of new business for most companies. If customers are not referring business, it's because they're not happy. Find out why. Pay close attention to what the customers are saying. Listen. Respond. And change, if necessary.

Do you know the number one reason why customers leave? Overwhelmingly, they leave because of an indifference toward customers. In fact, research shows that customers change for the following reasons: One percent die; 3 percent move away; 9 percent change for competitive reasons; 14 percent are dissatisfied with the product; and 68 percent leave because of lack of concern by salespeople, employees or the owner. Keep your customers' concerns as your concerns. Let them know you care. Happy employees will radiate a pleasant attitude. Pay attention. If you are losing customers, find out why. And find out quickly.

Advertising and promotion

Advertising takes money. Money is a limited resource to most women business owners. Most of us cannot afford the type of advertising we need, to make a difference. Still, advertising and promotion are integral parts of marketing. The key is to find the least expensive way to promote your product and yourself so customers know where you're located and why they should buy your product over the competition's. You must educate your consumers.

Here are some suggested steps to follow when establishing an advertising program for your business:

- Establish your goals and objectives for advertising.
- Develop a detailed program that meets those goals. Do not try to oversell by targeting in all directions. Be very specific.
- Determine what medium will be most effective for you.
- Establish a budget, and stay within it.
- Evaluate the success of the program periodically. If it is not successful, change it.
- Capitalize on free advertising wherever possible.
- Make yourself newsworthy.

When determining your goals for advertising, look carefully at your total budget and your desired objectives. Most often, your desired objective is to increase sales. But, are your advertising efforts reaching your target market?

For my travel agency, during the first few years, I set aside a very small amount for advertising. I could not afford to wait for word-of-mouth advertising and referrals to support the overhead. Yet, I needed to remain fiscally conservative, especially during the start-up phase, since I knew there would be several unanticipated expenses. My primary goal was to stretch those advertising dollars as far as I could.

First, I looked at newspaper advertising, but I decided it wasn't right for my market. I was personally skeptical of many of the companies that advertised because of past travel scams. And I made the judgment call that my target market would be suspicious also. It would take too long and require too much money for me to convince enough new customers through newspaper advertising. I decided I wanted to concentrate on local markets and create name recognition there. Since there were several affluent neighborhoods close by, I purchased a mailing list for those zip codes.

My next advertising decision was determining what I should mail. Another indicator from my personal experience: I received numerous junk mail items each day, most of which I never opened. And, I assumed that my target market was similar. So, it was important to use my creativity and produce something that would be read. Otherwise, I was wasting my time and money. In talking with several different individuals, I determined that everyone reads the back of a postcard to see who it's from and where they went. I decided to try a mailing of postcards. I was able to get the postcards donated by cruise lines, which kept my costs down. With the assistance of a major cruise line and tour coordinator, I offered a travel destination seminar—open to the public.

The results were successful for attendance, but marginally successful for immediate bookings. I knew that it would take time and keeping my name in front of potential customers for results to materialize. Since the cost of the post-card promotion had been very reasonable, I repeated the mailing three more times in the next eighteen months. I listened carefully to why people had come to the seminar. I kept their names on another list and sent flyers concerning special destinations they had mentioned. But I knew that advertising of this nature would take up to two years to produce concrete results, and it did.

Consider volunteering to speak at luncheons or at schools by becoming a specialist in your field. Also, get involved in charity work, literacy programs or volunteering for community activities. The cost is your time. The rewards are priceless. Networking can bring in new business and promotes both you and your company.

Realize that business developed in this fashion may take longer to materialize, but money cannot buy the name and goodwill that community activity can. I once worked at a company that hired handicapped children to help with special mail-out projects. The pay was the going wage, but the reward was excellent media coverage and a good feeling around the office—neither of which you could put a price tag on.

Do not engage in these activities expecting to gain profits. Instead, the result is goodwill and name awareness. Profits are the by-product, not the means. When profits are used as the means, they not only cheapen the activity, but often fail in the process.

Public relations

Public relations is the overall impression you give to your customers and is expressed through business behavior and perspective. Since every business deals with the public, to some degree, every business is involved in establishing and communicating its image through public relations.

Public relations is relating to the public and gaining recognition in the process. It can be achieved through various levels, the simplest being saying hello, learning your customer's names and sending notes of appreciation or congratulations for births, promotions, new business, referrals, etc. Or it can be more complex and orchestrated by having a customer appreciation day or a parade. Public relations is the sum total of everything that creates a favorable impression of your business name.

Surprisingly, the most overlooked aspect of advertising is the free or inexpensive tactic of making yourself newsworthy. Get to be known by local journalists so that when they need quotes from specialists in the field, they remember to call on you. Donating your time and money to a local charity can make you newsworthy. Also, offering free training is a way of becoming newsworthy. The opportunities are endless; your imagination is all that is needed.

Publicity can be a very effective marketing tool for both new and existing businesses. It costs virtually nothing to the owner. Yet, the rewards can be extremely high. The focus of publicity must be intentional, however, for the benefits to materialize. It doesn't just happen. Take the time to learn to write press releases. Getting the information to the media will get you recognition. And press releases are information that you control. Here are some ideas of how you can create publicity:

- Always send customers thank-you notes for referral business. This is a most inexpensive and rewarding marketing tool. And it shows your customers that you appreciate them, that you care.
- Become an expert in your field and give free seminars or talks at business luncheons or special events.
- Adopt a local class of students. Get involved with their needs. Mentor to

them from your own experiences. Teaching is the best method for learning.

- Pick a charitable event and get involved in a major committee. Be active.
- Get your employees involved with local charities. Perhaps time off during working hours can be arranged. They will enjoy the benefits of contributing to the community, and as an added benefit, your company will get excellent publicity.
- Wear a name badge. Have name badges for your employees as well. Make sure people know your name and the name of your company.
- Write a letter to the editor, either for your local paper or a national magazine. You'd be surprised how many people read editorials. Remember to keep your company's image positive when writing letters.

- Hire mentally and/or physically challenged adults to help out around your company wherever possible.
- Celebrate your company's anniversary.
- Get involved with local community events and special holidays.

Marketing is integral to small business planning. But, it doesn't have to be expensive to be profitable. In fact, originality and sincerity will go far towards keeping your name and image in the public's eye. Realize that you are always representing your company, whether or not you are selling your product, as are your employees. Be certain that you are consistent in what you say and what you do. Consumers are skeptical when they discover inconsistencies.

Chapter 8

Funding the dream: finding capital sources

"Clearly, the biggest need any small business has is access to capital. You can have the greatest idea in the world, but if you don't have the funds to buy the time to prove this idea, then you have no chance of success."

Erskine Bowles, Former Head of Small Business Administration

The need for money

You've looked at your own abilities and matched them to a potential business opportunity, or maybe several opportunities. Before you plunge forward, however, carefully analyze the facts to determine if you can financially support this venture.

The majority of educators select undercapitalization as the single most common death trap for startup businesses. But that, in fact, may not be the case at all. There are individuals who actually take the opposite view. The most famous is Paul Hawken, author of *Growing a Business*, who identifies too much money, not too little, as a major problem for small businesses. Hawken recommends that for your first venture you "start slowly and steadily, preferably using your own money." He asserts that limited financial resources causes entrepreneurs to resort to much more creative means of achieving results. This is the essence of the true entrepreneurial spirit. And one I strongly agree with.

Because of the difficulty women face in obtaining financing, this advice can be a blessing in disguise. In fact, many women are following this advice with great results. They are starting slowly, with whatever means they have, and growing cautiously. As profits are generated, they are reinvested into the business to begin building it up. They are flexible to grow as quickly or cautiously as they see fit. They use such creative measures as bartering and networking for increasing revenues and exposure.

You do need to understand your capital needs, however, whether using your own investment money or someone else's, you need to calculate startup costs, overhead and revenues. Estimating costs and revenues not only assists with deciding whether or not to enter a market, but can also determine how quickly you can anticipate a return on your investment.

One key to business formation and expansion is your ability to obtain and secure financing. You may have heard that small businesses have a difficult time borrowing money, or you may have had a similar personal experience. The difficulty is enhanced when you add gender or race barriers. The process can be tedious and frustrating, but there are several steps entrepreneurs can follow. First, know your financial needs. Second, present your financial request in the most professional, direct way possible. Next, look, act and talk the part of a successful business owner. And finally, know exactly how the money will be spent and how it will be repaid.

Capital estimations plague new business owners. The rule of thumb for estimating costs for new businesses is first to determine, as thoroughly as possible, the individual costs anticipated and then *double* that amount. No matter how often this advice is rendered, novice entrepreneurs still fail to accept this guidance. Instead, they feel they have a better handle on estimating expenses and projecting revenues than previous entrepreneurs.

Remember that estimating costs also includes determining how much of a loss you can sustain and for how long. Pro forma evaluations estimate how quickly revenues will be generated and your rate of growth. Chapter 9 details the financial statements needed in business operations, including projections. Again, the conservative rule of thumb for the new entrepreneur is to project the anticipated revenues and then reduce that figure by half. Yes, it will cost more than you estimated and profits will be generated more slowly than projected. If your business is the exception, it simply means you will be profitable sooner than expected. But time and again these cautions have proven to be sound advice.

Capital

The word "capital" can be confusing for women because it is used loosely in the business world. It may mean the total of a company's finance. It might also refer to long-term funding injected into a business. Yet another meaning might be the total of equity in the company, or maybe just the amount of money contributed by owners and stockholders. Unfortunately, you will have to determine the exact meaning by the context! There is no easy solution.

The amount of money a business needs varies. Capital (the company's total finance) can be broken down into three basic types, depending on its use and the business's operational needs. Assets retained for a long time are classified as *fixed capital*. These include land, building, machinery, equipment and furniture. *Working capital* represents those assets that may readily be converted into cash, such as inventory or raw materials to manufacture your product. Working capital includes cash reserves and accounts receivables. *Operating capital* refers to the money needed to cover overhead expenses necessary to operate your business. These overhead items include rent, utilities and salaries.

The actual requirement of fixed and working capital depends on your specific industry and personal needs. Less money means more creative resources must be used to grow the business. Retail businesses typically require more capital investments, whereas many service type firms and freelance operations can be started on a shoestring.

To determine your total cash needs, you will first need to project revenues. Revenue projections should be conservative. If possible, break sales down to a monthly basis so you can anticipate growth, especially identifying seasonal trends. Realize that many of your friends and family who have encouraged you thus far and promised their business and support will not materialize as customers. Or, they will expect to receive special treatment and discounts.

A safe calculation is to consider their revenue potential as guarded at best.

Next, look at your monthly (or quarterly) overhead operating expenses. These are often referred to as recurring costs. Rent, leased equipment, monthly utility bills, taxes, salaries (including yours) and inventory purchases are just a few types of recurring costs. List overhead expenses that you can identify. This is probably the one area in which you will greatly underestimate your expenses. Have others review your estimates, especially other small business owners, and make suggestions. Accurate projections is key to having sufficient cash flow to operate and grow on.

Subtract your expense figure from revenues to determine how much (if any) shortfall will occur for the first year. Very few businesses make a profit during their first year operating. But I suspect that most project a profit. Now, take those figures and divide your revenue figure in half while doubling your expenses. Keep this in mind:

Business is more likely to be slower to develop than you anticipated, and costs are more apt to be higher than projected.

Prepare a projected cash flow statement based on this information. Some businesses are seasonal. Others require larger cash investments initially. Each business is different. This is where an industry mentor can be very beneficial. Your cash flow projections will show how much extra cash you need each month, or how much cash (if any) will be generated from profits. If cash shortages do exist, they must be covered by capital injections.

In calculating your other cash needs, decide what type of equipment and inventory are necessary to maintain the quality and standards of your business. Determine whether used equipment is appropriate for your needs, or whether technology changes so rapidly that used equipment would produce an inferior product. Try to cut corners wherever possible with used or leased equipment, but maintain your high standard. Sometimes a high investment in technology can save you money in the long run by lowering salaries, improving quality and allowing faster production. Do not cut corners if the result will impact your service or product.

Potential suppliers are an excellent source for determining equipment and inventory costs. They may even supply you with names of people who want to update their old equipment, which may not yet be obsolete, and may still be in good working condition. Keep strong, open communication lines with your suppliers to gain the inside track.

The next step involves determining unusual expense items, including redecorating the office, installing equipment, deposits and painting signs. Don't forget to factor in grand opening costs if you plan on a big party or celebration. These costs occur only once or at least infrequently. Then there are also business cards and stationery printing; both are important for name recognition and networking. These costs are necessary to open the business and do not directly affect its operation. Total this figure.

Don't forget the monthly expenses you will incur when you operate a business. These are often the most difficult to project because some expenses will increase with additional sales. These are called *variable* expenses and include money spent to increase sales. Once sales increase, you may need to spend additional funds to handle the volume.

On the other hand, many monthly expenses will be *fixed*. Whether or not sales happen at all that month, you will still have to pay the rent, utilities, phone bill, insurance, business taxes and licensing fees. Estimating carefully these costs requires researching typical costs in your region. It involves making several phone calls to find out what current rental rates are. Once you have a good idea about the size of your building, you will be able to call the utility company and get ranges for monthly bills. Check with the phone company, electricity company, rental company and so on concerning the need for security deposits. These will be part of your operating expense figure.

However, the bulk of your expenses will have a semi-fixed/semi-variable quality about them. They may increase, but not necessarily in proportion to sales. Sometimes the increase is a stair-step increment; other times it will be varying in proportion. Realizing that these relationships exist between sales and expenses can help you project budgets at different sales levels and better see what volume of sales is needed for you to begin to see a profit.

For home-based businesses, operating expenses can be greatly reduced. These may be expenses you incur already. But, do not forget about your salary, additional telephone lines (whether or not dedicated) and budgeting for advertising, accounting and legal services. Home businesses have many advantages, but be careful when determining your capital needs that you identify as many potential costs as possible. All businesses have operating expenses, including freelance home-based service businesses. Your ability to anticipate these expenses is a critical piece in estimating your capital needs. Take your time and be thorough in your investigations.

Now, you are able to calculate the total capital required to start and operate your venture until profits are able to support its continuation. Total capital includes fixed asset purchases such as equipment, automobile and fixtures, plus startup costs, working inventory and working cash for operation. It is easy to overlook some of the necessary costs that may occur in starting a business, so I have listed several of the more common expenses associated with opening a new operation. This list is not complete. Review industry data and talk with other small business owners to get a better handle on your anticipated expenses.

Fixed capital: Business vehicles; equipment in office, shop and/or garage; computer; desks and office furnishings (don't forget a refrigerator or microwave for your kitchen); and other leasehold improvements.

Working capital: Starting inventory; material; inventory (for replacement).

Operating expenses (overhead): Rent and security deposits; utilities, installation and deposits; auto expense, insurance, tag and title; training; licenses, permits, tax deposits; legal fees; insurance (property, casualty, liability); interest on any borrowed monies; advertising and promotion for opening day; cash on hand; reserve cash for unforeseen situations (and they will happen); salaries; payroll taxes; accounting charges; advertising/marketing; office supplies; printing and duplicating; and equipment rental and repair.

Single item (unusual) expenses: Outside signage; interior decorating and fixtures; installation (i.e., computer, telephone).

Startup costs: Incorporation fees (if you are a corporation); accounting fees to set up books.

Insurance: Discuss your business and home insurance policy with a professional.

Licenses: What license you need will depend on the type of business you operate. In some areas, a locally obtained business license is all that you need to get started. In others, federal and state or provincial licenses are required as well.

Where to find seed financing

Once you have determined how much the business needs for capital, then come the creative opportunities for developing resources. Unfortunately, the most obvious source—banks—are often the least receptive to female entrepreneurs. Banks seldom lend money to startup businesses. Fortunately, however, there are numerous other sources to pursue, such as personal resources, credit cards, friends and relatives, SBA guaranteed funds, life insurance policies, credit unions, other financial institutions, grants, venture capitalists, corporations, personal loan companies, vendors or suppliers and business incubators.

Be patient. Be persistent. Be prepared. Financing is difficult to obtain, especially for women. But it is not impossible. If one source turns you down, keep knocking on doors until someone says yes. When turned down, ask each lender or investor why so you can improve your presentation. Listen to their suggestions. Be open to their comments. And learn from their experiences.

Most outside investors will ask to see a detailed business plan (this includes bankers). Your presentation to potential investors needs to be professional and thorough. Your confidence and enthusiasm will score points in these areas. Strive to convince others that you have the *knowledge, expertise* and *determination* to make your business work. You must also present your financial needs precisely, showing exactly where the money will be used and how it will be repaid. The key to financial independence is financial responsibility. At a very minimum, have the following information ready for the presentation:

- A detailed explanation of your business idea.
- The purpose of the loan.
- The exact amount of money needed.
- Details about how the loan will be repaid.
- Collateral offered to guarantee the loan.
- Financial information about the owners, partners and/or key employees.

You may want to have someone else, experienced in preparing business plans, review your proposal before making the presentation.

Most lenders, especially banks, are conservative in their lending policies. Common reasons for denial include insufficient owner's equity in the business, lack of established earnings record, a history of slow or past-due trade or loan payments or insufficient collateral.

Service companies usually lack great amounts of tangible assets (machinery, equipment, inventory or real estate), and tangible assets are what investors look for as collateral. Investors seek collateral that can be readily marketed, that is owned by you and to which you have a legal title that can be transferred. This lack of collateral adds to the difficulty in obtaining financing for women who have primarily concentrated in service businesses.

A lender is *not allowed to ask* you for information about your spouse unless your spouse has connections to the business or unless you are relying on your spouse's income to support your credit application. All creditors are subject to the Equal Credit Opportunity Act (ECOA) and Regulation B (issued by the Federal Reserve Board), which contain specific rules governing credit transactions. All business applicants have certain protections against discrimination. The ECOA makes it illegal for lenders to deny your loan application, discourage you from applying for a loan or give you less favorable terms than another applicant because you are a woman or a minority group member. That does not mean that lenders must assume additional risk by making a loan they consider unfavorable, however.

Credit history

You must understand that your personal credit history is an indication to lenders of how you will handle your business finances. Many women have not created individual credit histories, relying instead on the creditworthiness of their spouse. If you have not already done so, you need to establish credit in your own name. Do this by borrowing money and then paying it back (when due). Apply for a charge card in your own name if you do not already have one. Banks look very strongly at an individual's credit history. And unfortunately, we live in a society that penalizes you for paying by cash.

There are several major regional credit reporting agencies. Your local bank will know the names of those that service your area. It is important for you to frequently get a copy of your credit history and verify the reporting for accuracy. Credit bureaus are notorious for errors. Often, months of letter writing and phone calls are required to clear up mistakes. You do not want derogatory information to keep you from getting your loan.

Personal resources

Women sometimes are forced to rely heavily on their personal investments to start businesses. This has been a blessing. When you invest your own money in your business, you invest cautiously, carefully and with conviction. If you honestly believe in your company and prove it by risking your own money, outside investors will look favorably upon you for taking this risk. Personal investments should provide a higher return on your investment than interest or dividend returns if your business is a success. In addition, your investment is making it less risky for lenders; in case of bankruptcy, you—as the owner—would be the last to receive any cash from liquidated assets. In most cases you will assume the greatest proportion of risk for your business.

Credit cards

According to recently published SBA statistics, "70 percent of women business owners are financing their businesses with their credit cards." This is a very costly financing alternative, but proves a point: It isn't that women don't need cash, it's that they can't get it. Use this source of financing only if less costly sources are not available. Try more conventional methods first. Because women are starting businesses that frequently require less capital infusion, many of the conventional alternatives have been slow to respond to the lower loan amounts women need, often arguing that these small amounts are not profitable risks. This has resulted in limited access to smaller loan amounts (often under $5,000) and has created more dependence on credit card financing.

Friends and relatives

Friends and relatives have been another major source of financing for women business owners. Ask people you know personally if they are interested in lending you money, perhaps even at a lower interest rate than a bank. Friends and relatives look to the individual and beyond the numbers. They often do not assess the financial risks as thoroughly as outsiders. However, if the new business is not successful, personal relationships are often permanently damaged. Be cautious about mixing business with personal relationships. You may lose a friend or have a relative who never forgives you. Is it worth the price? If you do borrow money from friends or family, it is extremely important that you repay it on time and in full.

SBA Programs

The SBA is a well-known but misunderstood source of financing for small businesses. The most common loans are funded through the SBA 7A Program, which is designed to provide lenders an additional tool for constructing long-term packages for small businesses. The SBA rarely lends money directly. The primary lending function of the SBA is as a guarantor to financial institutions. This is designed to encourage banks to accept the higher risk associated with smaller companies and to offer more favorable terms. To be eligible for SBA

lending (or guarantees), businesses must meet the following criteria:

• Size limitations for industry.
• Be independently owned and operated.
• Be a profit-making venture.
• Not be dominant in the industry.
• Not discriminate in employment.

The SBA will guarantee a loan of up to 90 percent (to a maximum of $750,000). Terms depend on the type of loan requested. Working capital and inventory loans can be financed for up to 7 years, while real estate loans can extend as long as 25 years. The SBA also sets limits on the maximum interest rate banks can charge for these loans.

Currently, there is no official minimum on SBA lending programs, but in practice banks have imposed voluntary minimums (often $50,000 or higher). Completing an SBA loan package requires patience, a lot of time and sometimes professional assistance to accomplish. This was true for all loans until the SBA implemented a new program (effective July 1994) that reduced the amount of paperwork required on loans under $100,000. Referred to as the *Low Doc* program, it requires business owners to submit one form, along with up to three years of tax returns. Bankers and business owners welcome this change. For loans over $100,000 the tedious and somewhat intimidating paperwork is still required, often requiring documentation reaching 50 to 75 pages.

Unfortunately, statistics show that while women represent 38 percent of all businesses, they account for less than 10 percent of SBA loans. The SBA is trying to increase this figure to a minimum of 15 percent, so there are new opportunities emerging for women to seek SBA support.

For instance, the SBA is testing a pilot program in select markets that has loan packagers pre-screening female applicants and presenting their credit requests to SBA officials. When the borrower qualifies, the SBA issues a pre-qualification letter that can be taken to participating local commercial banks. Call your local SBA office to see if this program is available in your area. After the SBA evaluates the success of this program, it is anticipated that they will implement a similar program nationwide.

Another new program is the microloan program. Banks and the SBA have begun to address the need for microloan programs, which are designed to assist entrepreneurs in the inner city and rural areas form small (often home-based) enterprises.

Call your SBA office to find out about the variety of options they can assist you with. The SBA is a great resource and friend to have.

Life insurance policies

Life insurance policies that have cash surrender values are another source of money to borrow because often the interest rate is lower than market rates. Be sure you understand the conditions outlined in the insurance policy *before* borrowing against it. Since you purchase life insurance for its protection, borrowing money and missing payments may cause the policy to become void and leave you unprotected. Understand what risk is involved and then determine whether you are willing to accept that risk. Not all life insurance policies have cash value.

Credit unions

If you or your spouse belong to a credit union, approach them about borrowing money. Since most credit unions are member-oriented, you will have an advantage. You may have already established a borrowing history with the credit union, which often is sufficient to qualify you for additional loans. And the cost to borrow money may be lower at credit unions than at other lending institutions.

Commercial banks or savings and loan companies

Financial institutions include both commercial banks and savings and loan institutions. Banks do not have a good reputation for lending startup capital. Banks are generally a more conservative source of financing, and they often characterize startup ventures as "too risky." Anticipate having to provide sufficient collateral if they are even willing to look at your request. Unfortunately, most financial institutions look for at least a three-year profitable track record. If you are in an industry that has been plagued by problems, lending institutions may red-flag you at the outset. Banks and savings and loans usually require stronger financial positions than smaller loan companies but may offer a more favorable interest rate. It is important to establish a friendly relationship with your banker or loan officer. Expect to be asked to maintain all deposits and handle other banking relationships at their branch.

Grants

Grants represent monies borrowed that do not have to be repaid. Grants are supported by several sources, including federal and state government and private corporations. The research involved may be tedious and the application process lengthy, but this remains an excellent source of capital and one that is frequently overlooked. There are several excellent books available concerning grant funding. Check your public library for copies. Grants are used to support a wide array of businesses, such as those representing minority ownership, those in high unemployment areas and those retraining employees for new career positions. Processing grants may often be slow and painstaking, but worth the time. Finding the source is often the most difficult part. Start by calling several state and federal agencies to determine if they have money available in your area. It is wise to take a professional course and learn the art of writing winning grant proposals. Women who have followed this advice are having great results. Learn how to play the game and profit from the experience.

Venture capitalists

Venture capitalists can be either individuals, groups or corporations that invest startup money in risky ventures, but expect something in return. Often the tradeoff is stock or part ownership in your company. New business enterprises, however, are finding that venture capital is hard to come by, especially within certain industries. Talk with your accountant or attorney first. Because of the nature of venture-capitalist financing, all documents should be approved and negotiated through your professional advisors. If stock is the bargaining chip, then you would need to form a corporate structure, if you haven't already done so. In other words, if you were a sole proprietorship or partnership, you would not be able to sell stock in your company because there is no such thing. Venture-capital firms look for companies with top-notch management, a waiting market and key products for that market, along with a fast turnaround time on their money. Venture capitalists look for talented people who are "hungry" for success and have the ability to make it

happen. The degree of involvement by the venture firm varies according to the perceived need. The ultimate goal of most venture-capital investors is a ten-fold return on their investment within five to seven years. Rejection from a venture capitalist frequently is based on the assessment that the entrepreneur lacks the management finesse and capabilities to make it happen. Your belief in yourself and your ability to communicate effectively are crucial to gaining access to these funds.

Corporations

Today, many corporations are looking to invest in companies that are either complementary to their product line or offer benefits desired, especially employee benefits. While some corporations offer assistance in the form of grants, others are looking at investment opportunities. It never hurts to approach companies you think may benefit from your product to see if they are interested in offering some financial assistance. However, have a well-prepared and well-orchestrated presentation ready to sell your company. A large corporation wants to know, first of all, that you have management skills and that you know what you're talking about. This requires selling yourself, your company and product.

Personal loan companies

While financial institutions may provide lower rates and other banking services, another option is small loan companies. This is an expensive way to get financing, though, and it is generally used as a last resort. Perhaps you need more money than is available on your credit cards. Small loan companies often charge the highest legally allowed interest rate to startup businesses. Your loan may be classified as risky, and to

The Smart Woman's Guide to Starting a Business

compensate, the loan companies charge anywhere from 24 to 42 percent interest (depending on individual state usury regulations). Although this is not a recommended source of financing, you cannot deny its existence or effect on small businesses. When seeking any form, but especially this form, of financing, business owners must anticipate the cost of borrowing funds. Profits must be able to support this added expense.

Vendors or suppliers

While vendors and suppliers can help a startup business significantly, it is generally not in the form of direct financing. It is, however, more common for them to offer longer terms on purchased items, a practice that can help a new company's cash flow. Sometimes these terms may be negotiated interest-free. These relationships are normally developed slowly over time. Vendors and suppliers succeed when you succeed. They have a vested interest in your business growth. Ask for more lenient terms. You may never know unless you ask.

Business incubators

The latest craze in business financing has been business incubators. There were over 500 incubators across the U.S. as of 1992, and the numbers are rapidly increasing to meet demand. Incubators have had great success in stimulating economic development and can help create a positive entrepreneurial mind-set. They have been organized to bring new businesses together to increase the probability of success.

Business incubators do not guarantee success. Typically, they are office complexes offering a host of special benefits to startup and existing small businesses, encouraging growth, lowering costs and providing assistance. Some of the services that might be offered include office space at below-market rates, shared overhead costs, such as utilities, computer services, labs and receptionists, support services, such as shared secretarial pools, and professional advice. The purpose is to lower costs to encourage stronger cash flows for startup ventures during those difficult first few years. Many incubators are targeted toward niche areas, including high technology, biotechnology/medicine, international trade and light manufacturing. Your local SBA office will probably be aware of incubators in your area and their specific markets.

The five Cs of lending

When seeking financing from beyond your personal resources, there are certain expectations and requirements that will be placed on you. Most loan requests are judged on the five Cs of lending. These are credit, credentials, character, capacity and collateral.

First, almost without exception, your personal credit history will be reviewed. Credit includes your personal and business credit history. As a startup company, you will probably not have established business credit history, which places more importance on your personal history. Always pay your bills on time. The importance of knowing your credit history and maintaining a good record cannot be overstated.

Lenders also will expect you to be very knowledgeable concerning your business and your industry. You must act like a specialist. You must present your package convincingly. Women have often felt that there was little need to convince others of their abilities. Unfortunately, this is a very misguided attitude. Credentials represent your experience and knowledge of the industry and how to run a business. Lenders must believe in you and your ability to make it happen.

Lenders look at the individual's character as a major factor. If you are an honest, fair person at home, then you will likely be an honest, fair person at work.

Capacity refers to the company's ability to pay the loan back, as agreed upon. Lenders must be convinced that the capacity exists to handle the debt structure proposed; otherwise they are making a bad loan from the start.

Collateral is the thing lenders like most of all. It represents something that has an assignable value and, preferably, a ready market. Although lenders are not in the business of taking over businesses, collateral represents their safety net.

Understanding and preparing for these five Cs will go a long way towards achieving your goal, the funding of your dream. Preparation starts long before you are ready to open the doors. Credit takes time to establish. Credentials must be mastered. Character is a life-long commitment. Yet, without these, financing will be difficult, if not impossible, to achieve.

Chapter 9

The numbers game: tackling the accounting process

"I spent a lot more time looking at the numbers and learning what it all meant than I expected. But, it was my money. And I wanted to know exactly what was going on."

Helen Burrus, Former owner of a specialty gift shop

The importance of numbers

Women have handled household budgets for years, and are applying the same concepts to business accounting. Numbers are important to entrepreneurs. The better you understand the interpretation of numbers, the more meaningful the collection of data becomes. However, most startup books concentrate more on record-keeping methods than on the interpretation of accounting or on financial concepts. This chapter delves into the interpretation and uses of information, lightly covering the steps necessary to produce the numbers. I recommend that once you understand the use of numbers, you sit down with your accountant and develop the record-keeping system she feels best meets your specific business needs.

To successfully compete in today's marketplace, female entrepreneurs need to understand how to interpret financial statements. It is integral to business survival and is the basis of prudent decision-making. As you grow with your business, you will become more astute at interpreting and utilizing data. The more financial knowledge you have to start

with, the shorter your learning process will be and the quicker positive results can be seen. If you currently have no accounting or finance background, do not become discouraged. Instead, simply begin gathering these tools as time permits. These tools are priceless for business owners. At the very minimum you need to have the ability to review data and determine if others are robbing you blind. Your ignorance and trust can cost you a lot of money.

This chapter is probably the most technical one in the book. Take your time to read, understand and absorb the information. A periodic review may also be helpful. Be patient with yourself. But don't give up. Having a basic understanding and appreciation of numbers is critical for small businesses. Think of record-keeping not as a necessary nuisance imposed by governmental regulations but as an important tool for your own use in managing your business efficiently. A simple, well-organized system of records, regularly kept up, can actually be a time-saver by bringing order out of chaos.

Some basic guidelines

The first rule of thumb is never overdraw your checking account. It creates bad credit and expensive insufficient funds charges. You can afford neither. Learn to follow your business cash flow statement carefully. In addition, always keep your personal and business money separate. The IRS frowns on the commingling of these monies; it also makes for difficult (if not impossible) record-keeping.

Next, understand that financial analysis is meaningless without a point of reference. Many business owners get caught up in the analysis of statements, never comprehending what they mean. Learn to interpret ratios within industries, by company size and based on historical data. Numbers alone are not sufficient for evaluation.

A constant objective of women must be to strive for balance. In the field of accounting, too little can be just as damaging as too much. Some individuals are such students of numbers that they feel this skill is enough to run a business successfully. It isn't. It is one of several ingredients necessary to create a successful operation. It is also important to know how to communicate effectively, manage a staff, listen to customers and have an intuitive sense about your industry. Either extreme, ignorance or obsession, can be detrimental to your business survival.

Keeping accurate records

Numbers scare many of us. Especially when their accuracy (or inaccuracy) translates into IRS penalties and higher payments. You can avoid problems with the IRS by keeping thorough records of your business expenses and by understanding what deductions are allowed under current regulations. Accurate record-keeping is an entrepreneur's best friend. Good records help to safeguard your assets. And good records let you know how the business is doing at any given moment. You can find shortages quickly when records are consistently maintained and then take action to correct the source of the trouble. The IRS requires a company's tax information be backed up by supporting proof through permanent records. Know what records to keep and for how long. Chapter 14, provides guidelines for maintaining tax records. However, state and local laws may differ, so verify your specific needs and requirements with your professional advisors.

Record-keeping is time-consuming. Consider this time an investment—one of the most important and rewarding investments you can make in running your business. The importance of accounting, finance and budgeting can impact the profitability of your company through wiser decisions, quicker responses and minimizing losses while maximizing profits. Understanding financial data can help you make well-informed decisions concerning future purchases as well as assisting with identifying cost-effective methods of operation. Your ability to understand and use financial data ultimately impacts your bottom line.

Accounting versus bookkeeping

Accounting is the compilation of financial information for use in making economic decisions. This is not to be confused with *bookkeeping*, which provides basic accounting data by systematically recording such day-to-day information as sales and expenses. Both are important features required in business operations. The method of bookkeeping you choose for your business will depend on the complexity of your needs. There are numerous bookkeeping software packages available if you decide to computerize. Or this function may be delegated to an employee. It is important, for whatever method chosen, that current record-keeping is maintained.

Accounting, on the other hand, is the art of interpreting bookkeeping information for informed decision-making. You need a strong understanding of accounting concepts to make better, more informed decisions. But don't try too much. As your company grows and expands, it may be more advantageous to relinquish this control to someone more knowledgeable and with more time to devote to this position. But initially, you will be in control.

Basic bookkeeping systems

Your bookkeeping system does not have to be elaborate or complicated to be efficient. In fact, it is better to set up (under the guidance of your accountant) the simplest system that meets your particular needs. Keep all receipts, and keep them in an organized fashion. Shoe-box accounting can be confusing and frustrating to those who work with your business. Your bookkeeping method will assist your accountant greatly in year-end calculations and save you money. Reconcile your bank statement as soon as it arrives. Banks do make mistakes (although not frequently). If an error is discovered, contact the bank immediately.

There are two forms of reporting income and expenses that the Internal Revenue Service recognizes: cash basis and accrual accounting. Your accountant will advise you on which method is recommended for you, based on current tax laws as well as your specific needs.

For *cash basis accounting*, no income or expense is recognized until cash is actually received or paid out. It is the simpler method. The *accrual method* reports revenues when they are earned (when a sale is made) as opposed to when cash is collected. Expenses are shown for accrual accounting when they are incurred, rather than when they are paid.

The IRS allows you to choose which basis to use provided that (1) it clearly reflects income and (2) you use it consistently. The exception to this rule is for companies where inventories play an important part in accounting for income. At that point, however, the IRS states you must use the accrual method.

If you are not utilizing computer software, the following are journals you may need to become familiar with: sales and cash receipts journal; cash disbursement, purchases and expense journal; accounts receivable ledger; accounts payable ledger; payroll ledger; general ledger; and your business checking account. The actual journals you use will be based on your individual needs. Because of the limitations of time and space, I am only providing brief explanations of each of these journals here. There are a variety of accounting and record-keeping books available that provide more details for these journals, if you need it.

Sales and cash receipts journal: Basically, this ledger shows the cash you take in for your business from sales. Keep an individual record of each customer's transaction. Checks and credit card sales are treated like cash, as opposed to credit sales, for this journal. It should be maintained daily.

Cash disbursements, purchases and expense journal: Shows items paid for by cash. Actual cash payments are identified by categories you have established, so the transactions may easily be transferred to financial statements later.

Accounts receivable ledger: Indicates revenues owed to your company from sales and not yet collected.

Accounts payable ledger: This ledger indicates the balance your company owes its creditors.

Payroll ledger: Includes a complete listing of all payroll information per employee, including gross wages, deductions and other withholdings. Payroll ledgers are used prior to writing payroll checks. The money withheld will be submitted at a later date. Do not assume that because this money is in your checking account you can use it for other expenses! That is a grave mistake made by some novice entrepreneurs. Know that filing for bankruptcy does not eliminate IRS payments. It is a good practice to deduct withholding amounts immediately from your checking account balance, even though they are remitted later.

Business checking account: Always keep your business monies separate from household expenses. This is a very important step in the maintenance of accurate record-keeping. As each check is written, be sure to complete the stub portion with date, payee, amount and purpose. A running balance is then maintained. The purpose line will help you to make the appropriate general ledger entries later. Each time a check is written or a deposit made, you will need to make a correlating entry to one of the above journals.

Maintaining records for general ledger

The information kept in the daily ledgers and journals above must be transferred into a combined form, known as the general ledger. Each transaction is expressed as either a debit or credit. These accounts are maintained to supply management with the desired information, in a summary form.

Debit and credit entries

Debits and credits are methods of accounting for general ledger transactions. What determines whether an entry is to be a debit or a credit is whether the transaction to be entered will increase or decrease the account. *Double-entry* bookkeeping shows the total impact each transaction has on the books. No matter how many separate entries are made, the value entered as debits must equal the value entered as credits. Otherwise you are out of balance.

Asset accounts normally have a debit balance. Liability accounts normally have a credit balance. The equity account will normally have a credit balance. Profits are shown as a credit to the equity account and losses are listed as a debit amount.

The information presented in the general ledger is correlated to form the income statement and balance sheet. These financial statements allow management to view the company's progress in a more complete format. Sample financial statements are presented at the end of this chapter to illustrate these relationships and how you can interpret the information presented.

Income statement

The income statement is the easiest financial statement to read and is the one most new business owners pay closest attention to initially. The income statement, also called a profit and loss (P & L) statement, shows the results of a company's operations *over time*. It is broken down into revenues, costs of goods sold, gross profits, itemized expenses, net income before taxes, taxes and net profit (or loss) for a given period of time. Income statements are prepared at least annually, although it is a good idea to prepare and review interim statements more frequently. This will allow you to recognize when expenses are getting too high and make the necessary adjustments to bring them back in line.

Most income statements are reported on a calendar year basis, January 1 through December 31. Some businesses prepare financial statements according to their opening date and file a short-term initial statement. Again, your accountant will advise you on when to establish your company's year-end. Sole proprietorships are limited to calendar year reporting.

Revenues show the total amount of sales to customers.

Cost of goods sold (Cost of sales) represents the dollars invested to buy a product or the material used in the manufacturing to sell a finished good. The cost of goods sold is calculated by determining the value of inventory at the beginning of the accounting period, adding the cost of materials purchased and subtracting the value of the inventory at the end of the period. The difference is the cost of goods sold associated with revenues for the period being reviewed.

Service companies generally operate without a cost of goods sold category and their net sales amount is the same as their gross margin, less any refunds. Service companies often have lower profit margins than retail or product companies, but may have less risk associated with them because of lower capital requirements.

Returns and allowances. When this is a small figure, it may be included in cost of goods sold, which is subtracted from your total revenue figure. However, for companies with large amounts of returns and allowances, this figure is shown separately. This practice also includes service companies that offer money back guarantees.

The difference between revenues and cost of goods sold is your **gross profit.**

Expenses are outlined next on the income statement. Expenses include operating overhead (i.e., rent, utilities, salaries) and non-operating expenses (i.e., legal fees, advertising, subscriptions and taxes).

There may be some items purchased during the year that you are not allowed to treat as expenses during a single year because their relationship to revenues goes beyond one year. These *capital assets*, such as furniture, plant and equipment may be *depreciated* according to a variety of methods. Many entrepreneurs misunderstand depreciation and correlate it to providing for the replacement value of the asset. The act of depreciation has no effect on cash resources, present or future. However, it does reduce profits, which leads to lower taxes and more resources remaining in the company.

Expenses are totaled, and then subtracted from the gross profit figure to determine the income.

By itself, net profit (or loss) is not a meaningful gauge. However, when reviewed in relationship to both historical data and industry trends, the numbers become much more meaningful. Most startup companies require a few years before a profit is successfully generated from operations.

Balance sheet

The second financial statement women need to become familiar with is the balance sheet. Income statements only present part of the financial picture. While the income statement shows the results from a period of time, the balance sheet shows a snapshot or a picture of your business at a *specific point in time*. Since it is not feasible to stop a clock while a business is operating, the accepted "specific point" is at the close of a business day. The balance sheet compares all assets (things you own), liabilities (things you owe) and equity (what you have invested in the business) in a standard format.

The formula for items on the balance sheet is: $A = L + E$, where A equals Assets, L equals Liabilities and E equals Equity. The balance sheet, when prepared correctly, will always be in balance. And assets will always equal liabilities plus equity.

Assets

Assets are things the company owns. They are broken down into a current or noncurrent basis on the balance sheet. Current assets are assets that exist in the form of cash or that can readily be converted into cash or consumed within one year or less. Current assets include items such as cash, accounts receivable, notes receivable maturing in less than one year, inventory and raw materials (for manufacturing companies). On the other hand, noncurrent assets include fixed assets and assets that have a life or maturity of more than one year. They include buildings, plants, machinery, equipment and the balance of notes receivable beyond one year. Also included in noncurrent assets are intangible assets, such as goodwill, patents and customer lists. Although some balance sheet items, like cash, are easily measured for reporting purposes, the value of other items, such as equipment or intangibles, must be estimated. Plant and equipment items are usually represented by figures that are reduced by a certain proportion each year. This reduction is known as depreciation, and is reduced according to different (and approved) methods, based on the expected life of the asset. Intangible assets are reduced by a similar method, called amortization. In fact, assets may have no balance-sheet value remaining, but still retain significant monetary worth. Or the reverse could be true. Assets may be carried on the books as still having value, but, in fact, be obsolete or worthless. Technological changes typically impact values of assets in this way.

Liabilities

Liabilities, as well, are separated into current and long-term categories on the balance sheet. Current liabilities include such items as accounts payable, notes payable (due within one year), wages payable, interest payable and taxes payable. Long-term liabilities are those debts maturing beyond one year (or that portion due beyond one year).

Some stockholders may elect to make a loan to their company (in the form of a note payable) in lieu of a substantial equity investment. When the company begins to show a profit, the money can be repaid. Ask your accountant whether this is a beneficial investment tool for you.

Equity

The owner's equity for proprietorships, stockholder's equity in corporations or partner's equity in partnerships indicates the *net worth* of the business. Equity consists of the amount of money (or value) you have invested in the business, less any withdrawals, plus retained earnings (the reinvestment of profits). Losses, on the other hand, reduce your equity position.

Retained earnings are the profits (or losses) from the business that are left in the operation. Don't make the mistake of withdrawing more money than you earn, thereby depleting your initial investment. Continued losses from operations will also deplete the starting capital. A business cannot continue for long when this happens without replacing that equity, which means raising more capital or borrowing more money from other sources. During the early years, it is wise to try to retain (reinvest) all, or at least the bulk, of your profits back into the business operation. Money may be used to increase inventory, purchase additional equipment, or it may be left in cash to cushion cash flow.

For corporations, any distributions to shareholders from earnings and profits is generally a dividend. Ordinary dividends are taxable. Taxable distributions come first from current earnings and profits and then from accumulated earnings and profits.

Ratio analysis

Ratio analysis provides insight into financial statements. By using information you have collected on both the income statement and the balance sheet you can get a better understanding of how the company is doing. There are several important ratios that can be computed. However, numbers all alone, including ratios, provide no insight. To interpret the data, you must compare your financial picture to industry norms, to small business guidelines and to previous financial statements.

Ratios are divided into four main categories: liquidity, leverage, operating and expense to sales. Each represents a different measure of stability and soundness. Some of the more common ratio calculations are listed below, with brief descriptions and explanations of what they represent.

Liquidity ratios are the measure of the quality and adequacy of current assets to meet current obligations as they come due. They include current, quick, inventory and receivables ratios.

The *current ratio* shows a rough indication of a company's ability to service short-term obligations. It is calculated by dividing the total current assets by the total current liabilities. It varies among industries, but as a rule of thumb, a good ratio to strive for is between 1.5 to 1 and 2 to 1. Generally, the higher the ratio, the greater the perceived cushion between current assets and current liabilities.

The *quick ratio* (or acid-test ratio) is similar to the current ratio, except it realizes that the conversion of inventory to cash takes more time. It is a more conservative calculation. To determine the acid-test ratio, divide the total cash and net trade accounts receivable (less allowance for bad debt) by the current liabilities. The target ratio generally is around 1 to 1.

Inventory turnover in days is calculated primarily for retail companies who have large inventory investments. This ratio shows the frequency inventory is sold and then replaced in your store and is determined by dividing the cost of goods sold by an average monthly inventory. Turnovers will vary widely depending on the size and nature of the inventory. One shortcoming of this ratio is that there is no adjustment for seasonal fluctuations. High inventory turnover generally indicates quicker liquidation of merchandise.

Accounts receivable turnover in days is the measure of how well a company collects its accounts receivables, according to its credit policy. It is calculated by dividing net sales by the average amount of net accounts receivable. This figure will be in the number of collection days. If your credit policy allows for 30 day terms, but your accounts receivable turnover is 75, you have a problem. The higher the number of days, the greater the probability of delinquency and the harder accounts become to collect.

Leverage ratios are the measure of debt to equity of a company. A highly leveraged company (one with heavy debt in relation to net worth) is more vulnerable to business downturns than one with lower debt-to-worth positions. The ratios vary greatly depending on the requirements of particular industries.

The *debt-to-equity ratio* shows the proportion of capital secured from owners compared to other creditors. The more money you personally invest, the more you (the owner) are able to absorb continued losses and the less risk involved for other creditors. Investors, especially bankers, prefer a ratio of less than 1, where the owner is taking the greater proportion of risk.

Operating ratios are designed to assist in the evaluation of management's performance in the company's operation.

The *rate of return on total assets* is a measure of the company's efficiency, determined by dividing net income after taxes by the total assets. The rate should be higher than the rate paid for borrowed funds, and it should be higher than the current market rate for conservative investments. If not, then you need to consider another business that is.

The *rate of return on capital* reflects the return your investment has made. It is calculated by dividing net income by the average investment. For proprietors, the percentage will reflect a higher (and distorted) amount because the proprietor's salary is not included in expenses. Again, because of the risk involved in running a business, the rate of return should be greater than that obtained from a more conservative investment (i.e., certificate of deposit, stocks, bonds).

Expense to sales ratios comparisons are convenient for seeing how individual items affect revenues. Revenue remains a constant.

Net profit margin is the ratio of net income to sales. This percentage varies widely depending on the industry analyzed. It shows your mark-up on retail merchandise.

Expense items to sales is the situation where each expense item can be calculated separately as a percentage of gross sales. This is most helpful when comparing data for several years and to observe variances. Frequent review of these items allows for more control and quicker response to reducing figures that may have risen too fast.

Budgeting

A budget is a written plan of action in numerical form, which covers a specific period of time and against which actual performance can be compared. The purpose of budgeting is to establish goals, develop a plan that achieves those goals and provide a format for periodically checking to see how you are doing.

Budgets, also known as *pro forma* statements, can be prepared for revenue items as well as for expenses.

Controls are put in place when you periodically review and adjust the numbers. Discrepancies are shown through variances. These variances show items that have risen and are too high for the current sales volume. It allows management the opportunity to address these increases and justify the expense. They can also illustrate how well you are controlling certain costs.

Cash flow analysis

Cash flow statements are a type of budgeting. In this process you project (estimate) how much money you will receive and when it will arrive since you can control when your money goes out but not when it comes in.

A new company establishes its credit ratings by how it pays its bills. This is especially crucial in the early phases of business operation. Creating good credit is important to long-term growth. When you develop a solid foundation with suppliers, this may produce more lenient terms when cash may be tight later on. But, it is a relationship based on established credibility that comes from intentional cultivation and development. Favorable supplier terms are like interest-free loans.

From the day your first sale is made, you will have cash flowing in and out. Your primary sources of cash are cash sales and the collection of accounts receivable sales (if you allow customers to purchase on credit terms). You may also have income from the sale of an asset, money received from a lender or interest income. Accounts receivable occur when you extend credit on sales. And while you may offer terms of 30 days, that doesn't mean you will get paid in 30 days. Not all businesses need to extend credit to their customers. Offering terms of credit can be costly to small business owners when you consider the costs associated with handling the transaction and collecting overdue accounts. However, you are extending credit (whether or not it's your policy) any time a customer owes you money and does not pay.

Cash flows out mainly from accounts payable (paying your suppliers), operation costs (such as rent) and inventory costs. When you know your cash flow position, you can plan for any gaps in cash flow that might occur.

Poor cash management can be very costly to a business, creating the need to borrow, generating overdraft charges or resulting in the loss of potential accrued interest. Poor cash management has led to the demise of many small businesses through overdrawing the checking account or borrowing on a credit line and increasing interest expense. To avoid these possibilities, do not spend money before it's received, and look at the "cost" of borrowing money carefully. Cash flow analysis becomes more critical for those companies that handle significant amounts of cash.

Computerization

Modern technology provides the small business owner with an opportunity to almost completely automate her organization. Due to continuous changes within this industry, however, it is impossible to list specific programs or itemize costs. Personal computers (PCs) have become accessible to the majority of business owners, thanks to the continued reduction in costs and to constant improvements. What at one time was a major decision for business owners has now become easy with affordable prices.

The two major reasons for investing in computerization is to increase profits or increase productivity (or both). Labor-intensive tasks are the primary candidates for computerizing. Tasks such as payroll, invoicing, cash flow analysis, account tracking, budgeting, bookkeeping, customer lists and letter writing can all be done faster using computer technology. As a business owner weighing the cost of computerizing versus the advantages, you must first determine whether you have labor-intensive tasks that you want (or are willing) to have handled by the computer. Look at those jobs that are repetitive, time consuming and dreaded as excellent possibilities. Analyze each task to determine how computerization might save you time or money.

For example, if your business requires you to monitor large amounts of inventory, computers could quickly allow you to increase your control over the whereabouts, status and availability of goods. Most computer software for inventory will have the capability of generating reports to help you determine when and what inventory to purchase. While these functions can be done manually, the process is slow, subject to human error and often more costly in both salary and time than a computer, at least in theory. You will need to compare the actual cost of this technology to your savings in actual expenses, as well as time. Only then will you be able to make a final determination of the advantages and savings of computer technology in your business.

Also consider long-term growth. It is easier to integrate computer technology into a company when it is young and small. Resistance is less. Results can be seen quicker. And complications are minimized.

Managing finance is an important aspect of running a small business, especially one that is home-based. No longer are small businesses at a disadvantage when it comes to financial data. Now, small companies can access the same information as large businesses, thereby making better and faster decisions. By providing more efficient ways of handling information, computers can bring about major changes in your organization.

How do you find the right software package for your needs? Your accountant may recommend software she is familiar with. The recommended procedure is that you confer with your advisors to select the software, note its requirements and then purchase hardware.

A word about the examples

The examples on the following pages are hypothetical and are used to show the differences in accounting for retail businesses versus service companies. Operating expenses have been combined into one figure, not listed separately. The industry average comparisons come from the 1993 *RMA Annual Statement Studies*. Check the reference section of your local library for a copy.

Example 1: Assume that this is an incorporated retail clothing store. Comparative figures are from SIC (standard industrial classification codes) 5651, from the *RMA Annual Statement Studies*. For the balance sheet, the percentages represent the portion of total assets for the top half and total liabilities plus equity for the bottom half. The income statement percentages are based on net sales.

Balance Sheet

Assets	Year 1 (%)	Year 2 (%)	Industry Comparison %
Current			
Cash	$5,000	7,500	9.5
Trade accounts receivable	2,050	5,000	7.9
Inventory	32,000	65,000	60.6
Other current assets	1,000	1,500	1.3
Total current assets	40,050 (80%)	79,000 (83.6%)	79.3
Noncurrent			
Fixed assets	6,500	9,000	15.8
Allowance for depreciation	1,500	3,000	
Intangibles			1.5
Others, noncurrent	2,000	3,500	3.4
Total noncurrent assets	10,000 (20%)	15,500 (16.4%)	20.7
Total assets	50,050 (100%)	94,500 (100%)	100.0
Liabilities			
Current			
Notes payable, short-term	$3,000	$3,000	16.6
Currently maturing long-term debt			2.9
Trade payables	9,500	31,000	13.8
Taxes payable	500	2,500	.8
Other, current	500	1,000	7.7
Total current liabilities	13,500 (27%)	37,500 (39.7%)	41.8
Long-term			
Long-term debt	12,000	9,000	15.9
Other noncurrent	3,500	7,000	4.7
Total long-term liabilities	15,500 (31%)	16,000 (16.9%)	20.6
Total liabilities	29,000 (58%)	53,500 (56.6%)	62.4
Net Worth			
Stock	500	500	
Retained earnings	25,000	20,550	
Profits (loss)	(4,450)	19,950	
Total net worth	21,050 (42%)	41,000 (43.4%)	37.6
Total liabilities and net worth	50,050 (100%)	94,500 (100%)	100.0

Income Statement

	Year 1	(%)	Year 2	(%)	Industry Comparison %
Net sales	$250,000	(100%)	575,000	(100%)	100.0
COGS	129,000	(51.6%)	316,250	(55%)	63.5
Gross profit	**121,000**	**(48.4%)**	**258,750**	**(45%)**	**36.5**
Operating expenses	103,700	(41.5%)	213,800	(37.2%)	33.8
Operating profit	**17,300**	**(6.9%)**	**44,950**	**(7.8%)**	**2.7**
All other expenses	21,750	(8.7%)	25,000	(4.3%)	1.1
Profit (loss) before taxes	**(4,450)**		**19,950**	**(3.5%)**	**1.6**

What this all means

The balance sheet is in line with the industry averages. The company shows strong working capital ($226,500 and $41,500 in Years 1 and 2 respectively), but continues to be dependent on the sale of inventory. Trade accounts payable increased significantly in Year 2. The company needs to be aware of payable terms because cash is not currently available to cover these expenses. They are dependent on the sale of inventory as the primary source of cash. This is not necessarily bad, but something you need to be very conscious of. Industry comparisons reflect this as typical for your industry. In addition, fast growth often creates cash flow problems. It is important to make certain that inventory continues to turn over fast enough to pay current bills. Pay close attention to the cash flow statement.

Sales increased by 130 percent (from $250,000 to $575,000). A loss of $4,450 in Year 1 was changed to a profit of $19,950 in Year 2. Pre-tax return on sales (profits) were 3.5% in Year 2, much higher than the industry average of 1.6 percent. All are very positive signs. Look for why sales increased to better understand this trend. It may mean a future trend of continued growth, or it may have been the result of a marketing campaign you employed, or perhaps just reflective of a growing market.

The Cost of Goods Sold percentage increased from 51.6% in Year 1 to 55% in Year 2, but remained below the industry norm of 63.5%. The lower-than-average cost of goods sold may indicate that the business negotiated better buying terms than the industry average, or that you are able to mark up the price more because of the lack of competition, or because you are selling quality merchandise. This margin represents the cost of goods sold correlation to net sales. In any case, it transfers to the bottom line in Year 2. Another positive indicator.

Example 2: Assume that the business is a sole proprietorship day-care operation. Comparative figures are from SIC (standard industrial classification codes) 8351, from the *RMA Annual Statement Studies*.

Balance Sheet

Assets	Year 1 (%)	Year 2 (%)	Industry Comparison %
Current			
Cash	$3,500	$9,350	18.4
Trade accounts receivable	500	1,875	4.8
Inventory	150	675	.2
Other current assets	1,000	2,500	2.2
Total current assets	5,150 (19.7%)	14,400 (42.2%)	25.5
Noncurrent			
Fixed assets	18,750	18,750	62.4
Allowance for depreciation	(2,500)	(5,000)	
Intangibles (net)	4,000	3,500	4.6
Others, noncurrent	750	2,500	7.5
Total noncurrent assets	21,000 (80.3%)	19,750 (57.8%)	74.5
Total assets	26,150 (100%)	34,150 (100%)	100.0
Liabilities			
Current			
Currently maturing long-term debt	2,000		13.1
Trade payables	1,000	250	4.8
Income tax payable	500	250	.5
Other, current	3,000	500	15.5
Total current liabilities	6,500 (24.9%)	1,000 (2.9%)	33.9
Long-term			
Long-term debt	4,000		31.7
Other, noncurrent	2,500		2.0
Total long-term liabilities	6,500 (24.9%)	(0%)	33.7
Total liabilities	13,000 (49.8%)	1,000 (2.9%)	67.6
Retained earnings	8,150	13,150	
Profits	5,000	20,000	
Total net worth	13,150 (50.2%)	33,150 (97.1%)	32.4
Total liabilities and net worth	26,150 (100%)	34,150 (100%)	100.0

Income Statement

Assets	Year 1 (%)	Year 2 (%)	Industry Comparison %
Net sales	95,000 (100%)	125,000 (100%)	100.0
Gross profit	95,000	125,000	100.0
Operating expenses	78,000 (82.1%)	90,000 (72%)	93.9
Operating profit	17,000 (17.9%)	35,000 (28%)	6.1
All other expenses	12,000 (12.6%)	15,000 (12%)	2.7
Net income (loss) before taxes	5,000 (5.3%)	20,000 (16%)	3.4

What this all means

The company appeared to experience some cash flow problems in Year 1 (current assets were not sufficient to meet the current debt), but the firm improved its liquidity substantially in the second year. This is a very favorable improvement. If the company stays on this pace, the financial picture looks very good.

Sales increased by 31.6% from Year 1 to Year 2. All margins on the Income Statement surpassed industry averages. And the margins improved significantly from Year 1 to Year 2. This is a strong indication that the company is doing well. Operating expenses increased only $12,000 from Year 1 to Year 2, but decreased significantly as a percentage of sales. This strong improvement carried down to the bottomline.

Profits from Year 2 were used to pay off debt (short- and long-term), and the balance of the profit is shown in current assets. This reduces interest expense charges for future years.

Chapter 10

Growing concerns: the nuts and bolts of operating a business

"I kept saying, 'Sam, we're making a good living. Why go out, why expand so much more?' After the seventeenth store, though, I realized there wasn't going to be any stopping it."

Helen Walton
Sam Walton: Made in America

Sam Walton was a visionary, no question about it. He seized opportunities for his small company to grow, and grow, and grow. Helen Walton, however, was also a very important ingredient in the Walton success story, and one often forgotten.

Growing a business is risky. First, bigger is not always better. Yes, it worked well for Sam and Helen Walton. But for every success story there is a company whose profits were depleted at the risk of expansion. The growth came too soon and got out of control. Besides, not every one wants to be another Sam Walton.

Also, simply because you *want* to grow doesn't mean the growth potential exists. It is important to evaluate your market and listen to the customers. Are they willing to buy your product or service if...? Can you meet these demands and still make a profit? Why has no one else done this? Is it too costly? Too risky? Or not really what the customers are saying?

This chapter delves into the routine business procedures many entrepreneurs face, including some of the mundane and less glamorous operational decisions. Depending on your industry, some of these operating decisions may or may not apply. I have tried to include a variety of operating guidelines common to most small businesses.

Product life cycles

Products, like people and businesses, have a life cycle. They are born, they grow and eventually they die (or become obsolete). This is a natural process and one that cannot ultimately be altered. However, it can be enhanced with attention to certain details. And that is what your goal should be, to give attention to the details of prolonging your business life and success as long as possible.

As a business owner, it will be your goal to observe and predict where you are in the cycle. At times you will be able to prolong your product life cycle by responding quickly to changing market conditions. At other times, simply identifying where you are can assist in pricing philosophies and promoting your goods or services. These are the times you are unable to control, but they are not without responsibility and action.

Each product has a different and unique life cycle. Life cycles are affected by society, from public expectation and perception, as well as by economic measures. Local trends play a significant factor in determining this cycle. Many marketing experts applaud California as a more progressive atmosphere in which new ideas are born and readily accepted. Californians may accept change faster than perhaps the more conservative south; this does not mean the south will necessarily ever accept the new, innovative idea.

While sushi bars and gourmet coffee shops may succeed on the West coast and in large metropolitan areas, many small towns are less inclined to support such businesses. Even though the market may be growing, it does not guarantee that *your* market will participate in this growth. And your market (wherever and however it is defined) is your main concern.

Understanding how your local market reacts to change is important if you are selling locally. Some areas that were strongly supported by military bases have witnessed this firsthand. Base closings produce a ripple effect, causing small businesses to feel the consequences of such actions. Your product may not be obsolete, but if there is no one left to buy it, your business life may quickly be shortened.

Knowing where your product is in its life cycle will allow you to address circumstances commonly experienced at various phases of the cycle. When a product is new, in its birth or infancy stage, you can expect a lot more educating of the public to be required. During the growth stages, you can look for new ways for customers to use the product, innovative measures that will help prolong its life. A perfect example of prolonging the life of a product by creating new ways of using it is *baking soda*. When baking soda was

first introduced, its primary use was in cooking. Today, you can find numerous uses of the product outside the kitchen. And its marketers are constantly seeking new ideas from consumers. This innovative approach has created additional sales and added years to the life of the product by expanding potential markets.

There is often increased risk associated with new, emerging markets. The life cycle may be very short, and companies may be at risk to lose a lot of money. Yet, the potential for earning the highest rewards is the greatest in these emerging markets. That was part of the Walton formula.

Examples of emerging markets include those concerned with environmental products, as well as a variety of services for the older population. Both of these markets show significant growth potential, but may be impacted by governmental regulations. Actually, numerous environmental (green) products have been created to meet some of these stricter regulations. As for the aging population, it continues to grow and baby boomers continue to create demand for new products and services, such as elder care services (day care for elderly). The marketing of these products and services requires attention to educating the consumer.

While a product or service is in its infancy, the number of potential consumers is constantly expanding. Education and promotion expenses may be higher, but often companies succeed merely by riding on the coattails of others. This happens when there is more demand being created than there are businesses to meet this demand.

A more conservative, less risky approach can be achieved by entering a market that is reaching its growth and maturity levels. The length of time a product requires to reach this stage ranges from months to decades. When a product is in this life-cycle stage, you will find a more competitive environment. The earning potential for each owner is less, but because the market is more predictable (and somewhat stable), the risk is greatly reduced as well. Pricing products during this stage requires more attention to differentiation. How are you different from your competitors? And what are your customers wanting in their product that others fail to supply?

For example, both restaurants and printing companies are considered to be at their mature-growth market level. Entering these markets requires attention to product differentiation and offering new services because of the amount of competition that exists. Location often plays a significant role in retail businesses at this juncture. Educating the consumer is not as much a factor as creating name recognition.

As the life cycle begins to decline, many competitors will decide to get out of the business. This may be due to forced closings or it may be based on the lack of potential customers. For those companies that survive, since capital investments—such as large equipment purchases—will have been recouped from earlier sales, the potential to continue making money exists. But, only for companies that are run very efficiently and priced competitively. It is during this stage of operation that companies often find themselves lowering their prices to maintain or create sales. The effect of the lower prices is reduced profit margins. This is not the time to enter the market. But it is the time to expand to new or complementary markets.

Declining markets include companies faced with significant amounts of automation and technological change,

such as the computer-manufacturing industry. Entering this market, dominated by a few companies, would be costly and gaining profitable market share would be difficult. Because of rapid changes in technology, these companies are constantly expanding their product line as products become obsolete. In fact, many of their products have very short life cycles because of these fast changes.

To prolong or maintain product life, you can diversify. Diversification can mean the introduction of new products that are just emerging in their life cycle. Or it can be finding new ways of using the old product, like baking soda, and creating new markets from one product. In either case, it's important that women pay close attention to product life cycle and to their customers. Change, when identified early, represents new opportunities.

Consequences of fads

Fad items are those products that have a very short life and reach great sales volume in that period. The success of these items is often unexplained as their sales mushroom. During their life span there is the opportunity for a few business owners to make a lot of money.

The risk of entering fad businesses is great. It is not that you should avoid fad items; rather, you should identify and work within the constraints presented by such products. If it can be done at minimal cost, then you might entertain the notion. Given the short life span, your costs will need to be recouped very quickly. Otherwise, you could potentially lose a lot of money.

Who would have ever projected the success of items like the pet rock, Slinky or Cabbage Patch dolls? Yet, they did succeed. But they also declined as quickly as they rose. You don't want to get left holding a lot of unwanted inventory.

As new markets emerge, sometimes it is difficult to determine whether an item is a fad or a new way of life. The answer will be based on research as well as on instinct. Many thought that yogurt was just a fad. But they were wrong. Use your best judgment and proceed according to your findings.

Deciding to grow or maintain the status quo

When a company reaches the crossroads between capacity and growth, between profits and losses, between a static and dynamic state, there are a lot of questions that must be evaluated carefully before a realistic growth policy can be determined.

Growth, in this sense, pertains to areas that can be controlled by the owner. In reality, however, growth is actually the result of items both controlled and uncontrolled. The question then becomes, "How much control do you have over growth?" The answer varies from company to company. But there are certain steps you can take that are more likely to affect growth. Moreover, many entrepreneurs have said that not growing a small business means a fast and certain death for the company.

Most entrepreneurs do not have the luxury of saying, "This is the volume I want to handle" and stopping there. An exception might be a home day-care operator who wants to handle six children, has six children already signed up and has a waiting list. However, most of us must constantly seek new business opportunities. Otherwise, the business may eventually wither away as customers leave one by one for a variety of reasons. Not every step will produce

new business. It is important to consider all possibilities and to evaluate the outcomes with each option.

Some of the steps you might take to grow a company include increasing exposure and finding and exploring new markets. For example, increased advertising and promotional expenses should (when done successfully) achieve increased sales. Increased sales may mean the need for a larger location. This is especially true for retail and manufacturing businesses. But service businesses must also evaluate existing space available and determine whether additional staff will be needed and whether the current location can accommodate these additions.

If you operate out of your home, you may find growth limited. There may come a time when you want to rent office space away from the house. Along with such relocation comes not only a larger office but higher rent. Larger space means higher utilities bills, higher taxes, increased inventory needed, costs associated with renovations and wiring, and other costs. But these are not the only costs incurred in growth.

Some of these costs will have a high price. Others are psychological in nature—namely that you must be willing to let loose of your tight rein. As the company grows, you must be willing to let others have the authority and responsibility to act appropriately for their job functions. Many successful businesswomen cite this as the single most difficult aspect of growth—learning to let go of something you have worked so hard for, to share and support others' decisions, and not watching over their every move. But it is a necessary step for growth to lead to success.

Hiring additional employees to handle the growth will also translate into costs other than increased salary expenses.

There will also be higher taxes the companies pays on wages, not to mention the purchase of new desks, additional phones (and phone lines), plus office supplies. In addition, there are costs associated with training these new employees.

The decision to aggressively grow must entertain both the positive and negative aspects before a final decision can be reached. On the positive side should be that with increased sales will be increased profits. It may also mean that you are able to garner more favorable buying rates from suppliers because of the increased volume. But the downside may be that the increased expenses incurred may be higher than the increased profits. Or, that the expenses come much sooner and the profits lag months (if not years) behind. Do you have the money today necessary to grow the business? Your option may be to grow it at a slower rate, one that can support its own growth from operating revenues. Women have found great success in this alternative.

Credit policy

Credit is one way for some businesses to increase sales by reaching larger markets. When you see that potential customers are not buying from you because they do not want to pay for the product (or service) all at one time, you should look at the possibility of offering credit terms. Or, credit sales may be the norm and consumer expectation in your industry. In these instances you may be forced to offer credit to customers just to stay competitive.

As a new company, you should establish very specific guidelines for accepting credit sales. Many small business owners have lost everything because of poorly defined and inadequate credit policies.

The first step in establishing a credit policy is to set up your basic guidelines. What terms can you offer and still make a profit? What is the industry norm, in number of days? In actual collection? (The two may not be the same.)

Offering credit terms allows others to use your money interest-free. This is money you could be using to reinvest in inventory. Or money that could pay current bills. Consider how quickly your inventory is turning over (being replaced) as well as your gross profit margin for each item. And then decide whether your cash flow supports credit terms.

If you are operating on a very thin margin to start with, offering credit terms may put you in the red. Make sure that credit sales will increase sales and increase profits.

The next step is to have each customer complete a credit application form. Verify the accuracy of the information provided. Collecting the data doesn't do any good unless you verify and analyze it. Determine the applicant's credit rating with other companies. Local credit reporting services can produce this information.

The end of this chapter has a sample credit application form you can use for an individual. It can be adapted for use as a company application with minor changes. Realize that the amount of information you request will directly relate to the amount of credit being sought and its risk to you. For small amounts, and in communities where you feel a credit application could be perceived as insulting, use your judgment. Your attorney will advise you specifically on your needs based on your exposure, climate and local regulations.

Next determine how much credit you want to extend to particular customers and the terms. This may vary, like pricing, from customer to customer, based on volume or creditworthiness. Keep in mind that some customers, like government agencies, may be a great source of income and a low credit risk but a notoriously slow payer. It is important to consider this fact when you bid for government contracts. You don't want to ruin your credit with your suppliers because a large customer continues to be late in paying you. Credit problems cause a trickle affect. Learn to anticipate and resolve potential problems early.

And finally, establish appropriate steps within your organization to follow when accounts become delinquent. Assign the phone calling and letter writing to one person. The sooner you address these slow accounts and begin working them, the better your chance of collecting the money. You can't afford to carry large, delinquent accounts receivable balances, especially as a young company.

The following guidelines may be adapted to your company's needs to assist in establishing your credit policy:

- Develop a clear credit policy.
- Communicate payment terms to customers.
- Date every invoice to eliminate confusion.
- Send bills out quickly.
- Have a specific number of days for your grace period. Once the grace period has been reached, start collection steps immediately.
- Train your staff to handle collection matters; these are crucial to the well-being of your business.
- Begin collection action with a reminder letter; then proceed with letters that demand action in specified number of days. Once letters have been sent,

follow up with a phone call. There is no need to be rude or hostile during the collection process. Promptness and politeness have proven to be more effective in gaining results.
- If no money has been received, advise your clients when you will be turning the account over to a collection agency or attorney to handle. And then follow through on your warning.

Know the law concerning collection practices and techniques. It is very specific, and state regulations may require strict adherence. Know that phone calls often get better results with companies than with individuals. Being firm doesn't mean being rude. You can be pleasant and firm at the same time. Keep in mind that if you anger a customer, your payment may be delayed even longer.

Credit card sales

The acceptance of credit cards in your business is another method of helping it grow. Nearly one-third of all sales today come from the use of credit cards. The use of credit cards affords small business owners the opportunity to grow in volume without the risk of extending credit. Credit card sales are treated like cash for both banking and accounting purposes. Cash, checks and credit cards all have costs associated with them that must be considered, analyzed and factored as one of the costs of doing business. Accepting credit cards has a direct cost associated with it as well. Therefore, if credit cards don't increase sales, you may not want to take on this additional expense.

Major bank credit cards, such as VISA or MasterCard, have monthly service fees that average between three and five percent of the net credit card sale. American Express fees are usually higher. If you have small-ticket items, credit card sales may not be profitable. Service fees may be too high for your low profit margin. However, the larger the items you sell, the better terms you can often negotiate on credit card fees. Home-based business owners may have difficulty in finding a bank to approve credit card transactions, but it is not impossible. Banks consider home-based businesses a higher risk because they have gotten stung by fly-by-night operators. This again underscores the importance of creating a positive personal relationship with your banker early on. A few more tips on accepting credit cards:

- Each card company will determine your floor amount, that amount you can accept without approval.
- Make sure that you call in for your approval code when you accept a credit card for purchases above your floor amount.

Check local consumer regulations to see what information you are allowed to request on credit card approvals.

Accepting checks

Not all businesses accept checks as a form of payment, but many do. Accepting checks can, in effect, become an extension of credit terms. If someone writes you a check for payment and that check is returned because of insufficient funds, then you have sold your product or service without collecting the money first. You have offered credit terms, even if you had not intended that to happen.

There are steps that can be taken to lessen the risk in taking personal (or business) checks. First, it is always an advantage when you know your customer. Although this doesn't guarantee

that the funds will be good, it does reduce the risk. When knowing your customer personally is not an option, you should have established procedures on accepting checks—what identification you will require, whether bank pre-approval is necessary and so on.

Accepting or not accepting checks is a delicate affair because the vast majority of businesses do accept them. A great deal of intuition and gut feelings are factored into the equation. In addition, you should look at your risk verses reward. If you are selling small-ticket items, and you are in a community where everyone knows everyone else, you may not require additional identification for checks, assuming instead the risk of returned checks in exchange for not offending customers.

On the other hand, if you are selling items that are very costly and if one returned check could have a very strong impact on the financial future of your business, then you should establish procedures to reduce that risk to an amount you are comfortable with. Some companies require two credit cards for payments by check, others accept local checks only and others require the state driver's license as a form of identification. The most conservative measure is to employ an outside company (for a fee) to guarantee your checks when you call for an approval. Again, the cost for this service is high and recommended only if you are in an area where there is a high transient population or great risk of checks being returned marked "insufficient funds."

Special pricing considerations

When liquidating inventory, it is often better to assume a pricing posture that is very different from the usual.

Inventory that has been sitting on the shelves too long is money that is tied up—money that is unavailable for the purchase of more popular inventory items. Most small business owners should look at the total cost of that shipment, earn the cost back on the front-end of sales and make their profit at the end.

Let's assume, for example, that you own a woman's dress shop. Naturally, you would carry inventory according to the upcoming or current season. And, because of limited space, you might be unable to keep out-of-season clothes in inventory. In addition, the style may change so that those items become less desirable and even harder to sell. As a new shipment for the upcoming season arrives, you would price your items according to your predetermined profit margin (mark-up). Let's assume that your mark-up allows for costs to be covered after you have sold half the inventory. This will actually vary, depending on competition and demand. If the inventory moves quickly, changing the pricing formula may not be necessary. However, for inventory that remains on the racks for an extended period of time, you may begin lowering prices slowly, eventually going below what you actually paid for the item. But, since you have already sold half of this particular inventory item, you actually are looking at making some profit versus none while inventory sits on the shelves. This pricing consideration should only be used as an exception, since it does not take into account overhead and related business expenses.

Your ability to lower prices will depend on a lot of variables, but don't be afraid to change as you need to. In other words, lower the price to whatever it takes to sell the item. Some money in hand is better than inventory sitting around collecting dust on your shelves.

Often, novice owners want to make (at the very minimum) their cost back on every item. But if most of the inventory has already sold, you should not evaluate each product on an individual basis. Instead, look at the total picture. Move old inventory using whatever pricing formula it takes.

Look to the future and learn to identify and cut your losses quickly.

Integrating computers into today's business

You may be surprised to think of computers as another way of growing a business, but they are. While computers may not actually increase sales, they can contribute to both the efficiency of your operation and to lower expenses. Either (or both) of these measures will free you up to handle more business and perhaps save you from having to hire additional staff to meet these increased demands.

By increasing efficiency, computers reduce the amount of human error in labor-intense jobs. These errors can be costly and often take hours to uncover (or weeks).

Computers can allow you to create an in-house mailing list from existing or potential customers. Then, with one of the easy merge features available in most word-processing programs, you can write one letter and have it personally addressed to each individual on your mailing list. This is a very personal approach to staying in contact with your customers, and it is less costly than purchasing a mailing list.

With the introduction of computers, some job duties can be combined, thus lower costs can be achieved by eliminating the need for additional staff. This salary reduction frequently can pay for the computer many times over.

Computer technology is rapidly changing. Through these changes are born opportunities for new businesses to emerge. Whether or not you participate directly in these markets, you still can achieve numerous benefits from computers in your business.

Computer terminology can be confusing and cumbersome to many first-time owners. Often, those in the know forget about the learning process and can intimidate you by tossing around terms and industry jargon that are foreign to you. Before you begin shopping for a computer, you may want to familiarize yourself with some of the frequently used terms listed below.

System Unit: Is the box that houses the "brain" of your computer.

Microprocessor: Is the heart of the system unit. This is the place where your computer interprets and processes information.

Memory: Determines how much information the computer can process at one time. Software programs usually have minimum memory requirements. Computer memory is measured in kilobytes and megabytes. One kilobyte, usually expressed as 1KB, equals 1,024 bytes and one megabyte, expressed as 1MB, equals 1,048,576 bytes.

Disk Space: Refers to the amount of information you can store on a disk. Disks are either enclosed in your computer (hard disk) or inserted into the computer each time you access the information on it (floppy disk). A hard disk drive contains a nonremovable disk built into your system, whereas a floppy disk drive holds a removable floppy disk; it has considerably less storage capacity than a hard disk.

Monitor: This is the screen that displays the information in your computer. Choices are either color or monochrome, although monochrome monitors are uncommon in standard systems. Quality in color monitors continues to improve considerably providing greater definition and range.

Printer: A printer prints the information processed by your computer. Choices center on the quality of output needed and the speed required. Laser printers, bubble jet printers, and dot-matrix printers are the primary categories, in descending order of cost. Prices range widely, as do features. Consider who will see the finished product before deciding on the quality you need.

On-line communication

On-line communication is not only the wave of the future, it is a reality of the present. On-line communication refers to two or more computers "talking" with each other. It requires having a modem, software that operates the modem and a telephone line to transmit the signals.

Popular commercial on-line services include Prodigy, GEnie and CompuServe. They offer services ranging from bulletin boards, where you can share information and ideas on a variety of topics, to e-mail (electronic mail), where you can send and receive individual messages, to services that give you the capability to make travel bookings. These services provide a great opportunity to network with other small business owners. But, as with all networking, to get the most benefits, you must participate.

Many commercial on-line services offer connection to the Internet. The Internet has been around for more than two decades, but its popularity has grown exponentially in recent years. In a nutshell, the Internet is a worldwide web of interconnected university, business, military and science networks. It is the fastest global network around, reaching millions of people around the world in seconds. Some of the information accessible through the Internet includes texts, files, bulletins, reference sources, statistics, electronic journals, research reports, government information...and much, much more. Another feature is that it can provide numerous on-line catalogs from most major U.S. academic and research libraries, along with access to government research.

Business owners are beginning to realize the importance of being well-connected in order to remain competitive in the global marketplace. Women should eagerly explore the Information Superhighway, realizing that on-line communication networks can bring greater amounts of information, in more detail, faster than other sources.

Look for classes and workshops about the uses of on-line communication. Because information sources are so diverse, the uses and benefits vary from person to person. You do not have to be a computer wizard to take advantage of these applications. However, you do need a commitment of time to learn how to maneuver a complex system so that you access the information you want.

Embrace these changes. Take advantage of the benefits. On-line communication opens up an array of mentors and specialists that were not easily accessible for our predecessors. But our good fortune can only happen if we use the system.

Credit application (individual)

Name of applicant _____

Current address _____

City, State, Zip _____

Telephone number (day) _____(evening)_____

Length of time at current address _____

Previous address (if less than five years) _____

City, State, Zip _____

Driver's license number _____

Date of birth _____

Social Security number _____

Employer _____

Employer's address _____

How long _____ Position _____

Bank _____ Types of accounts _____

Account numbers _____

Additional credit references (name, account number, balance)

1. _____
2. _____
3. _____

Personal references (name and telephone number)

1. _____
2. _____
3. _____

Have you ever filed for bankruptcy? _____ If so, when?_____

I declare the foregoing information to be true and correct, and I am hereby authorizing you to conduct an employment and credit check and to verify my references.

Signed _____ Date _____

Chapter 11

The all-important banker: friend or foe?

"The banking industry's past troubles are in large part responsible for its present unwillingness to lend to small businesses....Consequently, getting a loan to expand or improve a small business is difficult; getting a loan to start one can be next to impossible."

Stephanie Barlow
Entrepreneur Magazine

Meeting your banker

Because women are often intimidated by numbers, they may also be intimidated by bankers. Don't be. Bankers can be very helpful in starting and growing a business. The key to bankers is the same as for other professional advisors—finding the one who meets your personal needs. Not all bankers are right for you. Nor are all banks the same. Look for someone who cares about you and your business, someone you trust. Look for someone who has time to talk and listen. Look for someone with experience and stability (although that is becoming more difficult to find). And look for someone who can make decisions quickly, if that is a need you anticipate.

From the beginning, establish strong working relationships with your bankers. Notice, I use bankers in the plural sense. This is intentional. Putting all your eggs in one basket may be detrimental to your long-term growth. Bankers often ask for your total commitment to them as a condition of lending, but can be suffocating to you if they decide later not to grant your loan request. Of course, if you are starting very small, having two separate banks may not be feasible (or practical).

However, if you choose to favor a single relationship, bankers may be more receptive to you for your loyalty. There are benefits either way. It is better to establish your banking relationship before you have lending needs, if possible. Your goal is to have your financial needs met as quickly and as equitably as possible.

The first step is to find a bank and banker who meet your needs, goals and expectations. Banks are businesses, and as businesses they target specific customers as their primary market. Do not be offended if you do not fit into their general customer profile. Targeting customers is a business decision. Realize also that banks are in the business of lending other people's money. In this role, they respond in a conservative fashion.

Schedule an initial meeting and introduce yourself. (This may be difficult, since often loan officers only want to meet customers when there is a financial request on the table. If they don't have the time to meet you now, that may be an indication of how they view you—more as an interruption than as a valued customer.) Ask about the bank, its target market and the services offered. Establish a sense of how people are treated: as individuals or as statistics and numbers. Do they care about you, or are their interests more for themselves and how you can help them?

Consider those areas that are important to you and interview banks and bankers along those lines. For most small business owners, the banker will be the local branch manager. Some banks may have a small business department, in which case you should ask for an introduction. Other banks work small business loans in their commercial loan department. If you do not have any financial requests at the time, let them know.

Always keep your banker up to date on your business, how it's growing, its prospects, etc. Become more than a name to her. The first rule of banking is to realize that *people* pay back loans, not businesses. Your objective is to become an individual known and appreciated by your banker, whether or not you have a specific lending request. This will greatly enhance your overall relationship.

In evaluating banks and bankers, determine what services you anticipate needing and the costs associated with those services. For example, what are the fees for personal and business checking accounts? Look closely at business checking account fees. They are the culmination of a variety of charges, direct and indirect, that vary significantly from bank to bank. Are the hours and location convenient for you? Does the bank offer credit cards? What are the fees for merchant deposits? Are they an SBA-approved lender?

Without exception, establish a separate business checking account. This is important for all businesses. Keep business and personal money separate, no matter how small your business is or how good at record-keeping you are. Opening a separate business checking account is both professional and practical. Depending on your form of ownership and state regulations, banks will advise you as to the necessary paperwork and filings needed to open your account.

Bankers acknowledge (reluctantly) that money is readily available to those who need it least; if you need money, a bank is slow to oblige. I know. I was a vice president in commercial loans for many years. Banks are averse to taking risks. And because banking is still part of the "good ol' boy" network, it has been hard for females to gain credibility. There is no easy solution here, except to become known as an individual. I recommend sharing in your growth, asking for bankers' advice and keeping them informed each step of the way. Open communications will go a long way towards getting the system working in your favor, even if the news isn't always good news. Actually, it is as important, if not more important, to talk with your banker about the financial difficulties you are having as about your financial successes. The earlier you engage in these conversations, the more likely the banker is to lend a helping hand—although lending a helping hand may not equate to lending money.

Selling your ideas

Let's assume you need money. Having a business plan can be an invaluable tool in gaining access to money. Successful loan packaging and presentations do influence lenders. All that hard work is worth the effort, not to mention the benefits you received from the exercise. Prepare a very thorough and well-written business plan.

Find a bank that cares about you. It may not be the first bank you go to. It may take two or three or four times before you find the one that is right for you. But, keep trying until you do. And then present your needs.

If you are in search of seed capital, the money needed to plan, prepare, open and operate the business, anticipate some difficulty from banks and larger financial institutions. Do not write them completely off. Getting funds is not impossible. Nor is it even improbable. It's just more challenging. Your preparation, homework and ability to sell yourself and your company will be put to the test.

While advertisements claim banks love to help small businesses, the truth is they love to help small businesses with opening their checking accounts and by offering them free advice. They may even help entrepreneurs with secured loans, if the collateral is a strong mortgage with a lot of equity. Real estate mortgages are the collateral of choice for most lenders. Although real estate-dependent loans have cost the banking industry millions of dollars in recent years, they remain their preference.

Understand that banks are businesses too. They are in the business to make money by charging interest on the money they lend. This is the primary source of income for financial institutions. You are the customer. You want to "purchase" their product.

Be prepared to answer intelligently every possible question a banker might raise about your business and industry.

Rely on the market and industry analysis you have already completed to give you ammunition. Do not become defensive or overly zealous. Answer questions factually. Answer questions honestly. And answer questions to the best of your ability. Your knowledge and insightfulness will be impressive.

Still, that may not be enough.

Ask your prospective banker if they have loaned money to similar types of companies. Also ask if they have any upfront reservations about your industry. Ask about their minimum loan request for SBA guarantees and how many SBA loans they approved and funded the previous year. Knowing the number of loans sheds light on how supportive they are of small businesses.

Your detailed business plan will explain the fine points of your company and specific loan request. Remember that a business plan is the outline of your ideas, plans, marketing, location, customers, costs and projections. While some investors will prefer to read the business plan after you leave, others will want you to discuss the major points right then. Therefore, your communication skills should be polished and you should be ready to perform at all times. Your enthusiasm and attention to detail will color a plan that is laid out in black and white. You can bring life to paper through your presentation.

This is still no guarantee of a loan approval. Be prepared for rejection. Don't take it personally, though, and don't let rejection slow you down. A "no" is not a denial of your self-worth, nor of the validity of your business plan. You may have chosen a conservative or uninformed lender. Or your proposal may not fit the lender's current needs or abilities. Keep on until you get a yes. Be persistent and be positive.

Lenders' needs change as the economy changes and as the makeup of their outstanding loan portfolio matures. You may not be aware of the financial difficulties of your lending institution. Remember, they are a business just like you, and they have hardships and dilemmas just as you do. In addition, financial institutions are highly regulated, which intensifies their story.

I once worked at a bank that had typical business growing pains, which resulted in one area of the business growing at a different rate than another. The bank was strapped for cash and unable to assist existing customer's loan requests until it raised additional capital by bringing in new deposits. Unfortunately, when approached by a potential customer with a loan request, we had to graciously decline, for the time being. During this period loans were only made when urgent pleas came from existing customers who had no other alternative. Luckily, deposits increased quickly and the loans were made once again with regularity. In other words, you may not be aware of the whole story.

Preparing for borrowing

Regardless of the source you seek to borrow from, thoroughly prepare your application and supporting documents. Anticipate questions and have information readily available. When applying for a loan, you will probably be asked to provide business and personal credit information. Have these personal financial statements typed and with you at the time of the request, if at all possible. It will speed up the overall process. Copies are usually acceptable when they contain an original signature. Current financial statements should not be more than 90 days old.

Have a specific loan request. Determine an actual dollar amount needed and how it will be spent before you meet with the banker. Know how you arrived at the requested amount. Detail how the loan proceeds will be used and how they will be repaid. Bankers are especially interested in your projected repayment schedule. State your request for the loan's term and interest rate—not that you will get them, but start the offering process. These should all be factored into your repayment analysis. Be realistic in your request and be willing to negotiate (which may mean concede). You will have an advantage if you learn a little banking lingo. Bankers feel more comfortable lending to individuals who know the difference between a working capital loan and seasonal line of credit. You should know the difference between a debit and a credit, as well as how to read your financial statements. A banking officer will look closely at your financial picture, often commenting on the leverage position or amount of liquidity you have. Don't be intimidated or frustrated by their lingo. Instead, learn what it means by knowing and understanding your numbers.

And finally—and very importantly—look the part. Look professional. Act professional. Leave a great first, and lasting, impression. Banking is a conservative industry. Your goal is to instill confidence that you are a professional, a business person, a manager and financial planner.

Your business plan includes a balance sheet, listing all of your business assets and liabilities and a profit and loss statement summarizing sales, cost of sales, gross profits, expenses and net income before taxes. For established businesses, a minimum of two prior years' financial statements and income tax returns should be supplied. However, for businesses that have been operating longer, a banker may request three to five years of prior financial statements and tax returns to be presented with the loan request package. This will enable the lender to assess patterns and market potential more quickly. In addition, lenders almost always ask for personal financial information about the owners or primary stockholders.

State clearly how much you and your partners or directors are taking from the business in personal salary. Lenders do not look negatively on this figure, but use it as part of their business analysis calculations. It is thought of as profit that may not have to be withdrawn.

Checklist for requesting a loan

- Present a detailed business plan to show how you will use the financing to operate your business.
- Prove that you have a reputation for paying your obligations when due by supplying credit references.
- Show that you have had adequate business experience and are qualified to operate your company.
- Provide proof that you have sufficient financing of your own to warrant a lender's taking a reasonable risk by advancing part of your financial needs.
- Produce unfilled orders on hand, if possible, or potential business prospects that will result in a cash flow sufficient for loan repayment. Projections are viewed guardedly when they cannot be verified. Contracts and strong prospects add credibility and validity to your calculations.

Personal financial statements

Personal financial statements are very similar to company balance sheets. They show your assets, liabilities and net worth. Banks and other investors will probably want all primary owners of a business to complete a personal financial statement, which must be signed and dated to be authenticated.

Your personal financial statement will also include supporting detailed information on real estate owned, including appraised value, monthly payment and mortgages outstanding. In addition, notes receivable and payable should be included with their schedule of payments. There is a blank sample of a personal financial statement included at the end of this chapter. However, most banks have a form that meets their specific requirements. Inquire with your established bank first. But if you are in the interviewing stages, then prepare a personal financial statement following the format at the end of this chapter.

Taking the lead

Bankers often practice the art of negotiating. Do not be surprised if your original loan request goes through many changes and reductions during the negotiating process. It is just part of lending. It's not a matter of right or wrong. It just is. However, the more accurately and professionally your presentation is perceived, the fewer changes will occur.

Loans are often declined when the proceeds are to be used to combine existing debt or pay off other lenders. Banks do not like paying off other creditors, to be left as the only remaining risk taker. There are circumstances, however, when paying off a secured lender provides greater collateral positioning. In those rare situations, the bank may pay off another creditor to lessen its exposed risk, but this is rare.

Whatever conditions or requests are asked of you by a lender, you should, without exception, honor them. For relatively young or small companies, lenders often insist on restrictive or informative types of conditions, such as frequency of presentation of personal and company financial statements; maintaining certain ratios (liquidity ratios, leverage, bank balances); meeting with bankers quarterly for review of status; prepayment penalty; and exclusive banking relationship. Remember, if you agree to those conditions, honor your word. Trust is a major part of the financial equation. These conditions, if broken, may represent immediate default and may incur strong penalties, perhaps even an immediate demand to pay back your loan, regardless of the original terms.

Types of business loans

In presenting your loan package to a banker, know the type of loan you are seeking and how it works. The banker may consider a different type of loan and structure more fitting for your needs. Knowing loan types will allow you to negotiate and discuss on a more equal basis. Plus your banker will be impressed by your knowledge. The most common types of loans offered by bankers are: character loans, seasonal lines of credit, revolving lines of credit, term loans, collateral loans, cosigner loans, equipment loans, accounts receivable financing and factoring of accounts receivable.

Character loans. Generally, these represent short-term, unsecured loans (without any collateral) and are reserved for companies or entrepreneurs with the highest credit standing, business integrity and ability to manage the company. They are most commonly used within professional circles (for doctors, attorneys and accountants). As a new or young business, do not expect a character loan to be offered. And, depending on your industry, there may be such inherently high risk that a character loan is not feasible at all.

Lines of credit. These can be broken down into seasonal or revolving, depending on the nature of the industry, sales and trends. Both types are serviced in the same manner from a financial institution and require extending a total commitment amount, to be drawn in various increments, and under certain conditions. Interest is paid only on the amount of the line that is outstanding and for the number of days it is actually used. Often, financial institutions charge a loan commitment fee (the actual percentage varies), which is profit to the bank for servicing the line. Requests for seasonal or short-term lines of credit are better received by bankers since there exists an identified or normal repayment plan.

Seasonal lines of credit. A typical line of credit may be extended to a company that has seasonal sales fluctuation to purchase inventory for its peak selling time. Let's assume the commitment amount is $100,000. And let's assume the highest sales season for the company is the Christmas season. The company purchases $25,000 of additional inventory in September, an additional $50,000 in October and $25,000 in November at the peak of the season. As the inventory is sold and cash collected, the line of credit is paid down. The line may never need to be fully drawn, since inventory may move faster than anticipated and create a steady cash flow. The downside is that you may buy inventory you are unable to sell, or competition creates a price war and lessens your mark up, and you cannot pay off the line of credit when it is due. This is a time when maintaining open, honest communication with your banker, no matter what the news, is important.

Revolving lines of credit. Primarily, these revolve on an annual basis and are intended for a company whose sales do not reflect seasonal tendencies, or whose "off" season is one or two months of the year. The line of credit is therefore open for a twelve-month period. Basically, a revolving line of credit is a by-product of advancing profits before they are received to reinvest back into the company. Revolving lines of credit are very common among certain types of industries. Bankers will be careful to determine that your need is not actually long-term, permanent capital to grow on. Some ways of seeing a company's dependency on a line include requiring a 30 day pay-out period. What this means is that for 30 consecutive days the line of credit should be paid down to zero. If an annual clearance of debt is part of the arrangement, the business will ensure a buildup of funds by refraining from other outlays and purchases until the requirement is met. Bankers will generally review all your business payables to verify that you are not delaying current debt just to meet the 30-day bank requirement. That is a very bad sign to a banker and amounts to manipulating funds.

Term loans. *Short-term* loans cover periods of less than a year, often 30, 60 or 90 days. *Long-term* loans run more than 5 years, sometimes for as long as 10 to 15 years. Collateral, as well as a good credit rating, may be necessary to secure a term loan. The terms will depend

on how the funds are used and what sources of repayment are identified. Often, banks require payments monthly, quarterly or annually to reduce principal and pay out the loan. The repayment should coincide with how profits are generated. Short-term loans may be necessary when you have a large contract that needs additional inventory or material purchased to fill the order. On the other hand, long-term loans are frequently designed for permanent working capital loans, allowing the company to gradually repay the cash infusion from normal business operations.

Collateral loans. Inventory may be accepted as collateral for short-term loans. Longer-term loans usually are secured by real estate mortgages, stocks and bonds, cash-value life insurance or collateral that is substantive in nature (larger equipment, etc.). These loans often reflect less-desirable financial conditions and are substantiated by the liquidation value of the collateral and not by repayment from business operations. Since forced sale of collateral results in a less-than-desirable selling condition, the value is generally lower than in a competitive market. Therefore, financial institutions will only allow a percentage of what a conservative "fire sale" would bring, to protect themselves from unsecured debt as much as possible. The inflated real estate markets of the past few decades and the recession of the '90s have caused many financial institutions to be exposed when they thought they were well-protected by collateral value. When owners defaulted on loans and the real estate was liquidated for repayment, the banks found themselves short of cash to cover the loans. Banks shy away from collateral-dependent loans.

Cosigner loans or comaker loans are made to the borrower and to another individual, a cosigner or comaker. This second person is equally obligated to see that the loan is repaid, being responsible for 100 percent of your debt just as you are. A cosigner would also include a spouse asked to sign on your note. Try to gain credit in your own name. Unfortunately, it takes established credit to create credit in today's business world.

Equipment loans (installment loans) are generally five or more years in length that are established with a specific and steady repayment plan. The length of the loan often coincides with the life of the equipment, or a shorter period. Equipment loans are not thought of as collateral-dependent because the product from the equipment should generate sufficient cash to repay the debt.

Accounts receivable financing is primarily offered by commercial credit or finance companies and represents accepting accounts receivable as security for loans. Scrutiny of accounts receivable is high, and aging, names, and balances are reviewed prior to acceptance. With this type of financing, you remain responsible for the repayment of the loan when the proceeds of the accounts receivable do not cover the advance.

Factoring accounts receivable. This procedure is done through a factoring company, whose full time job is collecting and "working" accounts receivable. For a discounted amount, you sell your accounts receivable to a factoring company for cash now. The factoring company is responsible for collecting past-due accounts and usually absorbs any losses from charge-offs. High-quality accounts receivable are targets for this kind of financing. Factoring companies charge a substantial fee for their services, but these represent savings in administration and labor costs for you.

As a woman seeking funding, you will need to be prepared, knowledgeable and convincing in your presentation—perhaps more than you think necessary. It may not be fair, but it's a fact. And the sooner you accept it, the sooner you will see positive results. Your relationship with your banker can be instrumental to your growth and success as a small business owner. Find a banker you feel comfortable with, someone you trust and someone who believes in you and your business. Not all bankers are the same. Nor are all banks. Keep looking until you find the perfect match.

Personal Financial Statement

As of _____, ____

Name _____

Address _____

Phone _____

Assets

Cash on hand $_____

Savings _____

Stocks and bonds _____

IRA/pension _____

Life insurance (cash value) _____

Real estate _____

Automobile _____

Other personal property _____

Other assets _____

TOTAL ASSETS $ _____

Liabilities

Installment notes $ _____

Notes payable _____

Charge card balance _____

Mortgages _____

Loans on life insurance _____

Other liabilities _____

_____

_____

TOTAL LIABILITIES $ _____

Net Worth $ _____

Sources of Income

Salary _____

Investment income _____

Real estate income _____

Other (explain) _____

Contingent Liabilities

Endorser or comaker _____

Legal claims for judgments _____

Provision for federal income tax _____

Other debt _____

Have you ever declared bankruptcy? _____ If yes, when? _____

_____   _____

Signed   Date

Chapter 12
The art of networking: creating solid business opportunities

"Networking is an attitude, an approach to life."

Donna and Sandy Vilas
Power Networking

What is networking?

In the broadest sense, networking refers to alliances, relationships, bonds and interplay with other people on some common ground. It is a method of developing and using contacts that is mutually beneficial to all parties. It is your link to success. Everyone networks. *Megatrends for Women* calls networking "women's prime *modus operandi* in the work world." Effective networking helps us to keep our balance and perspective in a world that is constantly changing. It's how we keep our finger on the pulse of what is happening in the world of business.

Networking is more than just meeting people; it involves sharing, communicating and listening. You must be an active participant in networking for it to provide you with results. Women-owned businesses use networking as their framework. It is an ongoing, continuous process. It is your business lifestyle. In essence, it is who you know, what you know and who knows you.

Women must accept the fact that networking isn't automatic. At least not for most of us. You must be mindful and intentional of how and when to network.

You must seek opportunities to develop networks, even if they don't seem obvious. Networking can happen within small circles as well as in extended, larger and more obvious environments. Both are equally important avenues that women are utilizing.

The key to networking is to build a wide range of relationships, on different levels. You may have contacts within your industry, or develop contacts with other business professionals. Still other networks may be built strictly around female support systems. "Women-only" networks are one of the strongest and most productive alliances women business owners have created. The support found in these networks can help women over many of the hurdles they face, especially involving family issues and balancing hectic lives.

Networking is the most cost-effective marketing tool small business owners have available. It is a wise use of your time, which is a limited resource. No longer do you have to reinvent the wheel. No longer do you have to start each search at the beginning. Through networking channels you are able to gain contacts and leads that eliminate many preliminary and time-consuming steps.

There are numerous benefits to networking. Networking can help you gain new customers, locate new and less expensive suppliers, find subcontractors or employees for your company, help determine a fair market price for your product, discover a solution to a problem you have or recommend qualified professionals to complete your support system. Networking provides opportunities for mutual sharing, supporting and giving to others. It leads to new relationships, new opportunities and new ideas emerging. But for networking to "work," you must be willing to participate equally in the process. If you approach networking on the basis of what you receive from it, you'll find leads and ideas not being shared readily. Networking is based on mutuality. You must be willing and able to contribute to keep the system alive.

To gain these benefits, however, you must be the kind of person people want to help to succeed. Positive, real and honest motives will be rewarded. You must be willing to help others and share the knowledge you have gained through your contacts and experiences.

The importance of networking

Women know how to help other women. We have created very powerful and productive networking organizations. As a new female entrepreneur, take advantage of these existing systems. Tap into them at every opportunity you see. Join professional female organizations. But realize, joining isn't enough. You must actively participate to see results. Since you never know when doors will be open, position yourself to always be ready.

Networking is not easy, especially when you consider the long hours and multiple hats entrepreneurs wear. Networking often requires you to make the first move—to meet total strangers—and to enjoy yourself in the process. This may not come naturally to you. In fact, more than 70 percent of the population report experiencing shyness at some point in their careers and lives. Feeling uncomfortable in a room full of strangers is not unique. Learn how to assert yourself in spite of your feelings and inhibitions by creating a style and method of networking you are comfortable with. You set the tone and style of networking for you. It is better to meet a few people well than to collect business cards from everyone in the room without making any connections. Set a goal for yourself at each function. Then reward yourself when you reach that goal.

Networking is not simply a matter of going to a social event, chatting and meeting a lot of people. Nor is it simply handing out lots of your business cards. It's your opportunity to make connections on areas troubling you and to share leads and advice with others on topics that concern them.

Networking doesn't have to mean formal, business organizations. Networking can occur at volunteer gatherings, grocery stores, Sunday school classes or any place professionals gather. The potential for networking is everywhere. Keep your eyes and ears open to new networking opportunities you may uncover.

Networking provides leads that can produce tangible results. In fact, referrals are 80 percent more likely to materialize in results than cold calling. Although you cannot know what the result will be from any lead, the numbers are much more encouraging when referrals are involved. The investment in this process continues to prove beneficial and profitable. Appreciate every referral and lead. And always say thank you to the person who supplied the lead. Let them know how much you appreciate it and return the favor when you can.

Networking guidelines

When you are prepared for networking at every opportunity, you will not have a missed chance. You must be both patient and persistent in this journey, though. People know other people. While you may not know someone directly in a certain field, when you tap into networks, the chances are greatly increased that someone else can make that contact for you. It becomes an amazing web of names.

Don't abuse your friends by focusing exclusively on *your* agenda and *your* needs. Collecting meaningless stacks of business cards isn't networking. And inappropriate sales pressure at the wrong time can cause strong negative results. Be sensitive to the situation and be sensitive to others. A wedding is not the time to pass out your business cards. Nor is a funeral. Be conscious of your environment. In fact, the current techniques for networking are changing to meet today's growing needs.

Here are guidelines I have found helpful for succeeding at networking.

- Have your business cards easily accessible at all times, preferably in your pocket. Unfortunately, not all of our clothes have pockets, I know. But if you can get in the habit, keep your business cards in one pocket and those you collect in another. That way, you won't give away a card you just collected.
- Ask people what they do. Swap business cards. And listen for opportunities to share information and contacts. Sharing information is the key to successful networking. Provide leads and referrals whenever possible. The more you share, the more others will share with you. Always have the names and phone numbers of your key advisors handy (assuming you recommend their services).
- Learn to explain your business in one or two sentences. Brevity has a definite advantage.
- Have a pen with you so you can write comments on the back of business cards you collect, providing specific information about the person or names and phone numbers of leads they have offered. That way, you can remember who gave you what lead.
- Follow up on all leads and suggestions. Then, send thank-you notes to those individuals who have provided the leads and let them know the status. Always thank people for their help. This will have stronger impact when done in writing than the easier option of a phone call.
- Learn the art of listening. Listen to what is said and what is not said. Be attentive to body language. In addition, be sure to give supportive feedback through nodding, smiling and friendly eye contact.
- At social events, act like a host and not a guest. Do not sit around waiting for someone to come up to you and introduce themselves. Don't wait for others to serve you. Take a deep breath and take that first step. If you act like you belong, people are more likely to gravitate to you. But if you sit back and wait to be included, you may miss a great opportunity to make a potentially significant contact.

- Follow proper etiquette for introductions. Faux pas can be costly and make bad (and lasting) impressions. There are many good books available. My personal favorite is Lititia Baldridge's *Complete Guide to Executive Manners*.
- Learn to hold drinks in your left hand, especially cold beverages, so that when you shake hands, your hand will not be cold and wet.
- Wear your name badge on the front of your right shoulder. Since the majority of people are right-handed, most people tend to wear their name badge on their left side because of personal convenience. However, it benefits others if you wear your name badge on your right side. As your arm is extended to shake hands, your shoulder goes forward and your name can be easily (and discreetly) read. Also, make sure not to wear your name badge down on your chest because it will be hard (or awkward) to read.
- Be sure you're making the impression you want to make. You represent the image of your company to everyone you meet. Be consistent. Be positive. Be proud. In business, everyone shakes hands. A woman does not need to wait for a man to offer his hand before extending hers. Put your hand out first; introduce yourself and your company; and engage in conversation. Make sure you have a strong handshake. Nothing leaves a lasting impression like a limp handshake. Ask a friend to critique your handshake, and return the favor. I always do this in my classes. It's an excellent opportunity for building a consistent image. We are packaging ourselves, and we need to verify the image we are sending.
- Ask, then remember, names. Use a name. Introduce new contacts to your

contacts, even newly made ones. Calling someone by name makes a lasting, positive impression. It shows you care enough about others to make a mental note of their name and to use it.
- Learn the art of conversation. This means more than simply small talk. Be well-rounded in a variety of topics to discuss. Also, learn to sense when the conversation is coming to a natural close and don't drag it on. Don't stay too long with one person; you may be hindering their ability to meet more people. Besides, you need to work the crowd as well.

Networking means feeling good about yourself and your business. The art of networking involves the art of selling yourself. You are constantly marketing yourself and your business. Low-key marketing efforts are better received unless someone directly solicits information about your business. And, when your business is solicited, set up an appropriate time to conduct business, away from that particular event. Networking is not the time for selling your product or service. It is, however, the time for sharing ideas and concerns.

Women have a new spirit of networking. They are succeeding by building very strong and supportive networks. Our networks are built on a mutual willingness to share information. We are not as competitive as many men and therefore have grown, collectively and openly, together.

Sharing as the key to networking

Trust is the key to sharing. And the results of sharing will always be success, no matter how you measure it. The more you are willing to share, the more others are also willing to share with you. Sharing doesn't involve keeping score. Instead, it means you are willing to support and contribute to others while expecting nothing in return. Reciprocity will be the natural by-product when you participate freely. Share your knowledge. Share your ideas. Share your contacts. When you share openly with others, they will offer the same courtesy to you. And that's the very essence of networking.

Do not feel that you are giving away trade secrets when you share. The more comfortable you become with sharing information, whether with employees, business associates or competitors, the more information you will gain access to in the process. Sharing should begin with you.

I have heard several female business owners say they don't look at competitors as competition. Instead, they view them as business associates. These women are secure enough in their feelings to share information and knowledge within their industry and with each other. Everyone wins with this attitude.

Observing social graces

Letitia Baldridge refers to etiquette as a "quality of excellence, about the importance of details and how details linked together can create strong, effective executive presence." In essence, manners are the key to good human relationships. They govern how people treat each other. Manners are universally based on the concept of consideration for one another.

If you are not as polished as you would like to be, take the time to learn and practice the social graces. There are many excellent books on the market that examine etiquette in both personal and business settings, including those by Amy Vanderbilt and Emily Post.

In the world of networking, your manners will be observed and judged. Make sure you are not committing *faux pas* in introductions, dining and other areas.

Woman have replaced chivalry with a warm and collegial sense. We have replaced gender roles with treating everyone equally. And if someone needs help, we go to their aid and assist, however we can. No longer are there male and female executive manners. Women have donned "good manners for everyone." Women believe everyone should follow the same good-manners guidelines. Everyone should:

- Always be pleasant and agreeable.
- Always be on time.
- Be courteous and sensitive of others.
- Show compassion in business and personal situations.
- Never talk about another person in a demeaning fashion.
- Learn to give and receive complements with grace.
- Share the limelight with others.

The lost art of conversation

The ability to make conversation is just as important as what you are saying. Women must pay special attention to this skill. They have often let their lack of confidence and low self-esteem interfere with conversing. Networking demands that you know how to carry on conversations on a variety of levels. There is a time for small talk, a time for business talk and need for smooth transition between the two.

A good conversationalist can talk about a variety of subjects beyond her business. Discussing family and home life within networking circles is often successful because it is an issue many women commonly share. It is important to be able to adjust to the person with whom you are talking. This means listening for cues and not talking about yourself too much.

Some principles a good conversationalist should follow include:

- Have strong and supportive eye contact.
- Provide positive body language, including smiling and nodding your head.
- Don't interrupt while others are talking.
- Don't correct others in public.
- Use correct grammar.
- Address everyone within the group.
- Know how to include others in the conversation, especially shy individuals.

It is as important to know subjects one should avoid in conversations as it is to know subjects to talk about. Never talk about your health, controversial subjects, personal misfortunes or share stories in questionable taste or gossip that is harmful to others. Conversation becomes the natural cornerstone to communications in networking situations. Learn to use it to your advantage.

A board of advisers

One of the best things that can come from networking is the creation of boards of advisers. Your advisory board operates very differently from a corporation's board of directors. Because of the potential personal liability for directors, it may be difficult for small businesses to find a circle of advisers to join a formal board. A board of directors is required for corporate structures and is responsible for maintaining controls over major business decisions, especially financial concerns of the operation. The board can be held accountable for the mishandling of monies. Most small corporations have these boards more as a matter of formality than of function. A board of advisers, on the other hand, doesn't entail the personal liability, so it is much easier to put together. And any form of business organization can qualify.

An important feature of networking is being a part of others' networks. Whether your business is a corporation, partnership or sole proprietorship, you can still create a board of advisers. This board has no decision-making power in your company; instead it is an alliance for sharing ideas, concerns and information among other professionals. One method for putting together such a board includes having several professional (or semiprofessional) friends and acquaintances over for dinner. It's amazing what you can accomplish over a meal. At this informal gathering, suggest that the group get together monthly and allow each person to share one problem or concern. The size of the group will dictate how much time can be allocated to solving each person's concern. Realize that for this approach to work, everyone must get something. And for everyone to get something, everyone must give something. Creative solutions, new contacts and emerging markets are frequently the benefits of an advisory board. You may be surprised to learn that your stumbling blocks are not so unique after all.

Diversity in your group will produce the most diverse results. Think of people who have information to share, whether it is leads, professional advisers or marketing ideas. The group can consist of sales agents, customers and owners of other small and medium-sized businesses. Entrepreneurs may be new or experienced. The more varied the backgrounds, the more everyone will benefit. Keep the number of participants between six and ten for best results.

Rotate who fixes dinner. Other than the meal, there is no cost to participants. You simply have more opportunities to see and hear what events are affecting everyone and the opportunity to share openly in a safe, controlled environment. Obviously, confidentiality must be strictly observed for folks to feel comfortable sharing their problems or concerns.

Your circle of friends

For some reason, women business owners frequently lose contact with their current set of friends when they start their own business. Friends are important to all of us. To have friends means to be a friend. It means taking time for our friends.

Being an entrepreneur is tough. You are having to balance and juggle and maneuver around all sorts of obstacles. Everyone wants a part of your time. And time is what you have too little of already. While you may not have as much in common with your old friends as you used to, make it a point to schedule events with them once a month (or once a quarter). The time away from work will do you good. Enjoy the escape from the business routine and pressure. Listen to what's important to your friends. And relax and have fun.

In addition to your old friends, you will probably want to include some fellow business acquaintances and entrepreneurs in your social circle. Having people who understand your pressures is another aspect of your life you need to fulfill. These friends can help reduce the stress of being an entrepreneur by lending a supportive ear. They can serve as sounding boards for ideas. And they can help keep your sanity intact. Often it is a woman you met in your networking channels who becomes a close friend and confidante.

Business associates and professionals

Learn to meet a variety of business associates. Networking will prove to be indispensable at this level. Organizational meetings, conferences, seminars and workshops all provide excellent platforms for enlarging your network. Consider becoming active in your trade or professional association. Any place you find professionals together is an opportunity to network.

Business associates should not be viewed as the competition. When you view them competitively, you eliminate the opportunity to share and grow together. However, if you are willing to provide information and leads to others within your industry, they will return the favor. Not all customers are right for you. Once you accept this concept, the threat by others is dissipated. Know that you are providing your customers with a quality product. When your customers are satisfied, they will not easily slip away. When you are able to see that a project is too much for you to handle, recommend competing business associates you know and trust. Women who employ this tactic find the business environment much healthier and happier. Not many men have achieved this much confidence yet.

Charities and other outside activities

The outside activities you participate in are excellent sources for expanding your networks. Make it a point to volunteer for one (or more if your time allows) charity event. When you volunteer, however, your commitment is to get very involved. Serve on a committee or board of the organization. This participation will enhance your opportunity to grow and share in the process. You create more visibility for yourself while contributing to the success of the group. Charity and social functions are great events for gathering professionals who do not normally get together.

Another option for gaining additional publicity and name recognition while networking in this arena is to offer your product as a door prize. This way, people become aware of the product or service you represent. Make sure, though, that you get proper recognition for your donation. Otherwise, the opportunity for publicity is lost.

And remember, never go anywhere without your business cards.

Fears of failure and success

While you are creating networks, you must present a positive image of yourself. Your fears will be uncovered in conversations and they must be dealt with directly. Women have both the fear of failure and the fear of success. Both have caused stumbling blocks in our endeavors.

The fear of failure can be depicted by several things. First, women often have a perceived lack of skill. Women's work, primarily housework, continues to be undervalued by society and frequently discounted for providing a variety of business-related experience. Second, many women have low self-esteem. Women may seek others for constant approval and permission. And when they don't find it, they may assume incorrectly that it is because they are wrong or not worthy of support. Next, women may not fully understand what is expected in the business world because there have been few mentors to learn from. Women may have a distorted perception of reality because of limited experience in the upper realms of corporate management. And finally, women have shouldered the responsibility as caretakers. They are conditioned to pleasing everyone else. They are peacemakers. In business, sometimes a consensus cannot be reached, but decisions have to be made. Often these decisions are tough and require confidence in communicating the results. Women must realize they cannot please everyone all the time. Instead, they need to focus on what's important to the whole. Women must learn how to deal effectively with dissension and conflict. It takes time. And it takes practice. But, it's not impossible to achieve.

Women have an easier time identifying with failure than they do with success, for some reason. The fear of success becomes a self-sabotaging objective. It keeps us from achieving our potential. We don't believe good things should happen to us; therefore we destroy the opportunities. One way to help resolve this conflict is by listing ten reasons why you deserve to be successful. Be honest with yourself, since only you will see the list. If you are having problems coming up with ten, take more time to evaluate yourself. This step is essential. You must see your positive features in order to resolve your defeating actions. After you have completed the first list, jot down things you are currently doing that detour you from achieving your goal.

And finally, work to eliminate those things that are holding you back.

Success does not come without stumbling. Stay away from societal expectations of what it means to succeed. Instead, decide on your own goals. Define your objectives to meet your needs and expectations. Stay focused on what you see as your goals, not someone else's ideas of what your goals should be.

> *Success is a gift we give ourselves; not something others measure us by.*

When you perceive yourself as a professional, others will see you that way also. Your image begins deep within yourself and is manifested through your words, actions and presence. Believe in yourself. Become one of your best friends. Take some time for a quiet conversation with yourself and let that wonderful woman know how proud you are of her accomplishments. Let her know that she is not alone, that you are with her. And that you will not let her down.

Mentoring

Mentoring is a time of learning and sharing. It involves building a trusting, professional relationship. Mentoring can occur either formally or informally. To find a mentor, choose someone you trust. Someone you admire. And someone you respect. A mentor is someone who has gone through what you are going through and succeeded.

Men in the business world have been mentoring for years. When women entered the business ranks, they were not initially offered the mentoring role models. What we now know is that women's approach to mentoring is often different from men's. Lydia Swam, author of *Power Failure*, found that men approach a mentoring relationship with the goal of learning from and eventually equaling or surpassing their mentor. Women often feel uncomfortable competing with a mentor. Instead, women gain their strength from the relationship with another person, not the competition. Women see mentor arrangements as "we're in this together."

Look for different mentors to meet your different needs. Consider mentors as specialists. Have several mentors who specialize in various business aspects within your mentor circle. Always communicate your desires and make sure the mentor is willing to "teach." Just because someone does something well doesn't make them a good teacher. If your mentoring relationship isn't working, move on to find another one. Don't try to force it. If it doesn't click...it doesn't click.

As you grow in business, knowledge and experience, begin seeking opportunities to help other entrepreneurs, especially women. Bring someone along with you as you grow. Women are finding great personal satisfaction by offering encouragement to other women. Share your story. Offer words of encouragement and support. And also shed light from the wisdom you've gained through previous experiences. Become a mentor for young women in high school. Hire interns whenever possible to share in your knowledge and advice. Make it a point to teach as well as to learn through mentoring. It is a very rewarding process.

Chapter 13

Finding good employees: managing today's diverse work force

"Woman is woman's natural ally."

Euripides

Understanding your work force

Not every business needs to hire employees. In fact, approximately 75 percent of all small businesses do not have paid employees apart from the owner. However, if your business requires the employment of others, or if your business grows beyond your ability to manage effectively, then it is time to hire employees. The key to avoiding personnel problems down the road is choosing the right person up front. While this may sound obvious, it is as difficult as it is obvious. You must be able to communicate your expectations and needs honestly to potential employees. And your expectations must be realistic. Giving people false expectations about the job or your company only serves to create disillusioned, unhappy workers. It causes problems later that could have been avoided early on by direct communication.

Today, we hear a great deal of talk about empowering employees. Helping people help themselves has always been a strong suit for women. Women know how to nurture. Women know how to show caring. Teamwork can be synonymous with female leadership.

But managing in today's stressful, volatile marketplace takes more. It takes listening and sharing. It takes valuing others' opinions, their knowledge and ideas. It takes open and honest communication built on mutual respect.

Compensation and praise go a long way towards reaching these goals. When you share the glory and financial rewards with others, they feel a vital part of the team. Your reward comes from their satisfaction and contentment in your company. Dedicated, happy employees can make a huge difference to your company image, overall well-being and bottom line.

Salaries should be commensurate with job duties and experience of the employees. Women know firsthand the injustice of salary discrimination, having been on the receiving end too long. It is important to be fair and equitable to *all* your employees. It is a small price to pay for such high rewards.

Compensation and praise don't guarantee a trouble-free work force, however. Today, companies must guard against employees who may initiate lawsuits charging discrimination or based on other issues. By knowing and observing proper hiring and interviewing procedures, the requirements of affirmative action plans and other legal standards, you can avoid problems. Women-owned businesses are more apt to employ socially and economically disadvantaged females, allowing them to share both the responsibility and benefits. This attitude of inclusiveness helps ward off many problems, but it is not a fail-safe strategy.

As you grow, you may find you cannot control all the functions you once could. For many women, this is a frustrating and difficult time. Relinquishing control means trusting others' judgments. Without letting go, you cannot operate as efficiently or effectively as you could when you were small. Ideally, the decision would be yours to remain small and in control, or to grow and share the responsibility with others. However, realistically, you cannot always control your company's growth. Timing, competition, the market and other factors contribute to increases and decreases in sales. Identifying when it is time to delegate job duties is one of the most difficult aspects of growing. Your success in this task will set the example for handling other growing pains that might occur.

Deciding on your needs

First steps first. Before you can hire or even begin looking for potential employees, you must know exactly what their job duties entail. You should take care not to ask too much of employees for what you can afford to pay. If you are creating a new position, look carefully at what duties the new employee can handle. The smaller the company, the more versatile the employee has to be. Do you want to get untangled from a bottleneck you've created? Look at the duties you feel comfortable delegating. Make a list

of what is expected so that you look for the right person for the job. Also, know what the job might grow into and look beyond the immediate description.

It is much less expensive to hire the best now than to fire the worst later. Employee turnover affects morale, productivity and costs. At the same time you must keep a handle on all expenses and stay within your budget. Try to pay the most you can afford. Not only will this show your employees you care about them, but companies paying higher salaries frequently have lower turnover rates. Turnover is costly to any business, especially in training dollars. Also consider benefits that you can offer that cost little or no money. Maybe a flexible schedule is more important to a person than a higher salary. Can you operate efficiently with flexible hours? What about job-sharing? Or time off for classes? Even giving time off for charity in the community can have excellent benefits.

Know what you can afford. Be very specific about salary as well as other benefits, including vacation, sick days, insurance coverage, retirement plans, discounts, flex-hours, etc. Remember that not everyone is motivated by money. In fact, many people value respect, appreciation and input more than monetary rewards.

When you explore job descriptions, look at what the position might grow into as the company continues to expand. Are you looking for an employee who can grow with you? If so, identify that capability when you begin your search. Advancement options are often great selling tools.

It is better to hire an employee based on attitude than on skill. It is easier to teach new skills through training than to alter bad attitudes A person either has integrity or she doesn't. It is much more possible to teach adults specific skills and programs than to teach them morality.

Also remember that salary expense is not the only cost involved with the addition of employees. The cost for hiring new employees may also include such items as insurance, worker's compensation, withholding taxes and office furniture and supplies. Factor these miscellaneous expenses into the salary cost and then determine whether hiring a full-time (or part-time) employee is justified. It is better to hire part-time workers until you are absolutely certain sales can support full-time help.

Finding qualified potential employees

The best qualified person for your company is probably already employed with someone else. Seek them out and see if they are interested in a move. Ask other employees, friends and business associates to refer potential employees.

Many companies reward employees for referrals that lead to hiring. There are several benefits to this method. First, current employees will be honest and supportive about the company, especially if they are recommending the job to a friend. Second, they generally refer people who fit the company's image. Remember, their names and reputations are at stake as well. And finally, the initial foundation for team-building may have been laid. Getting to know the other employees and having mutual trust is a key element in team-building. When friends work together, they have this advantage.

Knowing the size of your job applicant pool is very important to the final outcome. If you are looking for a receptionist and you are in an area that has high unemployment, you will have an advantage. In addition, if several large companies recently closed or laid off a lot of employees, your applicant pool may be relatively strong. Of course, this depends on your specific needs and the qualifications of those unemployed. However, the current mergers and downsizing in big business have definitely been a plus to small business owners.

Application forms

Job application forms are advantageous for all businesses, especially small companies. Require all job applicants to complete your form. This includes applicants who have submitted a resume. Resumes may have gaps not easily detected. Resumes are controlled by the applicant, presenting what they want to present. However, job application forms allow you to gather the information you feel is important to make an informed, fair decision. On resumes, when information is omitted, it is because the applicant chose to omit it. But on a job application form, failure to answer correctly—or to answer at all—means the applicant may have misled you, or maybe even lied. When you accept "see attached resume" for answers on job applications, you allow the gaps to remain. Therefore, make sure all applicants complete your form in its entirety. And never hire anyone who lies (no matter how small a lie) on a job application. It is a red flag for future trouble.

Once the information requested on an application has been provided, your next step is verifying its accuracy. Talk with references and former employers. You may be surprised by what they say. Verify data. While time may not permit you to verify everything, spot-checking a few items on each application form will be a good indicator. If you fail to check any information, you've wasted your time and the job applicant's time by asking for the data.

Interviewing

Once you have determined your needs and created a pool of applicants, the next and most important step is the interviewing process. How well you communicate your needs and expectations can save you a great deal of time (and headaches) later.

Realize that interviewing is a two-way process. You will interview the job applicant, and the job applicant will interview you. Both sides need to reach a consensus for a good, solid working relationship to develop.

Carefully chosen interview questions can reveal important information about the candidate's strengths and weaknesses. Prepare yourself before the interview with a list of questions, expectations and general knowledge of each individual applicant. If you know what you are specifically looking for, you will be more apt to spot it when you see it. Interviewers must learn to *listen* carefully to the answers and be sensitive to the mood of those they are interviewing.

Define your role clearly in this process. If you have not interviewed job applicants previously, I recommend writing down a list of questions and taking notes on the applicants' responses. This allows you to judge each on a consistent basis. Yet, no matter how well the interview goes, in the end, the final decision is still largely based on guesswork. Someone who interviews well may not necessarily perform well. And vice versa.

When you ask interview questions, be sure you stay within the law. There are questions that are either illegal to ask or in poor taste. Illegal questions may center around race, creed, sexual orientation, age, ethnic origin, marital status, number of children, etc. Your questions should focus on the specific position being interviewed for, on the applicant's previous experience and on your company.

The following is a list of commonly asked interview questions. Although you should include specific questions designed for your specific position, this list provides a general foundation to incorporate into the interview process.

- What are you looking for in a new position?
- Why did you leave your last job?
- What skills best qualify you for this position?
- What are your greatest strengths? Weaknesses?
- Tell me a situation where you made a mistake and how you resolved it.
- Where do you see yourself in five years?
- Why should I hire you?

Document each applicant's interview (whether or not hired) and retain the records, for your operational needs and as a precaution. Even though you may be so small that regulations do not directly affect you, people can still bring lawsuits. The suits may be without merit, but they are still an inconvenience for you. By retaining complete records on everyone and everything, you are assuming a defensive posture, an unfortunate requirement of our time.

Decide what is important to you in potential employees. I firmly believe, for example, that all applicants should be dressed in neat, clean clothes and make every effort to look well-groomed. Hire people who fit what you want to say.

Listen to what applicants say in the interview. Do they sound too rehearsed? If so, try to get them off their script. Do they sound unsure of their answers? Maybe they are trying to exaggerate their experience. Delve further into work experience and knowledge when this happens. Are they hostile or negative about a previous employer? Stay away from those applicants; they will only be trouble for you. What questions do they ask you? Their questions will be an indication of what's important to them. Are the questions about benefits? Vacation? Advancement? Are they interested in the long-term growth potential of the company, or are they only looking for a job?

And, finally, don't let the interview go on too long. For most positions, interviews last no more than one hour. If the interview goes on for more than an hour, you have probably lost sight of the original goal and gotten sidetracked by idle conversation. Remain in control. Keep track of the time. There are exceptions to this rule, but make sure longer interviews are exceptions and not the norm for you.

Communicating beyond words

Listen to what applicants say as well as to what they don't say. Learn to interpret body language as an important tool for interviewing. Communication occurs by several methods. Only 7 percent is transmitted through the words we speak, 38 percent comes through sounds and 55 percent is transmitted by our body language. Taking a simple statement, such as "I didn't know that," you can change the meaning of the words by the inflection of your voice. It can be a question or a statement; it can be said in anger, in jest or in confusion. Body language can reinforce or dispute the words and tone. What a job applicant doesn't say may be more telling than what she says.

Nonverbal messages qualify the words people use and may even reveal discrepancies between words and true feelings. Nonverbal communication includes posture, body position, facial twitches, eye contact, head movement and tones in the voice. Your voice reflects the inner you, your character, moods, attitudes and emotions. Here are some basic nonverbal indicators:

- Speakers usually look away briefly as they're preparing to listen, rather than speak.
- A shortened, shallow breathing pattern may indicate frustration or anxiety.
- Tilting the head to one side and sitting forward in the chair usually indicates that the applicant is listening carefully.
- Job applicants who cross their arms in front of their chest may be defensive, angry, disapproving or aggressive.

Also review your own body language to see what message you are communicating. Are you comfortable in the role of interviewing? If not, it may be reflected in your nonverbal communications to the potential employee.

Do not, however, be overanxious to interpret nonverbal communications, especially when interviewing someone from a different culture. Body language can be interpreted very differently in different cultures. What Americans may think of as normal Western behavior may actually be quite offensive to someone from the Eastern hemisphere. Interviewees may not look you in the eye because it is a sign of disrespect. Or perhaps a picture or sign in your office offends someone or makes them feel uncomfortable.

It is important to be sensitive to all people. Sometimes this is a great challenge, because our ignorance suggests that we continue in the footsteps as those ahead of us. The world we live in is changing constantly. And, as business owners, women must reach out to understand and include others.

After reviewing what the applicant says and interpreting her body language, the final call is still very subjective. Follow your instinct. And yet, you will never really know the individual's capabilities until she is working for you. The more carefully you interview, however, the more likely the outcome is to be positive.

Hiring

Never hire anyone on the spot. Take time to reflect on the total process. Verify the information that has been provided. And review all the candidates. If you aren't completely satisfied with any of the applicants, consider one of two reasons. First, are you asking too much of any one individual? Do you need to reduce the job expectations or look for two candidates? Second, it may be that you just haven't found the right person yet. In either case, you must stop and evaluate your plan of action.

Having employees will result in an increase in the forms you must keep. Required paperwork can be required by either federal or state law. There are numerous records that must be maintained for all employees. Some of the more common ones are:

- The name, address and Social Security number.
- Amount and date of salary payments subject to withholding taxes and the amount withheld.

- Period of employment, including payments to employees during their absences, illnesses, injury, maternity leave, etc.
- W-4 and I-9 forms obtained from the IRS.
- Your employer identification number.
- Duplicate copies of tax returns that have been filed.
- Dates and amounts of deposits made with government depositories (your bank or Federal Reserve Bank).

Call your state and federal labor departments and the IRS for current forms and requirements.

Keep accurate and detailed records of all payroll information. Your accountant will help you set up these records. Accuracy in recording information will be beneficial on several fronts, including, but not limited to, taxes.

Training

Employee training programs are among the least expensive and most lucrative investments a company can make. And yet, they are a practice few small companies take advantage of.

The Special Report on Women Entrepreneurs (*Business Week*, April 1994) highlighted some of women's more common benefit packages as including "employee training, teamwork, reduced hierarchy and quality." The magazine went on to state that many women feel the investment in their employees translates into an investment over the competition.

The National Foundation of Women Business Owners (NFWBO) has found that women-owned businesses are apt to offer tuition reimbursement and flexible hours for their employees. They try to create worker-friendly environments by including employees' feelings and concerns in their discussions.

Businesses are more likely to succeed when they train employees in interpersonal skills, along with training for their job duties. Diverse training emphasizes the individual as more than just an employee.

You could offer training programs on etiquette, protocol, time management, stress reduction, financial planning, coupon clipping, car maintenance or budgeting. While all of these programs are excellent for home and family life, they also have strong implications for an employee's work performance. Building a strong work team means valuing an employee's whole self, both at work and at home.

You may want to pay particular attention to stress, the number one reason cited for poor job performance. Stress on the job can translate into claims on medical insurance and medical expenses. Job-related stress can lead to employee disloyalty, theft and sabotage. Some programs to help alleviate stress include exercise programs, relaxation time at work, massage therapy, career development, cross-training and mentoring programs. Inclusive management means letting your staff choose what programs they want, not deciding for them.

Telephone manners

Whether yours is a service business, retail trade or manufacturing company, every phone call means the same thing: *potential business*. How your telephone is answered says as much about your company as your advertising program. The manner in which a company telephone is answered gives a strong and clear signal to the caller how you view their importance. Telephones reiterate the character of the company.

I strongly encourage frequently checking to see how your system is working. It may be good to have a friend call in, someone whose voice is not recognized. You may listen in on the other line to determine the manner in which the call is handled and to decide how to improve the system. You need to know if phones are not being answered quickly enough. You need to know if customers are being put on hold for unreasonable periods of time. And you need to know that customers wanting information are directed to the appropriate person.

The following is a list of basic telephone etiquette that you might want to integrate into your training program. It is unfair to penalize people for what seems obvious to you if they haven't been trained properly or informed about expectations.

- A phone should be answered by the second ring—the third at the latest.
- When you answer a phone, always identify yourself and the company to the caller.
- Find out who is calling. And when taking messages, be sure to spell the name correctly. Few things are more embarrassing than asking for someone and using an incorrect name. Repeat the name to them to verify that you have it correct.
- If you have just gotten off the phone from a rude individual, don't take your hostility out on the next caller. If the call rattled you so much, get off the phones for a while. Take a break. Talk with someone else. Do whatever you have to so that you are focused on being positive for the next call.
- Smile on the phone; it comes across to the caller.

• Listen to what it is the caller is asking for. The person who's calling evidently wants something. Make certain that you know exactly what it is before you answer or transfer them.

Probation and performance reviews

Many companies start new employees with a probationary period. Frequently, a three-month time frame provides an adequate window for review. The purpose of the probation period is to ascertain that the new employee can do the job, is comfortable in the setting and is working according to expectations. Clearly explain what the expectations are during this initial period. At the end of the probation, review the new hire's status and share the information with her. Again, open and honest communication is integral to growing a business. Performance reviews are a good method of communicating, evaluating and sharing concerns and feedback among employees and management. Conduct reviews on a regular basis, preferably annually. This is a time for sharing concerns for both parties. And it is best achieved when the employee grades her supervisor as the supervisor grades the employee's performance. Both should talk over their findings and feelings. It is important to remain objective during this process. If employees feel they have no voice in the process, the process produces resentment. A review is a great time to reevaluate and help employees reach their career goals. Listen to their concerns. Advise on opportunities for personal growth and advancement. Be sure to document everything. Have the employee sign two copies of the evaluation, one to remain in their personnel

file and one for the employee to keep. Again, you are maintaining a defensive posture. This approach reduces potential confusion over what was and wasn't said. It maintains your open communication policy. And it allows everyone to keep a record of reviews. Personnel files, by law, are open for employees to review. By sharing information freely, you are establishing and reinforcing the company's philosophy on information and control. Everyone gets information. Therefore, no one has control to manipulate another. This review process is based on everyone's willingness to participate.

When it's time to fire

Sometimes employees just don't work out, and you are faced with letting them go. Ugh! This is definitely the worst thing about owning and managing a business. It's not an easy step to take, but ignoring the problem only magnifies it. The sooner the problem is addressed, the sooner everyone can breathe more easily.

Women tend to have more difficulty with firing people, although it isn't easy for anyone. The result has been that many women have kept bad employees a lot longer than they should have because they couldn't muster up the courage to fire them. That's not good management. It's not fair to the other employees. It's not fair to the employee involved. And it's not fair to you. Take a deep breath and proceed.

Women have found that firing an employee doesn't have to be a rude or hostile act. Actually, it can bring out sensitivity, caring and kindness. Kindness doesn't imply being soft. Instead, it means sharing the pain of losing a job, knowing that the pain is real and perhaps even steering that employee into work they may be better suited for. Every termination is an individual case. Be specific about why the employee is being let go. Be honest to yourself and to them. And when the firing is properly documented and previously discussed, there should be little debate (hopefully).

Letting good employees go because of lack of business is even more difficult. Talk over the facts with all employees. When they believe in the company, they may have some creative alternatives. Be willing to listen and stay open to new ideas for resolving the problem.

Managing diversity

Learning about other cultures will help you manage and operate your business. The concept of diversity in the workplace should be encouraged and welcomed.

Multiculturalism has often been identified with women and minorities. The discrimination and lack of understanding that women felt as they encountered the glass ceiling in business—the stereotypical roles and limiting expectations—are the same insensitive situations experienced by people who are culturally different from the norm.

According to government statistics, the 1990 U.S. population was 76 percent Anglo; 12 percent Black; 9 percent Latino; and 3 percent Asian. By the year 2050 the breakdown is projected to be Anglo, 52 percent; Black, 16 percent; Latino, 22 percent; and Asian, 10 percent. These statistics affect both the community and the marketplace.

Cultural diversity means enriching one another while retaining and sharing differences. It means accepting and respecting others who may not be like you. And it means including *all* people

in the decision-making process. There are both challenges and benefits for multicultural workplaces. Conflict may arise, but the open communication imperative for resolving these conflicts builds strong teamwork.

By recruiting, promoting and training a diverse range of individuals, women become more vital and accepting to their community and find success in reaching out to their customers. Through working within a wide range of ideas, you will gain a better understanding of different markets. It is a win-win situation.

Today, we realize that we are not all the same; our goals and objectives are different as well. This means treating individuals individually.

Now we are able to see the advantage of hiring a diverse work group. Joline Godfrey, author of *Our Wildest Dreams*, states that "women comfortable with a wider range of emotions tolerate a wider spectrum of behavior." Women seek and encourage individuality instead of uniformity and conformity. And Harvard professor Carol Gilligan, author of *In a Different Voice*, underscores that "while men represent powerful activities, such as assertion and aggression, women in contrast portray acts of nurturance as acts of strength." It is in women's nurturance that their companies have found the strength to survive in such high numbers.

Good management is largely a matter of caring. This is a word not normally associated with management. Proper management involves caring for people, not manipulating them. It centers on building community. And it is built on trust.

Co-leadership

A manager's success is wholly dependent on her ability to empower others to achieve their goals. The '90s term is "shared vision." The "who" we are of a company, the "what" and "where" we want to be, the "how" of getting there—these values must be shared and endorsed by employees at all levels of the organization. Any organization that wishes to achieve credibility and commitment with its work force must recognize that vision is the glue that holds it together. You can't have a vision without visionaries.

Make sure your employees:

- Have a clear vision of their work and are truly committed.
- Feel that the company has their best interests at heart.
- Know what's going on.
- Know and support the company's mission statement.
- Trust you.

Everyone has a voice. Your task is to let their voices be heard. Your ability to allow and appreciate others' ideas will directly affect how well you motivate your staff. Many of today's managers have frequent meetings involving a variety of employees. They have flattened out the organizational chart, so that everyone's job is valued. They do simple things like asking those in customer service for their input on how new telephone equipment can create a more positive and cohesive work environment. They respect differences. They work on consensus building. They teach by example and realize they will not always win. They learn to be a gracious loser and to compromise for the good of the team.

Rewarding hard work

While it is true that without customers you have no business, if you want satisfied customers you need satisfied employees.

If you want people to deliver outstanding customer service, you need to treat them as if they were more important to you than even your customers! This may mean having to "fire" a customer. Although this is a drastic measure, and hopefully not frequently necessary, sometimes customers cost you money, make unprofitable demands on you and are rude to your employees. This is not acceptable behavior. No employee should have to endure belittling comments. Train your employees well. Your training and hiring process should eliminate those individuals who are not worthy of your trust. Then always support them. Let them know they can count on you. Be willing to step up to their defense when necessary.

If you have happy employees, you will have happy customers. Otherwise, they will bring down the whole team.

When employees get what they want from their career, their morale goes up. When employees' morale goes up, product quality and customer service also go up and turnover goes down. All these factors affect the bottom line. There is a correlation between employee morale and profits. Never set making profits as your goal (or objective). Your goal should be employee satisfaction. Profits will be the obvious by-product of measuring success in achieving your goal.

You can reward employees by several methods. Not all employees are motivated by the same things. In the past, money was the thing most frequently used for rewards; second was giving employees titles. As a new business, you may be strapped for money, so you may not have that choice of reward. Also, not everyone is motivated by money. And titles may not be very fulfilling to your staff. Frequently time off, flexible hours and recognition can go far in gaining the loyalty of workers. Joline Godfrey decided to take her employees out for an afternoon movie, spontaneously, one day. She said the mental break was a great escape from the pressure everyone was working under. In addition, everyone was better able to contribute new ideas afterwards. The rewards were significant. Try something different to show your employees how much they are appreciated. But don't expect the rewards. Rewards come most often when motives are not tainted.

Independent contractors

Today's changing work force allows options beyond that of the employer-employee relationship. There may be times when hiring a full-time employee is not in your best interest. Or it may not be an alternative. For example, Sharon Lester, the builder in Chapter 2, uses contract workers to build her houses. She has no employees, other than herself, in her company. Yet she maintains very close relationships with numerous independent contractors so that she can provide consistency in her product. They are not her employees, but they enjoy working on projects she oversees.

Using contract employees can be advantageous, but it is not always an option. When you hire contract employees, they are independent of you. In other words, you cannot control the hours they come to work. A contract employee could not be a secretary who is expected to work from 8 a.m. until 5 p.m., Monday through Friday, in your office.

A contract employee may be used for a special project or consulting work. Because of abuse of the term independent contractor, however, the IRS has created a very specific test for qualifying under this rule.

Whether you use independent contractors or leased employees, make certain that you conform to the laws governing these types of employment. The law is specific about who qualifies as an independent contractor. If you pay someone as an independent contractor and the government views them as an employee, you will be responsible for their Social Security withholdings, unemployment insurance and other taxes. The IRS has created specific guidelines that must be met for a worker to qualify as an independent contractor. If you believe you are hiring the services of an independent contractor, verify this status with your local Internal Revenue Service office first. Mistakes can be very costly.

Basically, the test for independent contractor status is one of control. If you, the employer, control the hours, time and place of work, the worker is probably *not* an independent contractor. An independent contractor agrees to provide material and labor under a contract that binds that person to attain a specified result. Some of the tests for independent contractors question whether a significant investment in equipment has been made by the individual, whether they work for a number of individuals, whether their services are available to the general public, and whether they are legally bound by the agreement or contract to complete the job.

Leasing employees

Employee leasing began in the 1980s and offers specific benefits to small business owners. Check locally to see whether there are employee leasing companies in your industry. Leased employees are hired by a leasing organization, which provides employee services to you of a type traditionally performed by employees in your industry.

The major advantage of employee leasing is that you do not have to do all the paperwork involved in hiring employees; nor are you subject to the liabilities. Since the leasing company employs many individuals, they often have better benefit packages to offer at reduced rates, something many small business owners cannot afford. Under leasing arrangements, you are under contract with another firm, and you simply pay the company the agreed upon amount. They, in turn, are responsible for the wages, taxes and filings for employees.

Chapter 14

Complying with regulations: laws, laws and more laws

"We have not succeeded in answering all of our questions; indeed, we have not completely answered any of them. The answers we have found have only served to raise a whole new set of questions."

Anonymous

Know the law

As an owner/employer, you are responsible for complying with numerous state, local and federal regulations. These laws affect your hiring practices, your firing practices, collection procedures, taxes, insurance and retention of documents in your business.

According to Michael G. Trachtman, author of *What Every Executive Better Know About the Law*, "business is governed by a system of law that is either widely unknown or consistently misapprehended, not because of negligence on the part of business people, but because of its breadth and complexity." You must operate from a rule book, whether or not you believe all of the laws are just. Unfortunately, laws have gotten more complicated, a product of our time.

The purpose of this chapter is neither to discourage you, nor to overwhelm you with the enormous number of regulations that exist. The purpose is to educate and inform you about the number of laws that potentially affect business practices. Because these laws are constantly changing, subject to revisions and new regulations, the basic guidelines I have provided are on federal regulations currently in effect. However, you will need to verify the current regulations that might affect you before you open your business.

Unfortunately, there is not one single source that lists laws that potentially may affect you. Since new laws are always being written, this list is presented as representative, rather than complete. And while qualified attorneys and accountants should be able to provide counsel, you (as the business owner) are the one ultimately responsible.

You need to find out what laws affect your business and how to comply with the regulations. Start by calling the U.S. Small Business Administration. It can provide the framework for this research. Although the SBA will probably steer away from listing specific regulations, it can provide the agency names and phone numbers for initial research. Then, the next step is to call the U.S. Department of Labor as well as your state's Department of Labor to gather information on regulations concerning employees.

> *When state and federal laws differ, the most conservative (stricter) law is the one that normally is followed.*

Since the state regulation is often more conservative, contacting state agencies to gather complete information is imperative. Also call the Internal Revenue Service to see whether it offers educational classes for startup businesses. The IRS has received a bad rap. It is actually one of the most helpful government agencies I have found. It has many publications, which I have listed at the end of this chapter, that are excellent resource guides for small business owners. And they are free.

Your next calls should be to the federal and local EEOC offices, for information on laws they administer that affect your business operation. And finally, several state agencies manage areas such as worker's compensation, occupational safety and health and state unemployment tax. Call and get copies of these laws as well. Brochures are easier to read than the actual laws, but many of these agencies may not feel obligated to absorb the expense to make your job easier. And, ignorance is no excuse for not complying with these regulations.

Collect copies of these laws and ask about any pending changes they may be aware of. Again, the information outlined below is presented as a guide. *All of the requirements are subject to change.*

Fair Labor Standards Act

This law generally affects any business that has employees. Various aspects of the law are guided by revenue, size and interstate functions.

This federal law was established to set minimum wage, overtime pay, record-keeping and child labor standards. Workers covered by this act (nonexempt employees) are entitled to a minimum wage of not less than $4.25 an hour currently. Overtime pay at a rate of not less than one and one-half times the regular rate of pay is required after 40 hours of work in a work week. Salaried employees are considered exempt from the FLSA because their salaries are sufficient enough to allow for overtime hours when needed. Child labor laws affect youths from 14 to 18 years of age, limiting the number of hours and types of work they can do.

The FLSA requires employers to keep records on wages, hours and other items. Most of this information is of the kind generally maintained by employers in ordinary business practice and in compliance with other laws and regulations. Records required for exempt employees differ from those required for nonexempt employees.

You cannot work out another arrangement for nonexempt employees, even if they agree, concerning other compensation for overtime. The Department of Labor does not honor other arrangements. All hours must be documented. And all overtime must be paid at one and one-half the regular rate. Accurate record-keeping is a must.

Family and Medical Leave Act

This law was passed in February 1993 and became effective August 5, 1993. It affects businesses that employ 50 or more people (part-time or full-time) at locations within a 75-mile radius, for at least 20 work weeks. This means that if you have two or more locations within 75 miles of each other, you must combine the number of employees at those locations. It is estimated that

95 percent of U.S. employers are not covered by this law because they are not big enough.

FMLA entitles eligible employees to take up to 12 weeks of *unpaid*, job-protected leave each year for specified family and medical reasons.

Other labor laws

The Department of Labor also administers a number of other labor laws. The first three are considered government contract laws. The other laws are general labor laws. This is a sampling of some of the existing laws.

- The **Davis-Bacon** and related acts require payment of prevailing wage rates and fringe benefits on federally financed or assisted construction, such as public works, bridges, dams, etc. The act includes subcontract labor.
- The **Walsh-Healey Public Contracts Act** requires payment of minimum wage rates and overtime pay on contracts to provide goods to the federal government.
- The **Service Contract Act** requires payment of prevailing wage rates and fringe benefits on contracts to provide services to the federal government.
- The **Contract Work Hours and Safety Standards Act** sets overtime standards for service and construction contracts.
- The **Immigration and Nationality Act** reviews I-9 forms, on which employers are required to verify the employment eligibility of all individuals hired. Employers must keep I-9s on file for at least three years after an employee is terminated. This law applies to part-time and full-time employees.
- The **Wage Garnishment Law** limits the amount of an individual's income that may be legally garnished and prohibits the firing of an employee whose pay is garnished for payment of a single debt. Employers are responsible for maintaining the additional paperwork and reporting documents necessary according to the judge's request. However, this law does not stop you from firing an employee who receives two garnishments.
- The **Employee Polygraph Protection Act of 1988** prevents employers from using any type of lie detector test either for preemployment screening of job applicants or for testing current employees. In addition, the results from a polygraph cannot be used as grounds for dismissal.
- The **Equal Pay Act** prohibits wage differentials based on sex, between men and women employed in the same establishment, on jobs that require equal skills, effort and responsibility and that are performed under similar working conditions.

Equal Employment Opportunities Commission

The EEOC was created by Title VII of the Civil Rights Act of 1964. Its mission is to ensure equality of opportunity by applying federal legislation prohibiting discrimination in employment through investigation, conciliation, litigation, coordination, education and provisions of technical assistance. EEOC regulations apply to companies that employ 15 or more persons. However, small business owners should adhere to EEOC guidelines as good business practice. EEOC prohibits employment discrimination on the basis of race, color, sex, religion or national origin. This commission is also charged with enforcing the Age Discrimination in Employment

Act, which protects workers 40 years of age and older, and the Equal Pay Act, which protects women and men performing substantially equal work against pay discrimination based on gender. Sexual harassment claims are also handled by this office. In addition, the EEOC investigates claims filed under the Americans with Disabilities Act (ADA).

The Americans with Disabilities Act

This act covers employers with 15 or more employees (as of July 26, 1994). It prohibits discrimination in all employment practices, including job-application procedures, hiring, firing, advancement, compensation, training and other terms, conditions, and privileges of employment. It applies to recruitment, advertisement, tenure, layoff, leave, fringe benefits and all other employment-related activities. The ADA requires major changes in the way some companies operate. Because of the newness of this law, companies are striving for clearer interpretations and boundaries to operate within. The ambiguity of "reasonable accommodations" continues to be defined by evolving court decisions.

Employment discrimination is prohibited against "qualified individuals with disabilities." An individual is considered to have a "disability" if he/she has a physical or mental impairment that substantially limits one or more major life activity, has a record of such impairment or is regarded as having such an impairment. Persons discriminated against because they have a known association or relationship with an individual with a disability are also protected. Clearly, this act applies to persons limited by sight, hearing, speaking, walking, breathing, performing manual tasks, learning, caring for oneself and working. An individual with epilepsy, paralysis, HIV infection or AIDS, a substantial hearing or visual impairment, mental retardation or a specific learning disability is also covered. There are many gray areas surrounding the act's terminology, though.

The definition of discrimination does require that the individual be "qualified" for the position and meet the skill, experience, education or other requirements of potential applicants. This does not mean that an employer must give a disabled person preferential treatment.

While your company may be too small to be required to follow these current guidelines, it is advisable if you have five employees or more to have one individual designated as your ADA officer, someone who can listen to complaints and diffuse potentially damaging situations. Most often, situations can be handled by asking questions and listening to what is being requested. Confrontation may lead to possible lawsuits. It is much better to try to work out a reasonable compromise in the beginning than to put out fires later on.

COBRA

Rising medical costs have transformed health benefits from a privilege to a necessity for most Americans. The Consolidated Omnibus Budget Reconciliation Act (COBRA) creates an opportunity for persons to retain this important benefit for a specified period of time after employment. Group health insurance coverage can be available to terminated employees or those who lose coverage because of reduced work hours under COBRA. Employers with 20 or more employees participating in health care coverage are affected. Employers are required to notify former employees of this program, and the employee has up to 60 days to accept. Employees are responsible for the cost of the insurance, plus an administrative fee. The employer's responsibility is to provide information. Health insurance reform remains a hot topic. Its reform may change the role and requirements of employers.

ERISA

The Employee Retirement Income Security Act (ERISA) was enacted in 1974 to protect employees' rights to employer-provided pension and health and welfare plans. Neither the Federal government nor ERISA requires employers to provide such benefits. But when the benefits are provided, ERISA outlines the rules that employers must follow. ERISA is enforced by both the Internal Revenue Service and the Department of Labor.

For employers to receive a tax deduction for their benefit-plan contributions, they must comply with tax code provisions under ERISA. Failure to comply could result in disqualification from participation in the plan and could also lead to stiff penalties. Some of the requirements of ERISA include a summary plan description, the formal plan document plus amendments and the summary annual report and benefits statement. Each ERISA plan must have a named fiduciary charged with operating and managing the plan.

Administrative costs associated with the implementation of ERISA have discouraged many small business owners from offering retirement benefits. This is an unfortunate result of this legislation. Recent talks suggest the possibility of measures less penalizing to business owners that encourage employers to offer retirement benefits to employees.

OSHA

The Occupational Safety and Health Administration (OSHA) is designed to ensure safe working conditions for employees. Twenty-three states and territories have designed their own plans, which are at least as stringent as federal guidelines. The remaining states are covered by the federal plan. As with many of the laws and regulations, OSHA laws are constantly changing. OSHA requirements must be followed if you have one or more employees (either part-time or full-time). The General Duty Clause, which all states must follow, requires employers to provide a "safe and healthful place of employment" for all employees. Worker's Compensation Insurance came out of OSHA legislation.

Worker's compensation

Worker's compensation was started in Wisconsin in 1911 as a private-sector way to help employers and employees deal with job-related injuries. Congress set up the National Commission on Worker's Compensation in 1970. However, worker's compensation is handled on a state-by-state basis. There are no minimum guidelines that must be adhered to. Some states require business owners to have Worker's Compensation Insurance for one or more employees; for other states the minimum may be five or more employees. For all states, though, the cost has increased dramatically over the past decade because of weak regulations, higher costs for medical care, fraud and litigation. This higher cost of insurance directly affects small business owners. Added to the high price of premiums is the fact that many insurance companies are gradually withdrawing from the worker's compensation market, while those remaining are demanding higher deductions and limiting their underwriting services. This program is under current review to see how it can better serve employees. Changes are expected.

Federal and state unemployment tax

The federal unemployment tax system, along with the state system, provides unemployment payments to workers who have lost their jobs. As an employer, you must pay into your state's fund to help protect your employees when they become unemployed through no fault of their own. Unemployment insurance is mandated by federal regulations but administered individually through each state's program. Rates and requirements vary from state to state. This tax applies to all wages you pay to your employees. Most employers pay both the state and the federal unemployment tax. However, if you are exempt from your state tax, you may still have to pay the federal tax. The IRS will help you to determine the cost assessed your business.

More laws

Most business executives operate with the mind-set that so long as they treat employees fairly, do what's right and use common sense, they won't run into legal trouble. While this is a good foundation, ignorance of laws is no excuse. Businesses must keep abreast of changing laws in order to comply with recent regulations. Laws concerning employee's rights, discrimination and environmental liabilities are showing the most significant changes at the present time. Consider the following:

• The **National Labor Relations Act** prohibits firing employees for union activity.

• The **Fair Labor Standards Act** prohibits firing employees for making claims for minimum wage and overtime payments.

• **Title VII of the Civil Rights Act of 1964** prohibits firing employees on the basis of race, religion, gender or national origin.

• The **Age Discrimination in Employment Act** prohibits discharge based on age and covers employees beginning at age 40.

• The **Federal Trade Commission** administers many laws concerning garment labeling and requirements.

• The **Employee Retirement Income Security Act (ERISA)** prohibits discharges motivated by a desire to keep employees from obtaining vested pension rights.

Supervisors especially need to familiarize themselves with laws regarding company liability for employee injuries suffered outside normal working hours, discrimination against people with AIDS and the hiring of illegal aliens.

Small business owners must make sure that their payrolls conform to federal standards. The most common violation involves misclassification of nonexempt employees as exempt employees. This reclassification could mean huge amounts of back pay to employees, including former employees.

Fair Debt Collection Act

Although primarily targeted at collection agencies and attorneys, all companies that handle their own collections need to follow the procedures established by the Fair Debt Collection Act. It is administered through the Federal

Trade Commission. In particular, the law addresses the rights of consumers against debt collectors who may harass them, give false statements or engage in unfair tactics. Be aware of the following:

- Debt collectors may not harass, oppress or abuse any person.
- Debt collectors may not use any false statements when collecting a debt.
- Debt collectors may not give false credit information about anyone.
- Debt collectors may not send a creditor anything that looks like an official document from a court or government agency if it is not.
- Debt collectors may not use a false name.
- Debt collectors may not engage in unfair practices in attempting to collect a debt.

By prohibiting certain methods of debt collection, this law requires that debt collectors treat consumers fairly. The law does not, however, forgive any legitimate debt owed.

Fair Credit Billing Act

The Fair Credit Billing Act (FCBA) primarily applies to "open-end" credit accounts. Open-end accounts include revolving charge accounts, credit cards and overdraft protection on checking accounts. The periodic bills, or billing statements sent, are covered by this law. The act does not apply to loans or credit sales that are paid according to a fixed schedule until the entire amount is paid back.

If the consumer detects a billing error, she must notify the creditor in writing within 60 days of receiving the first bill containing the error. The creditor must acknowledge the letter containing the error, in writing, within 30 days after it is received, unless the problem is resolved within that period. Within no more than 90 days, the creditor must conduct a reasonable investigation and either correct the mistake or explain why the bill is believed to be correct. While the bill is being disputed, the creditor may not threaten to damage the consumer's credit rating or report the consumer as delinquent.

The Equal Credit Opportunity Act prohibits creditors from discriminating against credit applicants who, in good faith, exercise their rights under the FCBA. Consumers cannot be denied credit merely because they have disputed a bill.

Disputes about quality of goods and services are not necessarily "billing errors," so the dispute procedures may not apply. The Federal Trade Commission also enforces most FCBA violations.

Other collection laws

Some states forbid merchants to record credit or charge card account numbers on checks or to use them for other forms of credit verification. Merchants are permitted to simply note whether the buyer has a major credit or charge card as an indicator of creditworthiness. In states that do not restrict this action, merchants may still refuse to accept someone's check if the purchaser refuses to allow their card numbers to be recorded.

Many state agencies license and regulate members of various professions, including collection agencies. These regulations may also affect collection practices from any company. Contact the office of the attorney general in your state for more information regarding collection matters and credit policies.

Antitrust laws

Essentially, these laws prohibit business practices that unreasonably deprive consumers of the benefits of competition. There are three major federal antitrust laws: The Sherman Antitrust Act; the Clayton Act; and the Federal Trade Commission Act. The **Sherman Antitrust Act** outlaws all contracts, combinations and conspiracies that unreasonably restrain interstate trade. The Sherman Act also makes it a crime to monopolize any part of interstate commerce. The **Clayton Act** is a civil statute (it carries no criminal penalties) that prohibits mergers or acquisitions that are likely to prohibit competition. And the **Federal Trade Commission Act** prohibits unfair methods of competition in interstate commerce.

Employer number

You will need a taxpayer identification number so that the Internal Revenue Service can process your return. There are two kinds of taxpayer identification numbers: a Social Security number and an employer identification number.

A sole proprietorship does not need a separate employer identification number (EIN) unless she has a KEOGH plan, or files any of these returns: employment, excise, fiduciary or alcohol, tobacco and firearms. Instead, the owner's Social Security number is used as the taxpayer identification number. Partnerships and corporations must apply for employer identification numbers through their local IRS office.

Taxes

The type of business you organize and operate determines what taxes you are subject to. The major tax categories are: income tax, self-employment tax, employment taxes and excise tax. The Internal Revenue Service will assist you in determining which taxes apply to your business.

If you have one or more employees, you will have to withhold and submit federal income taxes from their wages. You may also be subject to Social Security and Medicare taxes under the Federal Insurance Contributions Act (FICA) and federal unemployment tax under the Federal Unemployment Tax Act (FUTA). Social Security and Medicare taxes, along with withheld income taxes, are reported on Form 941 and paid together. You must deposit both your part and your employees' part of Social Security and Medicare taxes. Businesses are considered either a monthly depositor or a semiweekly depositor. The IRS will send you a notice to confirm your payment schedule. Deposits are made to an authorized financial institution or to a Federal Reserve Bank. The penalty for a late tax deposit is based on the length of time the deposit is late. The penalties are stiff.

If you are self-employed, you will have to pay higher Social Security taxes and be responsible for paying estimated income taxes. The self-employment tax is a Social Security and Medicare tax for individuals who work for themselves. It is similar to the Social Security and Medicare tax withheld from the pay of wage earners, which employers must match. In essence, you are responsible for both the employer and employee portion. According to the IRS guidelines, you do not need to actually make a profit to be in a trade or business as long as you have a profit motive. You do need, however, to make ongoing efforts to further the interests of your business. Regularity of activities and transactions and the production of income are important elements.

Checklist for keeping business records

Unfortunately, there is no hard and fast rule as to how long you must keep business records. Your accountant and attorney will advise you on current retention requirements for your state and their personal preferences. Often, record retention depends on individual state statutes and federal requirements. The following information is presented as a general guideline.

Keep for two years:
Requisitions; general correspondence.

Keep for three years:
Petty cash vouchers; bank account reconciliations; personnel files on former employees; and expired insurance policies that have no cash value.

Keep for six years:
Employee withholding tax statements; employee disability benefit records and monthly trial balance.

Keep for seven to eight years:
All general canceled checks; vouchers for payments to employees, vendors, etc.; inventory records, payroll records and time sheets; payables ledger and receivables ledger; expired contracts and leases; purchase orders, invoices and others sales records; and operating cost ledgers.

Keep indefinitely:
Audit reports and financial statements; canceled checks for contracts, capital purchases or taxes; cash book; contracts and leases that are current; copyrights; patent papers; trademark registrations; corporate charter; minute books and bylaws; correspondence pertaining to legal and tax matters; deeds, easements, mortgages and property records; general ledgers and journals; insurance records; property appraisals; stock and bond records; and tax returns and all supporting papers.

Summary

Rights are defined in statutes or laws passed by the U.S. Congress and by state and city legislatures. They are also set forth in the written decisions of judges, both federal and state. To help administer those rights, Congress and state and local governments have set up numerous agencies to create and enforce regulations. Often agencies share responsibilities. Because there is not a single place to gather information about laws that affect your business, you will need to contact a variety of agencies to determine your compliance requirements. Take the time to make these calls. It can save you a lot of headaches and frustration down the road. Some laws are only applicable if you have a certain number of employees, whereas other laws apply for one employee or more. Start your business habits by knowing and complying with the regulations that affect your business.

The following IRS publications are excellent sources of information, providing examples for many individual situations. I strongly encourage you to get a copy of each of these publications. Ask the IRS about the Small Business tax kits it has prepared. These kits include many of the applicable publications listed. Call your local IRS office to order these *free* publications.

IRS publications

Chapter 15

Those golden years: planning early for retirement

"Remember always that you have not only the right to be an individual; you have an obligation to be one. You cannot make any useful contributions in life unless you do this."

Eleanor Roosevelt

Retirement planning

Women can only achieve economic security in retirement years by planning for it during their working years. Statistics show that women are living longer. And the longer you live, the more money you will need. While Social Security can help, do not count on it alone to support you in retirement. Instead, build your personal savings and investments to be a major source of retirement income. This is an area where women have fallen significantly behind men. However, it is the one area where you cannot afford to fall short. According to the *Working Woman's Guide to Retirement Planning*, by Martha Priddy Patterson, "only nine percent of women over 40 receive or expect to receive a retirement benefit, and if they receive a retirement benefit at all, it is usually less than one-third of that received by their male colleagues." Now is the time to plan for retirement. Don't wait. Start investing today, creating your retirement nest egg.

While the number of women participating in pension plans has increased by 1 percent over the past decade, the dollar amount of benefits has declined. To help educate women and promote retirement planning, a new campaign has recommended giving pensions, not posies, to women. Currently, only 29 percent of working women participate in some type of retirement plan, compared to 38 percent of men. And the gap widens near retirement age: For people 50 to 54 years of age, the gap increases to 14 percent more men than women participating.

Preparing for a successful retirement requires organization, planning, management and practice. You and your business must plan early to establish and contribute to a retirement plan if you want to retire in financial comfort. Do not assume that your business will sell, some day, at a premium and that you can live off those proceeds. Create your own nest egg and consider the possible sale of your business as icing on the cake, especially if you have a service business. A lot can happen to a business between now and when you retire. If you are gambling on that money as your primary retirement income, that is a very risky gamble.

In planning for your retirement, it is advisable to seek the assistance of qualified financial planners. Tax and estate laws are constantly being revised. These laws have strong implications for how you can best invest your money, reduce your taxable income and protect your investment. There is a web of federal regulations that govern these laws. The strategy is to calculate how much money you will need for retirement and then save accordingly.

The three keys to being happy in retirement are: financial security, good health and consuming interests. Unfortunately, women have been faced with financial insecurity at an alarmingly high rate. Currently about 33.6 percent of all households headed by women are below the poverty level. But you can change this statistic by taking charge of your financial future now. Second, good health means not only taking care of yourself physically but also emotionally. Follow the well-publicized advice of eating balanced meals and getting regular exercise and plenty of rest. And, finally, outside interests should ideally be a mix of physical and mental activities that absorb your attention for several hours at a time. Consider current hobbies and interests, as well as those you've never had enough time to develop. Retirement is the time when, hopefully, you have more time to do those things you enjoy.

There are a number of different avenues for saving money for a comfortable retirement. Individual Retirement Arrangements (IRAs), KEOGHs and company pension plans are ways to put money aside for your retirement. There are numerous variations on retirement plans, depending on your form of business, its size and your needs. *The language can be confusing*. Because retirement plans have become more complex over the years, this chapter is designed only as a guide. It is not intended to be a complete listing of all options currently available. Use this information as the beginning of building your foundation to sound retirement planning. Again, seek personal advice from a qualified financial advisor. No single plan is best for all people. But knowledge of options available can assist entrepreneurs in making informed decisions.

Some statistics

According to the U.S. Department of Labor, only 2 percent of individuals aged 65 and over are financially independent, while 23 percent continue to work, and 75 percent are dependent on family and friends for economic aid. Yet, 57 percent of employees as of 1992 did not have any retirement funds established other than Social Security. As baby boomers reach retirement age, the effect of these statistics will be staggering.

Currently, Social Security deductions average 12 percent of most employees' paychecks; it is estimated that by the year 2050 this deduction can represent as much as 43 percent of the pay, because of the greater number of people of retirement age, supported by fewer working people, as well as longer life expectancies.

There are three main sources of retirement money. First is *Social Security*, which normally doesn't start until you reach at least age 62 (under current regulations). There has been recent talk of raising the minimum age to 70 because people are living longer, and many are able to work. The second source is a *company's pension* and/or *employer-sponsored retirement plan*. Currently, government statistics report that 85 percent of U.S. firms do not sponsor any plan for their workers. And, finally, your *personal savings* will be a significant factor in your retirement income. Unfortunately, the typical American family reaches retirement status with a mere $7,000 in liquid assets, indicating we are not taking advantage of options that are available and that we continue to live in the present and not plan effectively for our future. Many retired people are forced to reenter the workplace out of financial necessity—not personal satisfaction. In addition, the income earned may reduce Social Security benefits.

The average breakdown of retirement income reflects that 18 percent comes from pensions, 22 percent comes from Social Security and more than 58 percent is the result of individuals' continuing to work or using personal investments. Depending on when you retire, your funds may need to last 35 years or longer. The earlier you retire, the more money you will need. Those choosing to retire at age 55 must save a considerable amount more than those planning to retire 10 years later.

Currently, the median annual income for couples over the age of 65 is $23,352, with 25 percent of those couples having income of $15,000 or less annually. The numbers are even less encouraging for aging single people, specifically women. Women must take control over their financial futures. And they must do it today.

How much will you need?

How much money you will need for retirement varies, but experts suggest that enough to cover from 60 to 80 percent of your preretirement expenses should be fairly close. Inflation is always a big factor in determining future needs. While this may seem a high figure, research continues to support this percentage range. Assuming an annual inflation rate of 6 percent, the cost of living doubles in about 12 years. What this means is that if your current

standard of living requires income of $40,000, in 12 years you would need $80,000, and in another 12 years (24 years from now), the figure would reach $160,000.

In retirement, your expenses may change. Your work-related expenses may drop considerably, as may auto, clothes and miscellaneous business expenses. On the other hand, health insurance often increases as an expense for retirees. Many spend more on travel and leisure activities and other personal expenses. Generally, a retired individual's standard of living doesn't change that much. Because of increasing life expectancy, when you retire at age 65, you may need to financially support yourself for another 20 years or more. Consider when you want to retire as important information in this equation.

Figure out what Social Security will pay you annually upon your retirement. Benefits are lowered if Social Security is applied for at an earlier age. To find out what you can expect in the way of Social Security benefits, request the Personal Earnings and Benefits Estimate Statement (Form SSA-7004), which can be obtained by calling the Social Security Administration's toll-free number, 800-772-1213, and requesting an application form.

With medical costs and life expectancy rising, pension coverage shrinking and uncertainty about the future of the Social Security system, women need to take control of their retirement planning. Because individual needs are different, you should select a retirement plan with your specific goals in mind. Design your plan based on your needs, taking into account your business's earnings history, cash flow and other important variables.

The aging of the baby boom generation will have a significant effect on the allocation of resources in the future. No one denies that fact. You cannot afford to ignore its reality.

The value of money and time

Each person will have a different objective in her retirement plan. However, the advice to diversify your holdings applies to all plans. Diversification reduces risk, which is especially important when it comes to your retirement assets.

The value of investing money over time has considerable implications, as the following table illustrates. I have chosen the compounding interest rates of 5 percent, 7 percent and 9 percent to show the difference time and rate make.

How $100 invested monthly will grow at various annual compound rates of return:

Years	5%	7%	9%
5	$ 6,801	$ 7,159	$ 7,542
10	15,528	17,308	19,351
15	26,729	31,696	37,841
20	41,103	52,093	66,789
25	59,551	81,007	112,112
30	83,226	121,997	183,074

For example, look at the amount of money earned over 10 years at 5 percent interest versus 7 percent, when you invest $100 monthly ($15,528 compared to $17,308). Then look at the 20-year interval for the same interest rates ($41,103 and $52,093, respectively). The amounts more than doubled in the double time period. When you consider the 9-percent interest figure, you see ever greater increases. You can interpret the returns shown in the table as varying returns from investments with varying degrees of risk. These figures reinforce the need for and advantage of diversification—gaining varying degrees of

returns on your investments—and time—beginning early, and saving for the long-term.

The younger you are when you begin your retirement plan, the more risk you can afford to take. And, potentially, the more you can gain. As you come closer to retirement age, you will want to invest more conservatively. Investing in stocks (if you are patient and have enough time before you retire) has provided the maximum growth in the past. The road to get there, though, is often bumpy. A diversified portfolio may include things such as stocks, bonds, mutual funds, certificates of deposit and annuities. Within each category the risk is wide-ranged. Blue chip stocks are going to grow more slowly, but they carry less risk. On the other hand, a mutual fund whose portfolio objective is growth will have a somewhat higher risk.

While each individual's portfolio objectives will be different, the following are guidelines based on trends and your current age.

If you are in your 30s. You can afford to take a modest risk with your savings in order to generate as much income as possible. You may consider putting as much as two-thirds of your retirement savings in stocks or equity-based mutual funds and the balance in bonds and bond funds.

If you are in your 40s. You may wish to invest half of your portfolio in stocks or stock funds and the rest in fixed-income bonds or bond funds and money market funds.

If you are in your 50s. At this point, two-thirds of your portfolio should be in more conservative investments, such as fixed-income funds or money market funds. The balance of your money could be in riskier investments, such as stocks.

If you are near retirement. Keep all but 10 percent of your holdings in conservative, low-risk investments. You cannot afford to gamble so close to retirement.

Retirement funds should always be viewed as long-term investments, not to be used earlier. Penalties and taxes for early withdrawal are often very steep on most retirement plans. Avoid these expenses by budgeting your retirement costs carefully into your current finances.

Basic vocabulary

It is important to have a basic understanding of retirement planning vocabulary.

Retirement plans: The term *retirement plan* includes all plans that make payments to retired workers, regardless of how the benefits are paid. This includes a one-time lump sum payment as well as systematic payment plans.

Pension: A pension is only one type of retirement plan and represents payments being made to an employee's retirement account. There is no current legal requirement that businesses must offer pension benefits, beyond matching Social Security taxes.

Qualified plan: A qualified plan is a written plan that an employer can establish for the exclusive benefit of her employees. Contributions may be made by you, your employees or both. To meet the qualifications, according to IRS guidelines, a plan must follow specific rules concerning:

1. Who must be covered by the plan.
2. How contributions to the plan are to be invested.

3. How contributions to the plan and benefits under the plan are to be determined.
4. How much of an employee's interest in the plan must be guaranteed.

There are two basic kinds of qualified retirement plans: defined contribution plans and defined benefit plans.

Defined contribution plans

The defined contribution plan promises to set aside a certain amount of money (up to the legally set maximum) each year for retirement. These plans provide for a separate account for each person covered by the plan. Benefits are based only on amounts contributed or allocated to each account. These plans are driven by fixed annual contributions. There are three types of defined contribution plans: profit-sharing plans, stock bonus plans and money-purchase pension plans.

Profit-sharing plans. This is a plan that lets your employees share in the profits of your business. The plan must have a definite formula for allocating contributions to the plan account for participating employees and for distributing the funds in the plan. Employees do not contribute to profit-sharing plans. And funding is based on a formula; if there are no profits, no money is contributed.

Stock bonus plans. The benefits in this plan are similar to those of profit-sharing plans. Benefits are payable in the form of company stock. Only a corporation can set up a stock bonus plan.

Money-purchase pension plans. Under this plan, company contributions are a stated amount, or are based on a stated formula that is not subject to your discretion. Your contributions to the plan are not based on profits.

Defined benefit plans

Defined benefit plans promise to pay a certain amount of money at retirement. The popularity of such plans is waning because of regulatory sanctions, increased costs in administration and nondiscrimination regulations. They specify the payment you will receive at your retirement, based on actuarial assumptions. Defined benefit plans tend to offer greater retirement security and higher levels of benefits than defined contribution plans.

Retirement plans for the self-employed

As a self-employed person, you can still establish certain qualified retirement plans. The available options include a KEOGH plan (HR-10) or a Simplified Employee Pension (SEP). In addition, you should also consider the option of investing in an Individual Retirement Arrangement (IRA).

KEOGH

The KEOGH plan is named for its congressional sponsor, Eugene Keogh. A KEOGH is a retirement plan for a self-employed individual. It can only be established by the employer and is limited to sole proprietorships and partnerships (but not to individual partners). Incorporated companies cannot participate in these plans. The plan allows the self-employed person to make a tax-deductible contribution to her own retirement plan as well as to her employees' plans. Most KEOGH plans follow a standard form, called a prototype plan, which has been approved by the IRS.

It is not necessary to have employees to establish this plan. However, if you do have employees, the plan must be made available to them if they meet age and service criteria.

The maximum that may be invested each year in such a pension plan depends on income, but currently cannot exceed $30,000.

KEOGHs are ideal for part-time workers. Even if you are employed by someone else and covered by a retirement plan through an employer, you may qualify for a KEOGH if you have free-lance income or income from part-time self-employment.

KEOGHs are especially useful for women. They are easy to set up and require little reporting until your account contains substantial assets. Unless the KEOGH is a profit-sharing plan, though, it must be funded each year or terminated. And the IRS looks unfavorably on plans terminated after only a few years, since their primary purpose is for long-term investment and retirement security.

Plans qualifying for contribution deductions and income deferral must be in writing and must be communicated to employees, maintained for exclusive employee benefit, and set up to prevent the diversion of plan assets for purposes other than providing benefits to plan participants. A KEOGH must also meet participation, nondiscrimination and vesting requirements in order to qualify.

KEOGHs use a net income method to determine contributions. In contrast, corporate plans use an income method. KEOGH contributions must be deducted before they can be calculated. Because of this difference, you may decide to incorporate for a larger financial savings.

KEOGH plans come in four varieties: a profit-sharing plan, a money-purchase plan, a combination plan and a defined-benefit plan. Defined-benefit KEOGH plans are more complex and are expensive to start up and maintain due to the legal and actuarial help needed. The simpler profit-sharing and money-purchase plans are much less expensive to start up and maintain and are more popular. Most KEOGHs are set up through savings institutions, mutual funds, or insurance or trust companies.

Simplified Employee Pension (SEP)

Although SEPs were established to help increase retirement plan sponsorship among small businesses, participation is surprisingly low. Yet the establishment and administration costs that hindered small business participation in other plans has been greatly reduced (often to zero), and there are virtually no IRS filing requirements. SEPs may be established by self-employed individuals, partnerships and all corporations.

A Simplified Employee Pension Plan (SEP) is a written plan that allows you to make contributions toward your own and your employees' retirement, without involving you in the more complex maintenance, filings and costs associated with other retirement plans. But some advantages available with KEOGH plans are not available under SEPs.

However, SEPs have many advantages not available under other plans. SEPs have virtually no reporting or record-keeping requirements. Also, each year the employer has the right to decide whether and how much to contribute to the plan. You are not required to make contributions every year. But if you make contributions, they must be based on a written allocation formula and they must not discriminate. Your plan must include both full-time and part-time employees. The contributions are made to IRAs in the name of the participants. Employees are fully vested

immediately and control their own account.

SEP-IRAs are set up for each qualifying employee who has reached the age of 21 years, worked for you in at least three of the last five years and received a minimum amount in compensation from you the preceding year. A SEP-IRA may have to be set up for leased employees, depending on the particular situation.

The contributions you make under a SEP are treated as if made to a qualified pension, stock bonus, profit-sharing or annuity plan. Consequently, contributions are deductible within limits. Your contributions (as employer) are not included in a participant's income when contributed. Your employees, therefore, cannot take a deduction for your SEP contribution. However, there are types of SEPs that allow for salary-reduction arrangements.

Under a salary-reduction arrangement (SARSEP), your employees can choose to have you contribute part of their pay to their retirement account. If you employ 25 or fewer employees, the SEP can permit salary reduction contributions from employees, much like a 401(k) plan. At least half of your employees must participate in the salary reduction plan to qualify. Qualified financial institutions can assist you in setting up such an arrangement.

Individual Retirement Arrangement (IRA)

Congress established Individual Retirement Arrangements with the enactment of ERISA in 1974. All taxpayers may contribute to IRAs and have dividends and interest accumulate tax-free. However, the Tax Reform Act of 1986 restricted the deductibility of contributions. Contributions are currently limited to $2,000 per year, with qualifying restrictions. IRAs are often overlooked when women analyze retirement investment opportunities. Always consider this option when making your retirement plans.

IRAs are set up by the individual. They are meant to be a vehicle for building retirement funds; therefore premature withdrawal is discouraged by strong tax penalties. You cannot currently begin withdrawing funds before the age of 59½ without penalty. The laws are continuing to change frequently concerning IRAs. Your financial advisor can explore this option with you in greater detail, based on your specific situation.

Other retirement options

There are other options available, depending on how your business is established. The 401(k) plan is frequently discussed; therefore I've included information concerning it. In addition, both ESOPs and annuities are gaining in popularity.

401(k) plan

401(k) is named after the section of the Internal Revenue Code that created the plan. It was designed so that the burden and obligation of providing for retirement wasn't solely with the employer, and it is an excellent way for the employer and the employee to share the cost of retirement funding. A 401(k) must be established by the employer and places limits on contributions. These plans are very popular with employees and employers. They have grown phenomenally over the last decade despite being governed by extremely complex tax rules. Funding may be from one or more of the following sources: employee salary deferral,

matching employer contributions or an employer profit-sharing contribution.

These plans enable both employer and employee to contribute tax-free money. Many employers who participate match employees contribution, although it is not required. The 401(k) is a defined-contribution plan, which means employees could receive a lump-sum distribution when they leave. Most often, these plans are administered by a third party contract, which increases the cost.

ESOPs

Under Employee Stock Ownership Plans (ESOPs) you let employees own a part of your company. ESOPs are the most unusual of all the retirement plans. They allow employees to purchase a portion of your company and allow you to sell a part of your company without paying taxes. As a retirement plan, employees receive their contributions in shares of the employer's stock rather than in cash. These stock contributions may be part of a profit-sharing plan or combined with a 401(k) plan. This method gives the employees ownership of your company and the effect is usually an increase in productivity and profitability.

There are voting rights that accompany ESOP stock transfers. Employees, as minority stockholders, must be permitted to exercise their voting rights, whether your company's stock is privately or publicly traded. For privately held companies, these rights can be limited to voting on major issues, such as dissolving, merging or selling the company. Small, closely held companies looking at selling a part of their business to their employees need to consider these ramifications. Your attorney will explain the benefits as well as how to avoid potential hazards.

ESOPs can be excellent for growing companies that have more than 30 employees and want to involve valuable staffers in the business. When employees become minority stockholders through ESOPs, they often become more productive and produce increased profitability for your business. But ESOPs aren't for everyone.

Annuities

An annuity is a way to set aside money during your working years and have it grow on a tax-deferred basis for your future use. When you are ready to retire, it can provide steady income that is guaranteed to last the rest of your life, regardless of how long you live. The way this works is that you invest money with an insurance company. The insurance company insures you against the risk that you will outlive your retirement savings. As an alternative, you can withdraw your money from your annuity in a single cash payment or in a series of withdrawals over a specified period.

Under current regulations, there is no annual investment ceiling, so you are free to set aside as much money each year as your retirement objective requires. (Other tax-advantaged plans, such as IRAs, shouldn't be overlooked for retirement savings, but the amount you can contribute each year is limited.) Since the tax on annuity interest is deferred, your investment will grow faster than in a taxable plan. If you wait until retirement to receive you annuity income, you may be in a lower tax bracket, further increasing the value of your investment. There are no annual IRS forms to file, and you won't need an entry on your income tax return until you actually begin to withdraw your funds.

There are three different categories for annuities:

1. **When income begins.** You can put money into an annuity and allow it to grow tax-deferred until some future date (deferred annuity). Or you can put funds into an annuity and begin to get a regular income from it right away (immediate annuity).

2. **How the annuity is bought.** You can choose to buy your annuity with just a single-sum payment, or you can make a series of periodic payments.

   Note: Immediate annuities are always purchased with a single sum. Deferred annuities can be purchased in either manner.

3. **Investment performance.** You can choose to have your annuity grow at a present interest rate guaranteed by the insurance company (guaranteed annuity). Or you can choose a variable annuity and have your funds invested in a family of mutual funds. Variable annuities are also referred to as self-directed annuities, because you have the right to direct into which mutual fund portfolio your money is invested.

Before you buy an annuity, carefully investigate insurance companies. Shop around. Most annuities are very safe investments, but not all. Look at the insurance company's rating with *Standard & Poor*, *Moody's*, and *Best* before deciding where to invest.

Establishing a retirement program for you

I have presented a variety of options in this chapter. It is not a complete listing of options, by any means. Instead, I have concentrated on some of the more common plans entrepreneurs are using. There are several steps you can undertake to establish a retirement plan for you and your company:

1. Talk with several financial advisors and planners. Always look for someone you are comfortable with.
2. Integrity, honesty and knowledge should be carefully evaluated.
3. Compare fees.
4. Ask what options are available for your particular form of operation.
5. Find out what the consequences are if you are unable to fund the contribution.
6. Ask how easily the plan can be dissolved and what the costs are.
7. Find out whether your plan allows for borrowing against it if the need arises.

Your personal retirement plan will be integrated with anticipated Social Security benefits. If you are single, your retirement plan may not allow your benefits to be transferred after your death. Often, if you take early retirement, your benefits are reduced. Getting money out of retirement plans varies with each plan. Verify the stipulations and conditions of your plan before you invest.

Estate planning

If you own any assets, you need to have an estate plan. A major part of this plan is your will. The importance of having a will cannot be overstated. There is no more important document. Writing a will protects your family and ensures that your wishes are followed. Because state laws affect estates so differently, you should seek the advice of an estate attorney who is experienced in writing wills and trusts in your state. While there are do-it-yourself kits available, I would not recommend them.

Estate planning looks forward to our future, given our current conditions. And in doing so, it forces us to look at our own mortality—often resulting in estate planning being neglected in the process. Equally important as dealing with our death, especially for women, is life. Given that women often live longer and statistically earn less than men, planning for the future is essential.

In fact, women over the age of 65 face a better-than-even chance of spending time in a nursing home, yet many have not planned for the realities of long-term care. The cost is not cheap. A recent study by the U.S. government noted that approximately two-thirds of single elderly persons and one-third of married elderly persons who pay for their own nursing-home care deplete their cash reserves within six months.

Estate planning is a method, when taken into account early enough, that will help you anticipate these financial hurdles. It should include looking at the current tax laws as well as at expected changes, what could happen to you before retirement, and how to plan flexibly for various outcomes, including long-term care for you, a spouse or other family member.

The benefits from estate planning assist women in anticipating (and, hopefully, lowering) probate costs, estate taxes, inheritance taxes and income taxes through saving, controlling debt and making calculated investments. With today's tax laws, it is especially important for women whose family net worth is more than $600,000 to do careful and thorough estate planning. Options available under current tax laws include giving cash gifts (up to $10,000) each year, or transferring discounted stock in your business to other (younger) family members. Your estate planner can help you discover legal avenues available to help lower your tax burden while providing for your needs.

Before meeting with an estate attorney, gather information concerning your personal assets and prepare your personal information sheet (including Social Security number, date of birth, information about your spouse and names and addresses of beneficiaries).

Next establish the financial worth of your estate. Assets that are not readily valued, such as your business interest, should be appraised. Include your car, home, boat and household furnishings, as well as stocks and bonds. Once you have valued your assets, subtract any liabilities (things you owe). The difference will be your net worth.

While financial planners can help make various investment decisions, there are some things you can do to assist in estate planning. Organizing your papers is a significant aspect of estate planning. By creating a master list with the location of all your important legal papers, you are communicating your wishes to others. This list should indicate which papers are kept where. For example, bonds and certificates of deposit, because they are negotiable items, should be kept in a safe-deposit box. On the other hand, insurance policies, burial instructions and your will should be in your home in a fireproof box. You should have copies with your estate attorney or a close relative. Be sure to indicate where the original is, since copies are usually not binding.

The following list indicates what papers might be kept in which location. The important idea, however, is to let everyone know where these papers are. We do not like to talk about the prospect of dying, but planning for our future is very important.

Safe Deposit Box.
Appraisals of personal property; birth certificates; bonds; certificates of deposit; copy of master list of important papers; deeds; legal agreements; marriage certificate; naturalization papers; personal property inventory and pictures; securities; stock certificates; and title policies.

Fireproof box at home.
Awards; copy of master list of important papers; financial records; income tax returns (individuals should retain for the past six years); insurance policies; living will; power of attorney; property tax receipts; warranties; will and codicils.

Attorney or close relative (or friend).
Burial instructions; copy of master list of important papers; living will; names and addresses for persons named in power of attorney, trusts and will; power of attorney; trusts; will and codicils.

Besides knowing your anticipated income from retirement investments, you should consider the importance of key-person life insurance and wills.

Key-Person Life Insurance
While many business owners spend a great deal of time and money insuring their business inventory and fixed assets, they often overlook their single most important asset—key employees. As a small business owner, you may be the single most important asset of your business. For partnerships, key-person life insurance is an invaluable way to protect each partner individually, as well as the business.

The loss of key people, frequently the business owner, can trigger a number of other crises concerning the continuity of the business, which must be addressed in order to preserve the business. To avoid adverse business consequences, key-person life insurance can be purchased as a protection for the business, for the survival of the business, or for the heirs.

Wills

Every woman needs a will. While wills are the most widely used tool of estate planning, statistics show that seven out of 10 Americans die without one, which is a very big and costly mistake.

Only you know how you want your estate distributed. If you die without a will, your estate is termed to be "intestate." And a state-appointed administrator distributes your assets without regard to your heirs' wishes. Dying intestate can also increase the tax burden for your heirs.

Most assets can be passed on through a will. Some money may be able to pass directly to beneficiaries without the delays of probate, which may be a big advantage.

As your assets change, you can modify your will through a codicil: an amendment to the original document. The codicil must be drawn up, signed, witnessed and dated to meet the same standards required of the original will.

The executor is the person (or institution) you choose to oversee your estate and its distribution upon your death. Executors are responsible to get the will probated, to collect the assets so they can be distributed according to the terms of the will, make sure the assets are valued, file the necessary tax returns, pay the estate's debts and distribute the estate's assets. The amount

of work involved will depend on the size and complexity of the estate. Choose your executor carefully.

Some words of advice: Never keep your original will in a bank's safe deposit box, since in some states the box may be locked upon your death and not readily accessible. However, do keep your will in a safe place. Make copies of your will and distribute them to various family members and legal advisors. Also, provide them with instructions on where they may find the original will, since copies are not legally binding.

A final word

It's hard to make long-term financial commitments when you do not know your long-range financial goals. It is important for women to become informed in this decision-making process. Take advantage of various retirement and estate-planning seminars when they are offered. Read educational material. And seek professional financial advice from individuals who are willing to take the time to explain your options thoroughly and who will oversee your investment portfolio with your needs in mind. Make sure you know what retirement benefits you will receive from Social Security, as well as from personal retirement investments, including other company pensions. Prepare for the future beginning today.

Chapter 16

Balancing work and family: managing stress and surviving

"Every working mother seeks a solution to her individual dilemma of how to balance and reconcile her competing roles."

Deborah J. Swiss and
Judith P. Walker
Women and the Work/Family Dilemma

"The need to integrate workplace and private-sphere responsibilities makes women's lives more complex, but also gives them a certain advantage."

Sally Helgesen
The Female Advantage

Seeking balance

Women have been the traditional caregivers of the world. We have been conditioned to make everyone else happy. Often, in the process we forget to make ourselves happy. Trying to be all things to all people can be exhausting. In the 1980s, Dr. Harriet B. Braiker coined the phrase "Type E Woman" as she described our need to be *E*verything to *E*verybody. Today, we see the repercussions of this lifestyle choice as many women face mid-life burnout caused by this impossible attempt. As we take control of our lives, we must take time to replenish our resources.

Creating balance in your life is not a simple process. It requires prioritizing and compromising. It requires honest communication, especially to yourself. And it requires work. But the result is a happy, healthy, sane you. And when you are happy, your happiness is contagious. Your family is happy. Your employees are happy. Your customers are happy. You radiate happiness.

Because of your role as caregiver, it is important for you to find a *balance* between giving and getting. A *balance* between stress and calm. A *balance* between home and work. Giving to yourself must be balanced with giving of yourself. It is not only wise to take time out for yourself, it is also healthy. This is much-needed and deserved time off for you to relax and reflect. To say you can't afford time off is myopic. In fact, you can't afford *not* to take the time off! It becomes your time of rejuvenation, a refueling of your energy. It's your prescription for sanity.

Communicating

The transition from work to home can be a challenging one for anyone. This transition requires time and patience. Integrating business and family takes a great deal of coordination. The key is communication. Talking and listening to feelings about work are at the foundation of a relaxing evening at home. You need to be able to acknowledge anger, disappointment and other fears in both yourself and other family members.

Not being willing to communicate leaves family members and friends outside your circle of trust. And it puts additional pressure on you—pressure you do not want, pressure you do not need, pressure you can avoid by communicating.

Spousal tensions

Couples are likely to encounter new pressures in their relationship when one becomes self-employed or an entrepreneur. These pressures result from changing roles. Starting a business is very stressful and demanding, because you may be spending less time on domestic chores and asking a spouse to help around the house more. You may start relying on each other more to pick up the slack. Jealousy and competition for your time may play heavily into these emotions.

Again, communication is important. While men and women communicate differently, you must make sure that communication remains open. Having your spouse's support is essential in lessening the tension of starting your own business.

You will have to evaluate your situation and decide how best to handle it. It may be necessary for you to continue with two full-time jobs, one as an entrepreneur and the other as homemaker. You may not wish to or be able to relinquish any of the domestic chores. Perhaps you prefer your own systems and methods, while others' attempts at helping don't suit you. Or, you may elect to use part of your self-employment income to hire part-time help around the

house. Or, you may find your spouse willing to help considerably in the domestic duties.

Time at home provides time to share with your mate on emotional terms. To value and appreciate him, practice sharing openly and honestly without attacking or becoming defensive. Learn to praise your mate and learn to become a gracious acceptor of praise. Both will take practice and constant attention to achieve.

According to Dr. Barbara Mackoff, in *The Art of Self-Renewal*, "Talking about fears and failures allows you to express a vulnerability that is the prerequisite for intimacy." Dr. Mackoff suggests following intentional steps concerning love and intimacy to build a strong marriage.

There is a significant risk involved with starting a new business. In healthier relationships, the common fears are discussed honestly and freely. Whether your fear is failure or success, whether your fear is financial responsibility or domestic sharing, whatever you are feeling should be shared. Understand that your spouse will probably have some very real fears as well. And together you must learn to build the bridges of communication and compromise.

Partner/spouse work relationships

The SBA reports that husband-and-wife businesses represented the fastest growing segment during the 1980s, increasing 83.9 percent from the previous decade. The National Family Business Council estimates that there are as many as 1.8 million entrepreneurial couples. There are definite benefits and hazards in this partnership arrangement. It takes a strong marriage to succeed. It can be demanding and draining on both partners and on the relationship. But the benefits can be sensational. The additional stress on the relationship is as individual as the individuals involved.

The term "copreneurs" has been coined to identify entrepreneurial couples. Women assume many different roles in copreneurial businesses. Research indicates that it is difficult for spouses to feel equally committed to a business unless they start out equally committed. Copreneurs know that the process represents a special extension of their commitment to each other. When they start the business, they realize it often drains them of a private life. Likewise, it can be devastating when couples bring unresolved personal problems into the workplace. It can be difficult for the copreneurs and for the employees affected by their tension or actions. Employees never enjoy being placed in the position of choosing sides. It is a no-win situation, they know.

Often, in copreneurial businesses the reality of family issues is integrated into the business life. Many owners create schedules around family activities, especially when small children are involved. In fact, owners often encourage and make allowances for employees to have a life outside the business. This aspect of copreneurial businesses has been very well received in the workplace and by the community.

There are some basic ground rules that married couples who want to work together need to establish. First, clearly define your roles within the business. Each person must know the boundaries and be willing to abide by those guidelines. Some companies divide responsibilities into sales and marketing for one and accounting and operations for the other. Find whatever combination works well for you and follow it.

Next, spousal partnerships require intentional and constant communications, which presupposes a mutual respect and trust for the other person. The advantage of a spouse as a partner is that, hopefully, in your marriage you have already created open, honest communications and gained mutual respect and trust for each other. If not, going into business will not be the avenue to build the relationship.

Be very supportive of your partner. Frequently, spousal partners say they feel more free to offer advice and suggestions to their mate than with another partner. Understand, though, that you will be more aware when your partner (spouse) has had a bad day at the office. The hope is that you haven't been the one to contribute to it. Business may well come home with you, even if you try to leave it at the office.

There are precautions to observe as well. Spousal partnerships do have a high rate of divorce. Partnership in business is *not* recommended for anything but a strong, sound marriage. Business is very demanding on both partners. When both spouses are working full-time in the business, there is also the additional stress caused by dependence on a single income.

Dennis T. Jaffe, Ph.D., author of *Working With the Ones You Love*, lists several prerequisites for success in copreneurial operations, beginning with a solid relationship, a mutual trust and respect and value for contributions. Copreneurs must share the same sense of mission and vision, have very defined roles, be good communicators and have complementary skills.

Try to decide ahead of time how to resolve conflicts. Develop a plan within these boundaries, and then stick with the plan. It is not easy, but those who have found success say there is no better way.

Including children

Don't try to keep your business and professional lives separate. It is both futile and unproductive. You live in both worlds. And the sooner you learn to integrate them, the happier you will be. Children are your natural priority. That doesn't have to change now that you're the boss. Accept both roles and work them together.

But realize that children may sometimes feel threatened by your new position. They may feel that mom doesn't have as much time for them as before. Or that mom is more interested in work than in what they are doing. To compensate for these feelings, it is recommended that you include your children in some aspect of your business. This assumes, of course, that your children are old enough to get involved and that they want to help. It also assumes that your business has some jobs for children to do. Depending on the child and the business, you may have them answering the phone, taking orders, opening mail, picking up supplies, packing orders, preparing the product or even cleaning up around the office. The important lesson is that you include your children and eliminate (or defuse) their fears of competing for your time.

Childcare issues

When your children are younger, childcare may be a major concern. Again, depending on your specific type of business, you may be able to take the children to work with you. Or you may be working out of your home, trying to work around their schedules and naps. There are other childcare options that you might consider, if you desire additional

help: family members, older children, someone to come to your home and keep the children, private baby-sitters (their home), day-care centers, childcare coops, trading baby-sitting with a friend or bartering for childcare with a customer. Evaluate all of your options before deciding which is the best choice for you.

When looking for childcare, ask the following questions:

- What are the licensing laws for day-care providers in my state? These laws may also include city and county ordinances.
- Can the provider give references? How many children does each adult watch?
- Is the facility (or home) clean? Are meals and snacks nutritious? Is there enough space inside and outside for children to play?
- What are the safety precautions in case of fire or other emergencies? Are the signs and procedures well-posted and visible for children?
- What about sick children? Do they stay at home?
- What are the fees for half-days, overtime, or sick children? Are you required to pay for days a child does not attend?
- How does the staff discipline children?
- How much of the day is filled with planned activities? Are the activities geared toward the child's age and development?

These are just a few of the questions you may want answers to before you select a day-care provider. If children are interfering with your working from your home, you will need to consider an outsider provider or another option. Not every business has the luxury of a lot of flexibility. If this is something you need, then you should look toward those businesses that can provide it.

A circle of friends

Friendships offer you the precious opportunity to separate yourself personally from your competitive and stressful professional world. Unfortunately, one of the most frequently identified dilemmas of women being in business for themselves is less time for friends. You may become isolated from your friends. Your business may put new demands on your social calendar, and friends may not understand why.

Friends are that safe haven where you can go to be yourself. You don't have to keep up your professional image. You can let your hair down, relax and have fun. Remember friends come for the pleasure of your company, not to judge or be judged by you.

Create some time for friends. It doesn't have to be with the same frequency as before you started your business. But the mental escape from the rigorous demands of your work will be a welcome change of pace. It will help keep your sanity in tact. All work and no play make for a very dull and exhausted person. You need a life, too. Try not to talk about work and how busy you are when you're with your friends. It lessens their importance. And it's rude.

Many women have broadened their circle of friends to include business acquaintances and other women met through networking. But don't forget your old friends. While you may have less in common than before, value those friendships.

You're the key

Are you feeling overwhelmed? I said you didn't have to be Superwoman to succeed. But you don't see how even Superwoman could do all of this. Well, she can't. And you don't have to either.

You hold the key to the jigsaw puzzle. You call the shots. You set the game plan. And you decide on the boundaries.

We no longer have to feel the pressures superimposed by others. We no longer have to adapt to their expectations, their qualities of life or their measures of success. *We are in control of our lives.*

This is a journey free of guilt because we know what it is we want, and we are striving toward its achievement. This book is a starting place, a place for exploring a lot of different options. It is a tool to assist and encourage you. Don't become overwhelmed in the process. Instead, stay focused on your goals. If you're not having a good time, then what's the point?

Time management

Your ability to establish priorities and to manage your time will be a key element of your success at work and at home.

Time management is simply the logistics of managing various aspects of your life. Realizing that your time is limited can be frustrating. But it's a fact. And the best way to handle the limitations of time is to manage your time efficiently. First, make a list of everything you would like to accomplish. Keep your list within the possible. Delegate what can be delegated. Delete what has been finished. Ignore the impossible. The object is to move it off your list. And with the items remaining on your list, set priorities. Realistically, you cannot do everything immediately. So, decide what item to complete first. Set a time frame and then begin working on it.

I usually work on both long- and short-term priority lists. This way, I see some immediate results (short-term accomplishments) as well as making progress on the larger items (longer term goals). I have found great success in organizing and utilizing my time by making and using lists.

Learn to effectively organize your hours. But be sure to schedule in your time off. Your special time for you. It's just as important as your time on, your time for everyone else.

Most of us waste more time than we care to admit. You may have a hard time getting down to what you need to be doing—particularly if the task is large or one you don't enjoy. A major requirement for running a successful enterprise from home is practical and efficient time management, a learned skill that requires discipline and commitment. No matter how disorganized you think you are, with a little effort, you can do it. Not only does it give you a feeling of control and greater sense of accomplishment, it also helps to keep you on track.

Every person puts her own value on time, either consciously or unconsciously. To practice sensible time management, that value must be consciously arrived at, analyzed, and then allocated. Remember that time doing one thing is always time taken away from another. Time is a fixed commodity and cannot be changed, no matter how much you try. You still only have 60 minutes in an hour; 24 hours in a day; and seven days in a week. Those are things you cannot change. That is why it is a good idea to assess how your time is used now before developing your time plan for your new business.

Attaining goals and managing your time are inseparable. If you don't want to accomplish anything, you don't need to concern yourself with how long it will take. But if you aspire to success (by your definition) in your business, you have an agenda, a full agenda. Your time cannot be idle or unproductive if you want your venture to achieve its full potential.

Try these steps to help you better manage your time:

• Keep it simple. Systems that are easy to operate will get used more often.

• Keep only one calendar and be sure to check it daily. This will avoid scheduling two events at the same time in different calendars. Always keep your calendar with you.

• Write it down. That will clear up your mind to work on the next project.

• Schedule quiet time and social time into your calendar, just like business meetings.

• When you call someone for information, work from a checklist. On the average, 11 calls are made per day. And one in eight is repeated for additional details. This can be avoided by writing down the information you need before you call.

• Handle paper only once, if possible. When mail is opened, act on it then. Separating it out and working on each pile later creates a second step and wastes your valuable time.

• Delegate responsibility and authority within your company. Learn to accept how others do projects. It will be different than if you had done it. In fact, it may even be better.

• Learn to say no without feeling guilty.

• Keep meetings to a minimum and make the most of the time together. Have a set agenda and stick with it. Let everyone know what will be covered in the meeting, prior to the meeting time. Start and stop meetings promptly on time. Be considerate of others' time as well.

- Work from a clean desk. Keep close to you only those items you use frequently; otherwise put it out of site. This also reduces stress by not overwhelming you.
- Plan tomorrow before you leave your office today. Also clear your workspace. This allows you to start each day fresh and with an agenda.
- Make a new "to do" list every day. Carry over what hasn't been completed.
- Don't let others steal your time away. Try to keep interruptions to a minimum.
- Know that interruptions and crisis will happen. Be flexible. Be prepared. But try to work around unforeseen obstacles.

Your agenda is your personal time plan. It will work best if you include both the business and the nonbusiness activities that will require your time and attention. And it must be something you believe in for it to work.

Stress

Everyone has stress in their lives. In fact, stress is not necessarily bad. Stress can add flavor, challenge and opportunity to life. The problem arises, however, when you have too much stress. And when you are unable to control your stress. At this level, stress can negatively affect your work, your home and your life.

We've all known people who worked better under pressure. Somehow the torture of the pending deadline manages to get them working harder and creates masterpieces. If that last-minute pressure excites you, then your stress level is different than mine. I am not a last-minute person. I am a list-maker. Lists have become my answer for managing stress. List-making only works if

you are aware of your goals, however, and if you take the time to make lists.

We are prone to stress from giving of ourselves to everyone else and not having any time or energy left for us. We are exhausted from trying to be all things to all people. We feel the pressure from the work and family collision course society has placed us on. Not all the news is bad though. Fortunately, we are beginning to understand the need for moderation, balance and prioritizing, especially in the pressure-cooker lifestyles we lead.

Stress can cause both physical and emotional repercussions when not managed properly. Too much stress can cause physical illnesses, such as high blood pressure, ulcers or even heart disease, not to mention sleep disorders, irritability and irrational thinking.

Stress can be magnified from a single event or be part of everyday occurrences. It can be heightened when you are starting a business because of financial concerns, others' expectations, and juggling more activities.

To handle stress, learn to recognize stressful situations. If you cannot alter the outcome of an event, learn to *let it go*. It will take some time and a lot of talking to yourself. But eventually, you can begin concentrating on those items you can control or change. *You control you and your feelings.* You cannot control others' feelings, actions, or abilities. Recognize and accept that fact early. It can save you a lot of grief and frustration later on.

Recognizing stress is an important step toward managing and avoiding burnout. Reactions from high stress can be manifested in a variety of symptoms, including physical symptoms, behavioral changes, emotional symptoms, and thought symptoms. Some of the common characteristics of these are listed below:

- **Physical symptoms:** Headaches, sweaty palms, sleep difficulties, restlessness, tiredness, stomach aches, racing heart, tightness in neck or shoulder area.
- **Behavioral changes:** Bossiness, abuse of alcohol, compulsive disorders (eating, drinking, smoking), grinding teeth at night, despair, inability to get things done.
- **Emotional symptoms:** Unexplained outbursts and crying, boredom, loneliness, anger, edginess, nervousness, feeling overwhelmed, unhappiness for no reason.
- **Thought symptoms:** Forgetfulness, memory loss, constant worry about everything, inability to think clearly, inability to make decisions, loss of sense of humor.

What you want to do first is get a handle on stress levels—the amount of stress that is comfortable and safe for you to operate within.

When you are faced with extremely stressful situations, learn techniques for minimizing the impact on your life. The U.S. Department of Health has provided the following guidelines for managing high-stress situations:

- **Try physical activity.** When you are nervous, angry, or upset, release the pressure through exercise or physical activity. Remember, your body and your mind work together.
- **Share your stress.** It helps to talk to someone about your concerns and worries. Perhaps a friend, family member or counselor can help you see your problem in a different light.

Knowing when to ask for help may avoid more serious problems later.

- **Know your limits.** If a problem is beyond your control and cannot be changed at the moment, don't fight the situation. Learn to accept what is—for now—until such time as you can change it.
- **Take care of yourself.** You are special. Get enough rest and eat well. If you are irritable and tense from lack of sleep, or if you are not eating correctly, you will have less ability to deal with stressful situations.
- **Make time for fun.** Schedule time for both work and recreation. Play can be just as important to your well-being as work. You need a break from your daily routine, a time to just relax and have fun.
- **Be a participant.** Sitting alone can make you feel frustrated. Instead of feeling sorry for yourself, get involved; become a participant. Help yourself by helping others in need.
- **Check off your tasks.** Trying to take care of everything at once can seem overwhelming and, as a result, you may not accomplish anything. Instead, make a list of what tasks you have to do; then do them one at a time. Give priority to the most important ones and do those first.
- **Must you always be right?** Do other people upset you, particularly when they don't do things your way? Try cooperation instead of confrontation: It's better than fighting and always being right. A little give-and-take on both sides will reduce the strain and make you both feel more comfortable.
- **It's okay to cry.** A good cry can be a healthy way to bring relief from your anxiety, and it might even prevent

other physical consequences, such as a headache. Take some deep breaths; they also release tension.

- **Create a quiet scene.** You can't always be away, but you can "dream the impossible dream." A quiet country scene painted mentally can take you out of the turmoil of a stressful situation. Change the scene by reading a good book or playing beautiful music to create a sense of peace and tranquillity.

- **Avoid self-medication.** Medications do not remove the conditions of stress. In fact, they may be habit-forming and may also reduce your efficiency, thus creating more stress than they take away. They should be taken only on the advice and under the supervision of your doctor.

Tying it all together

Congratulations! You have finished reading this book, and in all likelihood have begun starting the process for opening your own business. The most important thing I hope you have learned is to stay open to new opportunities for learning. Change is a part of our life. Information is being disbursed at such rapid rates that it is hard for most of us to make a dent in what's available. But, information is vital in today's workplace, wherever that is, at home or away.

Integrating your *female-ness* into your work life, providing a nurturing environment, supporting others and keeping your family as a priority can now be accomplished. It doesn't take Superwoman. It takes determination, desire and enthusiasm, plus your own personal set of priorities. Only you know what you want. Only you set your agenda. Only you can measure its progress. You are in control of your life.

Always keep a smile on. Keep the tough times in perspective. And learn to laugh a lot. Your sense of humor will be a great therapy. The road ahead may get bumpy from time to time. Always look for the lesson to be learned. And don't be too hard on yourself. You'll probably make some mistakes. I know I did. That's just part of the process. Learn to proceed.

I hope your business brings you joy and happiness. I hope it is everything you dreamed of. Remember, you—and you alone—decide the parameters for measuring success. And you—and you alone—evaluate it on those grounds. Do not let the pressures of society interfere with your game plan. You are on a mission. Continue on. And best of luck.

Glossary

Actuarial Tables: These tables calculate and state the risk and premium rates for individuals based on past statistical knowledge. They incorporate life expectancy and costs in these calculations.

Annuity: A way to set aside money during your working years to provide future income on a tax-deferred basis; usually established through insurance companies.

Asset: All the property, both real and personal, owned by an individual or business. Includes both current and long-term items, such as inventories, stock, cash balances, machines, equipment and buildings.

Audited financial statements: Financial statements that include an opinion from the CPA who performed the audit concerning the findings and the qualifications of the financial reports. These opinions are based on generally accepted accounting principles (GAAP).

Balance sheet: A snapshot view of a company's assets, liabilities and equity.

Board of directors: Elected by stockholders to run a corporation. The board is responsible to the stockholders for proper management of the corporation's business affairs.

Break-even analysis: A mathematical approach to determining the effects price changes might have on demand. All calculations are based on assumptions.

Budget: A financial plan of probable sales and expenses for a future period against which actual sales and expenses can be compared.

Bylaws: The rules of a U.S. corporation concerning its relationship with its board of directors and shareholders. Bylaws are filed with the state when the business is incorporated.

Capital: A word sometimes used loosely in business. It can mean an asset, a liability or equity.

Capital account: A statement of the amount and value of a business at a given time. On the balance sheet, it may refer to the equity.

Capital expense: Expenditures for permanent additions or improvements to property. Repairs are not included in capital expenses.

Capital gains: Profit from the sale of a capital investment, such as stock or real estate.

Capital goods: Material used in the business for the production of a good.

Cash flow: A type of budget that shows the amount of cash coming into or going out of a company. Cash flow statements are used for projecting how much money will be received and when, so that business owners can determine their upcoming cash needs.

Common stock: Securities that represent an ownership interest in a corporation. Owners of stock are referred to as stockholders or shareholders. The return on common stock is referred to as a dividend.

Copyright: Exclusive statutory right of authors, composers, playwrights, artists, publishers or distributors to publish and dispose of their works for a limited time, in limited states, for 28 years, with the privilege of one renewal for an additional 28 years. In recent years, copyright protection has been extended to computer programs and databases.

Corporation: A form of business organization that entails creating a separate entity under state regulations. Owned by stockholders and managed by a board of directors.

Creditor: Someone who is owed money. When someone owes you money, you are the creditor.

Debtor: Someone who owes money. When you owe someone money, you are the debtor.

Dividend: A sum of money from a corporation distributed to stockholders, based on net earnings. Unlike interest, which is paid to lenders, dividends do not have to be paid every year.

Equity: Value of assets in excess of liabilities for either a business or individual. The terms net worth and capital may be used as well.

Fiduciary: A position of trust and confidence of a third party, as that of an attorney, guardian or trustee.

Financial statement: Reports that show the financial condition of a business. The most common financial statement includes an income statement and a balance sheet.

Franchise: A business agreement in which one party, the franchisor, allows another party, the franchisee, to distribute a licensed product or service. A franchise is a licensing and distribution agreement between a parent company and an independent business.

Gross profit: The difference between total revenues and the cost of goods sold. From gross profits, one subtracts overhead and other operating expenses to determine income before taxes.

Income: Often used synonymously with the term profit, although income can also mean revenues or earnings.

Income statement: Shows a company's revenues (sales) and expenses, including costs of goods sold, for a period of time. It may also be referred to as a profit and loss statement.

Incorporation: The process of a business forming as a legal corporation.

Inheritance tax: A tax imposed on the passing of a deceased person's estate to her heirs.

Interest: Payment to a lender for the use of money. Interest is a compulsory payment and defaulting (not making payment) allows the lender to take legal action against the borrower.

Leverage: The degree to which a business is funded by loans instead of equity cash from the owners or retained earnings.

Liability: That for which one is liable; owing a debt. Liabilities represent things you owe.

Liquidity: The short-run financial health of a company; assets that are easily and quickly converted to cash.

Market: A place where merchandise is exposed for sale; or the state of trade as determined by prices, supply, demand and other economic factors.

Mortgage: A lien on property created by a secured note for repayment of the loan. A mortgage allows for transfer of ownership to the lender if the borrower defaults.

Mutual funds: A pool of funds from many people used to invest in a diversified portfolio of stocks and other investments that often are not available to individual investors who do not have substantial amounts of money to invest. Mutual funds range in risk and objectives.

Net income: The amount of money remaining on the income statement after all expenses and taxes have been paid. Also referred to as net profit.

Net worth: Another term for equity, it is the value of assets in excess of liabilities.

Overhead: General expenditures in a business that cannot be attributed to any one department or product. It does not include costs of materials, labor or selling expenses.

Partnership: A form of business organization between two or more individuals who combine their time, money, skills, expertise or property in the business.

Patent: Government protection to an inventor of the exclusive right to use a product or process that has been registered.

Preferred stock: A class of stock that possesses a claim on the company's earnings before payment can be made to common stockholders.

Press release: A bulletin announcing an event, development in a business, newsworthy decision, etc., sent to various interested parties, especially news media personnel.

Probate: The right or jurisdiction of proving wills.

Profit and loss statement: Another term for income statement.

Proprietorship: A legal form of business whereby an individual owns the business. All profits flow directly to the individual. In addition, all claims can go against the individual as well as the company. It is the least complicated form of business ownership to organize.

Public relations: Activities and techniques of a business that enhance favorable attitudes and responses by the general public or a specific group.

Retained earnings: For a corporation, the amount of profit earned in the preceding year and former years that has not been paid out as dividends.

Retirement plans: An employer benefit plan that allows for contributions to be tax-deferred until retirement. Employees as well as business owners may contribute, depending on the plan.

Sole proprietorship: See definition for proprietorship.

Stock (or share): The capital or funds of a corporation represented by shares. Stockholders have ownership in a company. More than one class of stock may be issued.

Tax-deferred income: Income that is not subject to current taxes, but is taxed at a later date.

Tax-exempt income: Income that is not subject to taxes.

Trademark: A name, symbol, design or word (or any combination thereof) used to identify goods and distinguish them from others. A trademark may be registered on either the state or national level.

Trust: A legal arrangement by which title to property is given to one party for the benefit of another (known as a beneficiary).

Working capital: The difference between current assets and current liabilities.